Mapping Hypertext

The Analysis, Organization, and Display of Knowledge for the Next Generation of On-Line Text and Graphics

Mapping Hypertext

**The Analysis, Organization, and Display of Knowledge for the
Next Generation of On-Line Text and Graphics**

by
Robert E. Horn

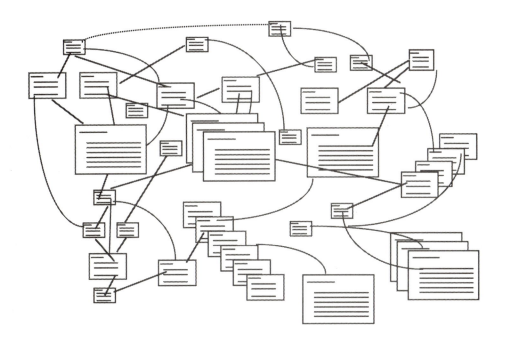

A Publication of The Lexington Institute

For Andrea and Jenny

To Order This Book
Call
(617) 890-7003
or Write
INFORMATION MAPPING, INC.
300 Third Avenue
Waltham, MA 02154

Library of Congress Catalog Card Number 90-060088

ISBN 0-9625565-0-5

Introduction

This Book: An Overview of Two Relatively New Frameworks for Thinking

For a number of years I have been working with two relatively new frameworks for thinking about and presenting information, which show a great deal of promise for improving human communication. They are:

Hypertext

a form of organizing text in computers that permits the linking of any place in text (or other media) to any other place and the rapid retrieval of information by following trails of these associative links.

Information Mapping's Method of Structured Writing

a methodology for analyzing, organizing, writing, sequencing, and formatting information to improve communication. It provides a way of describing the structure of subject matters that is very useful throughout the communication process.

Since no good description of these two methodologies exists in a single book, I have written chapter-length overviews of them. I also present extensive examples of their applications in business and academia.

Summary of the Argument

In addition to these overviews, I also make a case for the future importance of the coming together of these two approaches. The argument can be summarized as follows.

1   Hypertext will help knowledge workers to better organize the information they manage and to find it when they need to. Hypertext may even become the basis for a large new public medium of information exchange.

2   There are problems associated with the design, development, use, and implementation of hypertext knowledge bases. Some of these problems co-arise out of the very nature of hypertext and thus may not have completely satisfactory solutions. Other problems will be solved by the creativity and hard work of people in the field. Many of the major issues are resolved by the Information Mapping method.

3   Information Mapping's method is a mature, extensively tested, and widely used (in industry and government) methodology for analyzing, organizing and writing documents. It represents a new approach to thinking about the fundamentals of rhetoric (the study of the principles and rules for written and spoken composition). The method produces measurable improvements in human performance through better communication.

4   Modern argumentation analysis has been on the scene since 1956. When put into the context of the software systems described in this book, it can be regarded as an application of what I call structured hypertext. My claim in this book is that argumentation analysis will contribute to representing and solving some of the problems of analysis of disputes and that it can be used as a major linkage device to other domains of discourse we describe in this book -- experimental (the domain of empirical science) and the domain of relatively stable subject matter (that which we place in our textbooks, procedure, policy, training, and documentation manuals).

5   I then propose that the ideas in Information Mapping's method and argumentation analysis that have proven so useful in other areas could be applied to certain parts of the communication of scientific information used in hypertext software systems. This point is illustrated with a sketch for the redesign of basic scientific reports and abstracts. I then provide prototypes of these documents so the reader can consider their usefulness.

6   Another implicit claim of this book is that Information Mapping's method and hypertext can be used in books like the one you have in your hands. So I have simulated *insofar as possible on paper* what this book might be like if it were actually being presented on a computer screen of a hypertext system of the near future.

7   Also implicit is the claim that the liberal use of graphics contributes to the effectiveness of communication of our ideas. In fact, in the last chapter I venture a forecast that such visual language will become a major communication methodology increasingly integrated with the words we use every day. (If a picture is worth a thousand words, then the approx. 600 illustrations in this book provide 600,000 extra words, which, if you figure about 300 words per page, is about 2,000 extra pages, which makes the book well worth its price.) I might mention that this book also demonstrates what can be accomplished with inexpensive modern computer graphics. All of it was done on the Macintosh computer with MacDraw II software.

Serve Different Readers

This book will be of use to many different readers:

 the general reader who wants to take a look at important developments in communication -- present and future

 managers who are planning to convert some text or graphic data bases to the computer for on-line access

 the knowledge worker who is planning to design, buy or implement a hypertext system, use the Information Mapping method or argumentation analysis

 scholars, scientists, teachers, students, writers or consultants who are planning to use hypertext, structured writing, or argumentation.

Advice for Reading This Book

One of the advantages of the Information Mapping method of structured writing is that it is written to be browsed. Readers are able to look at the headings (and the graphics) and get a broad picture of the content without reading every word.

So, I urge you to skip around in this book as much as possible and don't feel you have to read every sentence in order to use this book properly. There are summaries at the beginning of each chapter that give you a quick high level idea of what is in the chapter and review how the chapter fits into the overall book.

I have claimed that the combination of hypertext and Information Mapping is a very important way of enabling readers with different backgrounds and different interests to get what they need from the same text. This book provides an opportunity for you to test that hypothesis.

This book is *not*

☐ a report of comparison shopping on current hypertext software systems, for they change far too often for books to keep up (so watch your computer magazines for these consumer reports).

☐ a way of teaching you how to do either hypertext or Information Mapping's method (you can browse both well here, but if you want some minimum amount of competency or fluency, you will need to take a course or two and then practice).

☐ an analysis of the latest comments on the issues in these burgeoning fields (for this you need to go to the conferences and read your magazines). In this book you will find the more fundamental long term issues.

☐ an investigation of the specific computer interface issues that arise as a result of hypertext implementations on specific systems (for this, you need to become acquainted with the specific constraints of each hardware and software system).

Robert E. Horn
Lexington, Massachusetts
November 1989

Contents

Note: On these facing pages are two different views of the book -- detailed table of contents on this page and corresponding visual summary on the right.

PART 1. Hypertext - Hypermedia, New Opportunities - Detailed Table of Contents

Summary and Plan of the Book

PART 1. Hypertext - Hypermedia, New Opportunities

Chapter 1. Introduction to Hypertext and Hypermedia

1

Hypertext

Hypertext is an important development
in the storage and retrieval of text and graphics
on computers...

It enables us to **link...**

...different places in text called **"nodes"...**

...with other nodes...

...through the use of **buttons...**

CLICK

button

nodes

...any place in a text...
...to any other place...
...any time...
...and get there fast...

Chapter 2. Current Issues with Hypertext

2

Issues in Hypertext

Among the major issues of hypertext
implementation and use are:

What shall
the nodes
contain and
the links
represent?

Overchoice
and Cognitive
Overload

Labor-Intensive
Maintenance

Some
Issues

Lost in
Hyperspace

Multiple Skills
and New Rhetoric
Needed

Serialist &
Holist Readers

...these issues
and others
are addressed
by the Information
Mapping method
described in the
next few chapters...

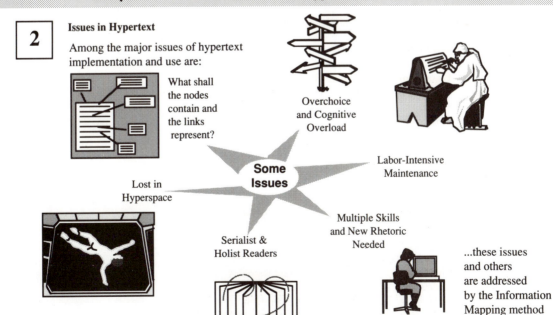

Note: On these facing pages are two different views of the book -- detailed table of contents on this page and corresponding visual summary on the right.

PART 2. The Method of Information Mapping - Detailed Table of Contents

Summary and Plan of the Book

PART 2. The Method of Information Mapping

Chapter 3. Introduction to Information Mapping's Method of Structured Writing

3 Information Mapping's method is a mature technology for analyzing, organizing, writing, sequencing, and formatting information. It introduces a novel way of modularizing information and provides a modern alternative to traditional concepts of approaching the writing of many types of documents in business, technology and academia.

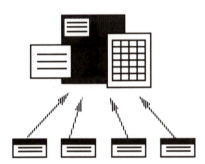

We show how four principles generate information blocks and maps. Then we show how the contribution of other principles and research enables us to build a systematic process for subject matter and task analysis. Finally we describe tools for the organization and presentation of learning and reference materials to users. The ability to analyze the structure of subject matters gives the method its particular usefulness.

Chapter 4. Navigating Structured Hypertrails

4 The larger structure of the subject matter can be shown to users by sequences or weblike structures of links called hypertrails. These hypertrails can also be used to specify various linear paths through the networks of hypertext. The nodes of hypertrails are information blocks and maps.

Chapter 5. Resolving Some Hypertext Problems

5 Using Information Mapping's structured writing method and hypertrails provides systematic guidance in the analysis and specification of nodes and links and in mapping the larger picture. Thus it enables us to resolve some of the major issues with hypertext raised in Chapter 2.

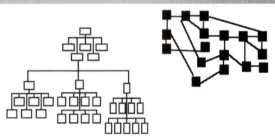

Note: On these facing pages are two different views of the book -- detailed table of contents on this page and corresponding visual summary on the right.

PART 3. Some Applications of Structured Hypertext - Detailed Table of Contents

Summary and Plan of the Book

PART 3. Some Applications of Structured Hypertext

Chapter 6. Relatively Stable Discourse: Documentation and Training

6 We present examples of the use of the Information Mapping method to analyze critical and complex documents in business and industrial situations, such as personnel and policy manuals, operations and training manuals, and product knowledge databases.

Chapter 7. Disputed Discourse: Argumentation Analysis

7 Argumentation analysis is a method of representing in a hypertext network sentences that are the components of a reasoning process about a dispute.

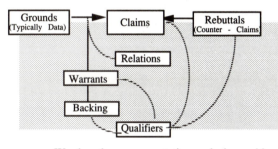

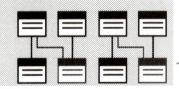

We show how argumentation analysis provides a linkage between relatively stable subjects and discourse about scientific experiments.

Among the examples presented in this chapter is an argumentation analysis of seven fundamental principles of Information Mapping methodology.

Chapter 8. Experimental Discourse: Scientific Information

8 We apply the principles of Information Mapping's method to a provisional redesign of scientific abstracts to improve their communication possibilities in a hypertext environment.

Among the examples provided of abstracts are some of the research papers and theoretical articles that support the principles and practices of Information Mapping's analysis and writing methodology.

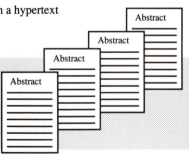

Note: On these facing pages are two different views of the book -- detailed table of contents on this page and corresponding visual summary on the right.

PART 4. So What? What Next? - Detailed Table of Contents

Chapter 9. Mapping Future Infospace: Summary and Trends

Appendix A. Some Historical Notes

Summary and Plan of the Book

PART 4. So What? What Next?

Chapter 9. Mapping Future Infospace: Summary and Trends

9 | **The Future**

Finally we combine all of these approaches to take a look at mapping and navigation of hypertext and hypermedia in the future...

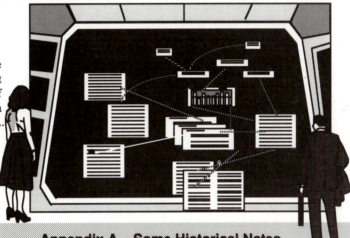

Appendix A. Some Historical Notes

A | **A Little Bit of History**

Where did hypertext come from? Who were the people who came up with the key ideas? Who were the people who first implemented the technology? When did all this take place?

From Vannevar Bush in 1945 who first suggested the possibility of hypertext, to Ted Nelson who named it hypertext and hypermedia, through Doug Engelbart who built the first system, through the other visionaries and builders who have given us the possibilities of hypertext.

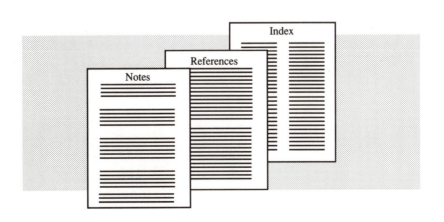

Chapter 1. Introduction to Hypertext and Hypermedia

Chapter 1
Introduction to Hypertext and Hypermedia

Essence of hypertext software

Definition of hypertext

Paper and computer metaphors for hypertext

In this Chapter ...an overview of hypertext and hypermedia

Definition of hypermedia

Dimensions and characteristics of hypertext systems

Paper metaphors for hypertext

Computer metaphors for hypertext

Navigation metaphors

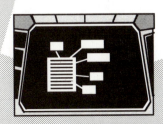

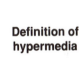

Overview of This Chapter

Introduction

Hypertext is a novel way of constructing computer-supported, non-linear writing. It can also be thought of as a new way of developing text databases. It provides many new capabilities for linking all sorts of electronic media. In this chapter we provide a detailed description of this important new computer tool.

Treatment: Textbook Chapter on Hypertext and Hypermedia

Since the concepts of hypertext and hypermedia have only emerged in the last 20 years and since they are still not well known to most people, our approach in this chapter is to present a relatively detailed introduction to this field.

Approach: Simulate the Look and Feel of Hypertext in Print

We all assimilate information in different ways and, hence, we often need different paths through a document in order to get the most out of it. Hypertext gets some of its power from the almost instantaneous ability to jump from one place in the text to another. In order to provide you with the best idea possible on the printed page of what hypertext looks and feels like, we have simulated computer screens and linkages in this book.

Commentary: Major Argument of this Chapter

This chapter will give you a broad picture of what hypertext is all about. As this book is written (in early 1989) there are only a few hypertext systems in operation. We are in a stage of technology development just before the rush.

Hypertext will emerge as a major way of organizing text and other media despite the obstacles that I spell out in Chapter 2. This obviously is not a startling hypothesis for those who have been following recent developments in the field. But for others, to contemplate having the flexibility and the choices of hypertext routinely available on their computers can be an exhilarating thought. (REH)

A Brief History of Hypertext

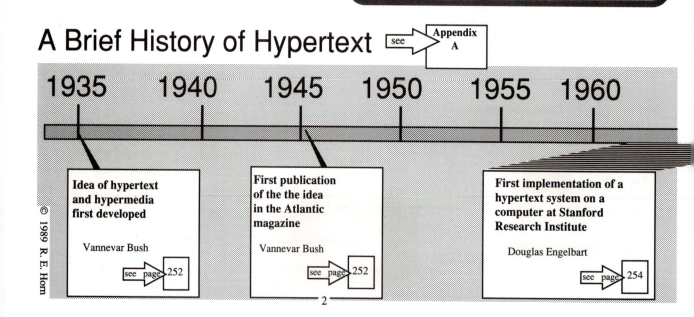

see → Appendix A

1935   1940   1945   1950   1955   1960

Idea of hypertext and hypermedia first developed

Vannevar Bush

see page 252

First publication of the the idea in the Atlantic magazine

Vannevar Bush

see page 252

First implementation of a hypertext system on a computer at Stanford Research Institute

Douglas Engelbart

see page 254

Author's Commentary: Personal Judgments

I faced a number of unique problems in writing this book. First, the goal of giving an introduction to hypertext, argumentation analysis, and Information Mapping implied a goal of "just the facts." But to give perspective on the issues, I needed to write more personal or more judgmental remarks like this. So I decided to simulate how I might "overlay" my comments on an otherwise somewhat more neutral approach to the subject. In this way, you'll be able to see how such commentary might work in a hypertext system where you and other people can add notes to the original text. We use a distinctive shade of border and sign the notes. In some cases, you will see that I have included quotes from other writers as if they were comments on my text. In these cases the author will be so noted and references can be found in the back of the book. My comments will be signed: (REH).

for example...

Forecast (1967) Multiple Ways to Read Hypertext

Ted Nelson, who coined the word hypertext, has suggested: "To be useful, the hypertext medium requires some ... variety in the ways and sequences that the same material can be connected together or explained. Indeed, these texts may be made big and diverse enough for study by specialist and beginner alike; with many entrances, tracks, and specially oriented meanders. Thus the user's previous background and level of knowledge could be taken beneficially into account by the author-editors." (Nelson, 1967)

In this book these little "see page" icons...

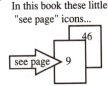

...simulate what in hypertext are called "buttons," places in the text on a computer screen you would be able to click your mouse, depress a key, or otherwise indicate that you want to go to the place indicated by the button.

see page 258

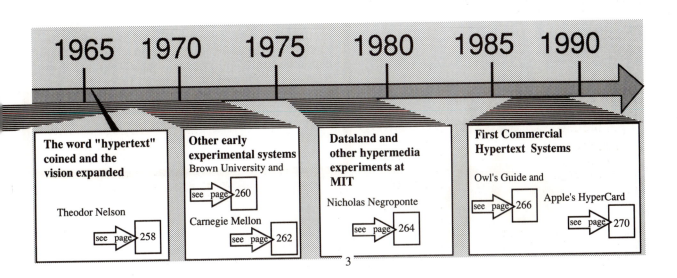

1965   1970   1975   1980   1985   1990

The word "hypertext" coined and the vision expanded

Theodor Nelson

see page 258

Other early experimental systems
Brown University and

see page 260

Carnegie Mellon

see page 262

Dataland and other hypermedia experiments at MIT

Nicholas Negroponte

see page 264

First Commercial Hypertext Systems

Owl's Guide and

see page 266

Apple's HyperCard

see page 270

Sources of Hypertext

Introduction: Human Thought is Multi-Dimensional; But Conventional Text is Linear

Human thought has many aspects, many dimensions. Our memories are associative; we connect many different things in quite unpredictable and idiosyncratic ways. And often our thinking appears as a kind of free association or even free juxtaposition. Other memory and thought is quite structured and hierarchical. We reason from goals to means. From causes to consequences. We plan rationally. We build large organizations on highly structured principles. The question this book addresses is: How do we best represent all this information and all these connections to ourselves and to others for communication, learning, and problem solving?

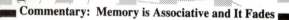

Commentary: Memory is Associative and It Fades

"Our ineptitude in getting at the record is largely caused by the artificiality of systems of indexing....The human mind does not work that way. It operates by association. With one item in its grasp, it snaps instantly to the next that is suggested by the association of thoughts, in accordance with some intricate web of trails carried by the cells of the brain. It has other characteristics, of course; trails that are not frequently followed are prone to fade, items are not fully permanent, memory is transitory. Yet the speed of action, the intricacy of trails, the detail of mental pictures, is awe-inspiring beyond all else in nature..."

Vannevar Bush, 1945

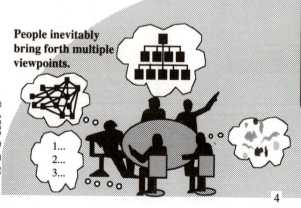

People inevitably bring forth multiple viewpoints.

1...
2...
3...

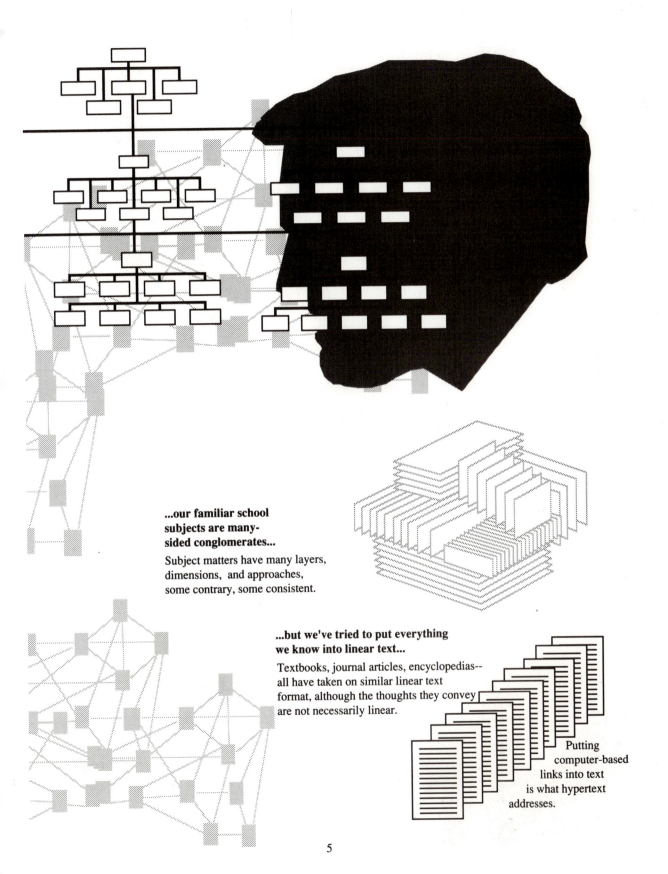

...our familiar school subjects are many-sided conglomerates...

Subject matters have many layers, dimensions, and approaches, some contrary, some consistent.

...but we've tried to put everything we know into linear text...

Textbooks, journal articles, encyclopedias-- all have taken on similar linear text format, although the thoughts they convey are not necessarily linear.

Putting computer-based links into text is what hypertext addresses.

What is Hypertext ?

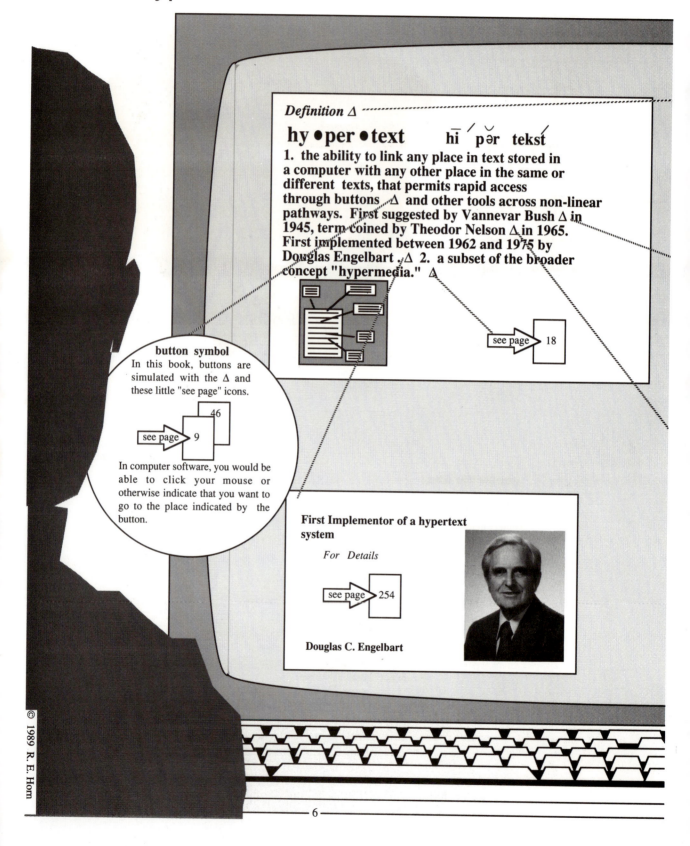

Definition △

hy • per • text   hī ′ pər tekst

1. the ability to link any place in text stored in a computer with any other place in the same or different texts, that permits rapid access through buttons △ and other tools across non-linear pathways. First suggested by Vannevar Bush △ in 1945, term coined by Theodor Nelson △ in 1965. First implemented between 1962 and 1975 by Douglas Engelbart △ 2. a subset of the broader concept "hypermedia." △

see page ▷ 18

button symbol

In this book, buttons are simulated with the △ and these little "see page" icons.

see page ▷ 9 / 46

In computer software, you would be able to click your mouse or otherwise indicate that you want to go to the place indicated by the button.

First Implementor of a hypertext system

For Details

see page ▷ 254

Douglas C. Engelbart

Commentary: Another Definition

"Hypertext is both an author's tool and a reader's medium. With hypertext software, authors or groups of authors will be able to link information together, annotate existing texts, and create footnotes that allow readers to see either bibliographic data or the body of the referenced text. Readers will be able to browse through linked, cross-referenced, annotated, footnoted texts in an orderly, but nonsequential manner: an automated encyclopedia of sorts . . . "

(Brown University, 1985)

Inventor of the concept of hypertext

For   Details

 252

Vannevar Bush

Commentary: Another Definition

"By 'hypertext' I mean
non-sequential writing."

(Theodor Holm Nelson, 1974)

**Coiner of the terms "hypertext"
and "hypermedia"**

For   Details

 258

Theodor Holm Nelson

Essence of Hypertext: Links, Nodes and Buttons

Three Important Features of Hypertext Software

The essence of hypertext software is

1. a network of nodes △ which may be text and/or graphics

2. software methodology that facilitates building of and access to nodes via links △

3. interface tools that facilitate the creation of arbitrary linkages in the text with buttons △ and (frequently) the easy manipulation of chunks of text and media through windows.

Links

Definition

Links connect nodes in the hypertext software by computer-supported relationships that permit rapid, easy movement across the network of nodes.

Examples of Some Kinds of Links

There are a great variety of links in hypertext systems. Here are some types of links:

- the internal document organization (e.g., connect two pieces of text in same document)
- the external organization (e.g., connection of one document to other documents)
- annotation via pop-up windows
- table of contents to document
- index to document
- local table of contents to a part of a document.

Buttons

Definition

Buttons are specific locations in the hypertext or on other media that permit the user to jump along a link to another node, usually with the click of a mouse or the pressing of a key. In one sense, buttons are the user-visible manifestations of links.

Example

Nodes

Definition

1. Nodes are the part of the hypertext network where the text or other media are located. 2. For some software implementations, a node contains one idea or one sentence; for other implementations the node may be a whole document as long as a book or chapter.

Comment

At present, the node is not a well defined concept except in certain very structured contexts. One node may include composite nodes where, for example, a node is a subnode. Nodes may have different display metaphors, such as cards, pages, windows.

Features of Hypertext

Introduction

Links, nodes and buttons are essential characteristics of hypertext. But there are other characteristics that give hypertext its distinctive flavor, and distinguish it from just another text database.

---

1 Focus on Rapid Browsing

Description

One of the values that hypertext theorists have always espoused is the ability of the user to conduct rapid browsing and navigation. The user must be able to get around in the hypertext quickly and easily. This means that the user interface must enable the user to navigate across the links in the system, usually with a couple of clicks of a mouse or a couple of key strokes.

Example

It is assumed that users will do something else when they get to the place they've jumped, i.e., to use the information for...

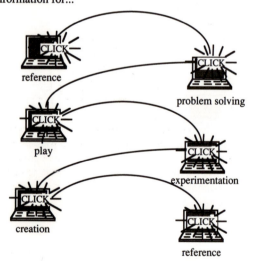

reference

problem solving

play

experimentation

creation

reference

Comment

Little is made of these other functions in the hypertext literature. Rather, in that literature, rapid browsing and navigation are often valued for their own sake.

---

2 Focus on Non-Linear Discourse

Description

Some hypertext software authors value highly the ability to have information partially or non-linearly structured. Here these distinctive definitional qualities enter the structure of the contents as well as the link-node structure of the software.

They celebrate the non-linear structure of the text and non-symmetrical organization.

Example of This Thinking

Not only is it possible that a story could have several endings, but it is claimed or implied that it is somehow better if it does have several endings.

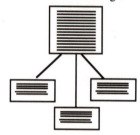

Authors Who Have Tried Non-Sequential Writing

These three authors have written novels with different paths for reading.

Hopscotch
Cortazar

Nabakov
Pale Fire

Dictionary
of the
Khazars
Pavic

Comment

The claim is made that, because human thought has the characteristic of being able to associate anything with anything else, somehow it is implied that all or most text should have "the freedom to associate."

3   Focus on Two Link-Making Options

A   Personalized Hypertext

Description

Many hypertext systems can be personalized. For example, the user can modify the hypertext database by making links and adding text, graphics, and numbers to the documents and windows.

Thus the document becomes increasingly the personal document of the user, rather than one solely produced by the orginal author. Different levels of security can be supplied so that access can be permitted or denied to different users.

The Original Document

Personalized Document (with User-Created Links)

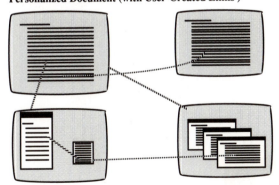

Comment

Little has been done to help readers figure out how they might want to organize such links, which could rapidly represent a large personal information management problem.

B   Read-Only Hypertext

Description

Some hypertext systems, particularly those used for policies, procedures, training and documentation in organizations, permit users to read and follow links without being able to write or make links.

Example

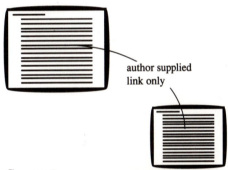

author supplied link only

Comment

You can't change the company's personnel manual unless you are the Vice President for Human Resources or somebody designated by the V.P. Similarly, while feedback may be welcome, you may want it to be private and addressed to the V. P. rather than posted on the pages of the manual.

Some Early Applications of Hypertext

Introduction

To what has hypertext been applied so far? What kinds of experimental and operational situations have been tried out? On these pages we note a number of the early explorations of hypertext. Bibliographic references in the back of this book will lead you to more detail.

A number of projects have been launched to put all of the documentation of given systems on electronic storage.

Aircraft Equipment Repair

There are several large projects to provide information systems for all of the maintenance manuals, costing, and troubleshooting of all of the models of a given make.

Auto and Truck Maintenance

Maintenance and Repair of Large Systems

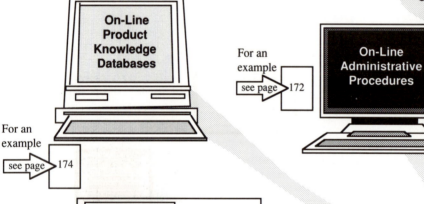

On-Line Product Knowledge Databases

For an example 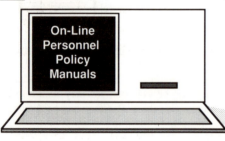 see page 172

On-Line Administrative Procedures

For an example see page 174

On-Line Personnel Policy Manuals

Business and Government Applications

Reference Tools

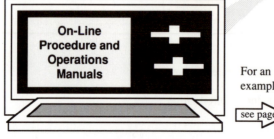

On-Line Procedure and Operations Manuals

For an example see page 170

On-Line help messages are now routine. Connecting them with hypertext links to more detail will improve documentation and training.

A current project at Harvard is linking all of the text on Ancient Greece.

Science, Technology and Academic Applications

Large Databases of Text or Graphics

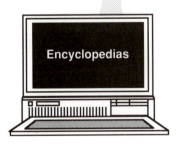

A couple of encyclopedia-size works have been organized with hypertext links and stored on compact disk storage.

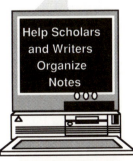

One of the early research programs focused on the metaphor of organizing the electronic equivalent of note cards.

Public and Private Hypertext Systems

Introduction

Hypertext concepts may be applied at different scales or sizes of systems as well as in public or private access situations.

Two Major Usage Contexts for Hypertext Systems

⒈ Private (or in-house) Systems

Definition

Private (or in-house) hypertext systems are systems in which the access to usage is limited to a designated group of users (usually within a single organization).

Example One *Company Reference System on Products and Services*

Sales and marketing could provide hypertext facilities that give sales people and customer service people access to hypertext databases on all the products and services of a corporation. ∆

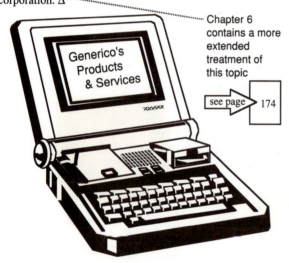

Chapter 6 contains a more extended treatment of this topic

see page ▷ 174

Example Two *Company Reference System on Research & Development*

A large research and development laboratory could provide a hypertext facility for the documents pertaining to various projects being worked on at the laboratory.

Example Three *Company Reference System on Personnel Policies*

Personnel handbooks and other human resource information can be built that enable all branches in a particular organization to access the hypertext that provides the information supervisors and administrators need to make decisions and take action.

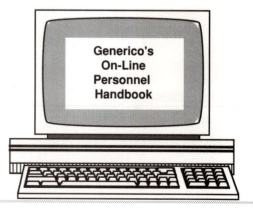

2   Public Access Hypertext Systems

Definition

Public access hypertext systems provide facilities for scholars, specialists, practitioners, and students in a particular field to share a common hypertext knowledge base system.

Example

A scientific field or sub-field could establish a hypertext knowledge base to provide up-to-date scientific information in hypertext form. This would provide significant improvements to the current science information systems.

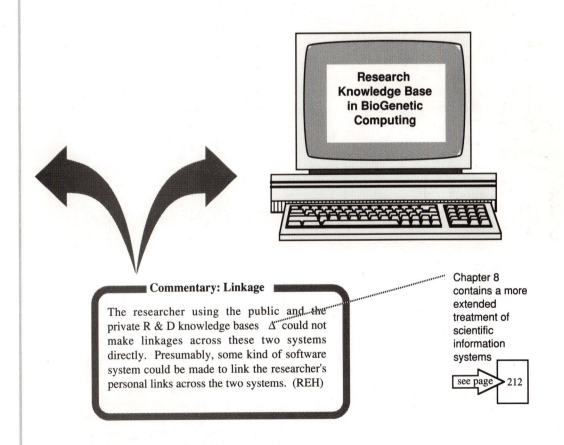

Research Knowledge Base in BioGenetic Computing

Commentary: Linkage

The researcher using the public and the private R & D knowledge bases Δ could not make linkages across these two systems directly. Presumably, some kind of software system could be made to link the researcher's personal links across the two systems. (REH)

Chapter 8 contains a more extended treatment of scientific information systems

see page 212

Navigation Through Information Space Metaphor

Introduction

Ted Nelson's gigantic vision of all the world's literature in one massive hypertext system has inspired science fiction writers to imagine what it might be like to maneuver around in all the world's electronic literature. The result is a metaphor based on the science fiction concept of "navigation" through hyperspace, that is, traversing through time warps that enable space travelers to cover vast amounts of time-space in rapid maneuvers.

Metaphor

Getting to the information you want resembles steering from the bridge of a spaceship. Various subject matters appear at different distances, e.g., (1) galaxies at a great distance, (2) huge abstract constructions at middle distance, and (3) vast integrated displays close up.

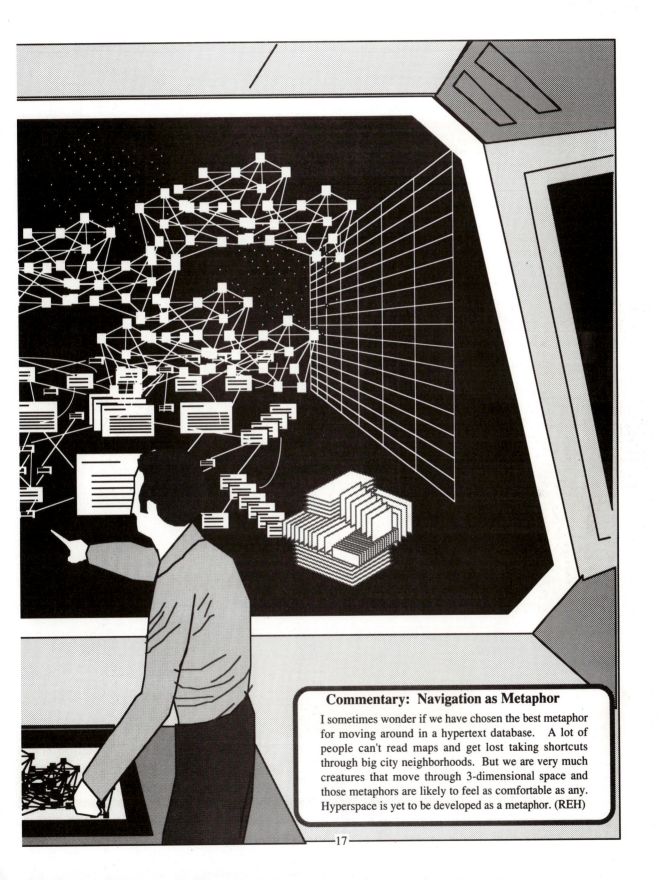

Commentary: Navigation as Metaphor

I sometimes wonder if we have chosen the best metaphor for moving around in a hypertext database. A lot of people can't read maps and get lost taking shortcuts through big city neighborhoods. But we are very much creatures that move through 3-dimensional space and those metaphors are likely to feel as comfortable as any. Hyperspace is yet to be developed as a metaphor. (REH)

What is Hypermedia?

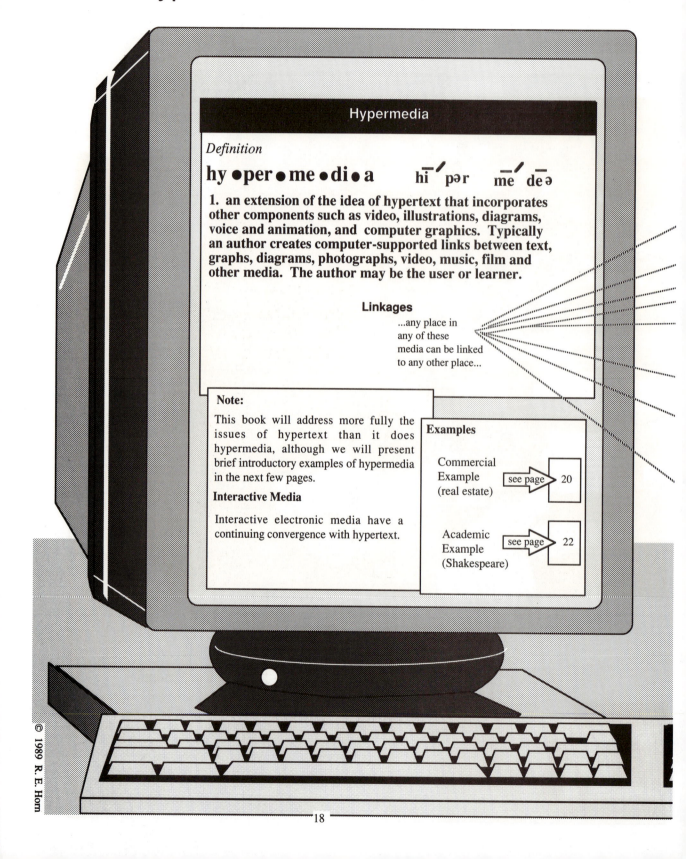

Hypermedia

Definition

hy ●per ● me ●di ● a $h\overline{i}'\,p\partial r$ $m\overline{e}'\,d\overline{e}\partial$

1. an extension of the idea of hypertext that incorporates other components such as video, illustrations, diagrams, voice and animation, and computer graphics. Typically an author creates computer-supported links between text, graphs, diagrams, photographs, video, music, film and other media. The author may be the user or learner.

Linkages

...any place in any of these media can be linked to any other place...

Note:

This book will address more fully the issues of hypertext than it does hypermedia, although we will present brief introductory examples of hypermedia in the next few pages.

Interactive Media

Interactive electronic media have a continuing convergence with hypertext.

Examples

Commercial Example (real estate) see page 20

Academic Example (Shakespeare) see page 22

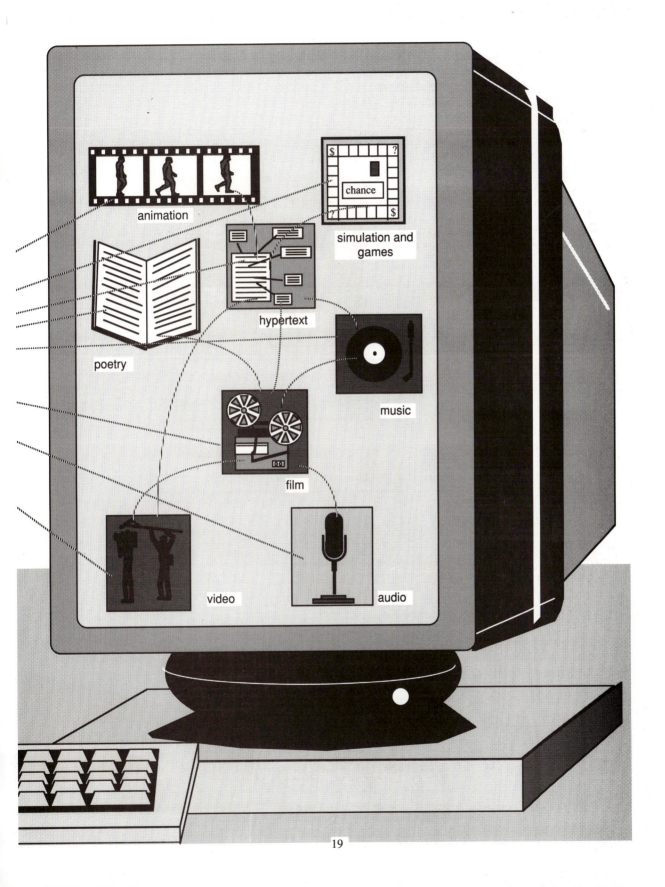

animation

simulation and games

chance

$

?

?

$

hypertext

poetry

music

film

video

audio

Hypermedia Application: New Product Marketing

Introduction

Hypermedia is finding a fair number of early application areas in the marketing of new products. Convention exhibitions and point-of-sale marketing are important areas where hypermedia concepts have been applied. Below we present a schematic of a new product release concept with hypermedia.

1 Potential clients use hypermedia software on computers to make choices about what they want to see on the laser disk and to get detailed text from the computer's memory.

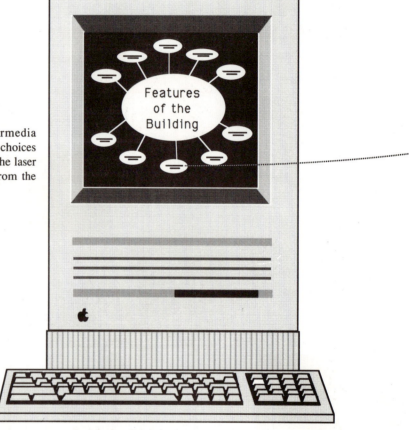

4 Clients can see still photos of different parts of the building and its spaces. They can also see animations and movies of movement through the building to visualize their space. All can be stored on the same disk and controlled by hypermedia links from the computer.

2 Clients view video film, animation, and slides on video disk. In this example, commercial real estate can be explored for leasing before or while it is being built.

3 Commentary and music can accompany both the computer and laser disk displays. Any segment is available in any order on the disk and in the computer.

Case Study: Hypermedia for Shakespeare

Introduction

Hypermedia is also beginning to make a mark in education. On these pages we present a brief schematic overview of what hypermedia course materials might be like. The subject is Shakespeare's plays and their historical and critical context.

see → | Notes

1. | **Begin by watching the play scene by scene on videodisc...**

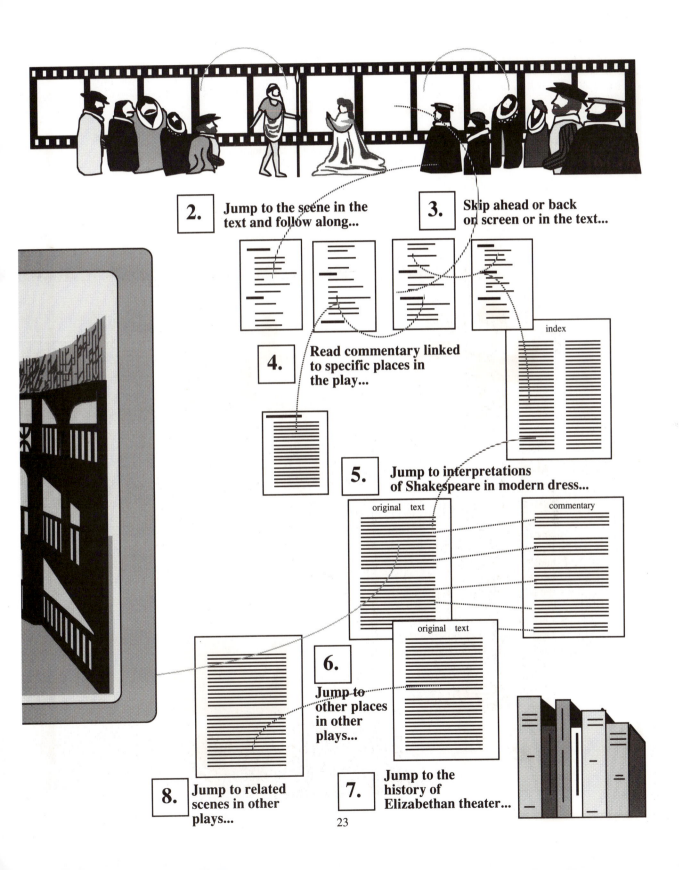

2. Jump to the scene in the text and follow along...

3. Skip ahead or back on screen or in the text...

index

4. Read commentary linked to specific places in the play...

5. Jump to interpretations of Shakespeare in modern dress...

original text

commentary

original text

6. Jump to other places in other plays...

8. Jump to related scenes in other plays...

7. Jump to the history of Elizabethan theater...

Next -- More Detailed Dimensions of Hypertext

Chapter 2. Some Issues with Hypertext

In chapter 2, we look at four different kinds of issues having to do with hypertext:

1 System Design Issues

- What size shall the nodes be and what shall they contain and why?
- What shall the links connect?
- Characteristics of links
- Where to put how many buttons of which kind?

2 Development Issues

- Labor-intensive creation
- Labor-intensive database maintenance
- Additional skills needed for hypertext authoring
- Relating hypertext to other on-line documentation and training

3 User Issues

- Normal reading cues may be inadequate in hypertext and these are often missing
- Poor metacognition skills may hinder usefulness of hypertext in business training
- Serialist readers may have considerable difficulty when forced to branch
- Lost in hyperspace
- Overchoice and cognitive overload
- Chaos in titles for documents and their parts

4 Implementation Issues

- Managing the creation of different versions
- Rewrite or convert to on-line text "as-is"

This Chapter So Far

We have looked at
- what hypertext is
- what its main features are
- some examples of applications
- what hypermedia is
- and some typical examples.

These are the basics. Now you have a choice point.

Author's Commentary: Choose Your Detail Level

Go to Chapter 2 and start looking at the major issues concerning this new medium.

Choice Point

Other Options

Continue reading this chapter which now will go into a lot more detail about some of the characteristics and dimensions of hypertext systems.

Of course, you always have the option to browse, skim, and dip into whatever you choose. (REH)

The Rest of This Chapter

The rest of this chapter focuses on the following topics.

1 **What are Some Types of Links?**

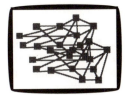

2 **Dimensions of Hypertext Systems**

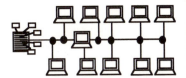

3 **Computer Metaphors for Hypertext**

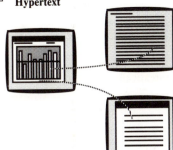

4 **Paper Metaphors for Hypertext Linkages**

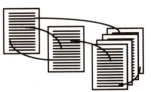

5 **Ways of Using Hypertext**

Browsing   Briefing
Learning   Grazing
Referencing   Analysis & Writing

What Are Some Types of Links?

Introduction

We now turn our attention to a more detailed level of examination of hypertext. We revisit the concept of links to observe some of the kinds of links that have evolved in some of the systems developed thus far.

Three Types of Hypertext Links

1 System-Supplied Links

Definition

System-supplied links are those that are automatically supplied by the hypertext software at all times or are created by the software according to predetermined criteria.

Examples

Here are some examples of the system-supplied links:

1 **command and control pathways through the textual knowledge base (e.g. , next buttons)**

2 **automatically created tables of contents**

3 **automatic tracking of what user has seen and showing this track upon command**

4 **automatically created user profiles and suggested sequences**

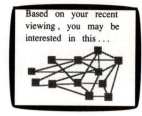

2 User-Created Links

Definition

User-supplied linkages are those links created by the users (using system-supplied facilities) to link text for their own purposes.

Examples

Some examples of user-created linkages include:

1 detours and shortcuts

2 notes, commentary and reminders

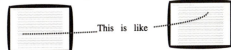

3 analogical linkages

4 new text

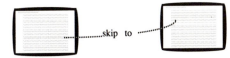

5 links to other knowledge bases

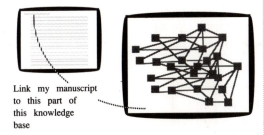

Link my manuscript to this part of this knowledge base

Note: These links are described from the viewpoint of the reader. They may be implemented in the software in quite different fashions.

3 Author-Created Links

Definition

Authors. We refer to authors as those who create text and hypertext for others to read to distinguish them from end-users.

Author-created linkages are links which authors insert in text that are "pre-prepared" for the user to traverse. Usually they are links that authors anticipate users will need frequently.

Examples

Some of the major types of author-created links include:

1 links to prerequisite knowledge

see page 128

2 hierarchical links based on classification of information

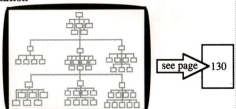

see page 130

3 chronological links

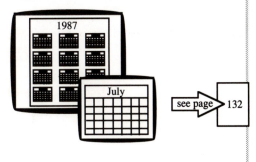

see page 132

Dimensions of Hypertext Systems

Introduction

The concept of hypertext covers a fair amount of territory -- any way you can segment text and any way you can link text is of interest to hypertext theorists. So, clearly we need some ways of characterizing the dimensions of hypertext and its software. Different systems have been built (and imagined) from small, single user authoring systems for a single task, to large, multi-purpose networks with a large number of users.

Three Dimensions of Hypertext Systems

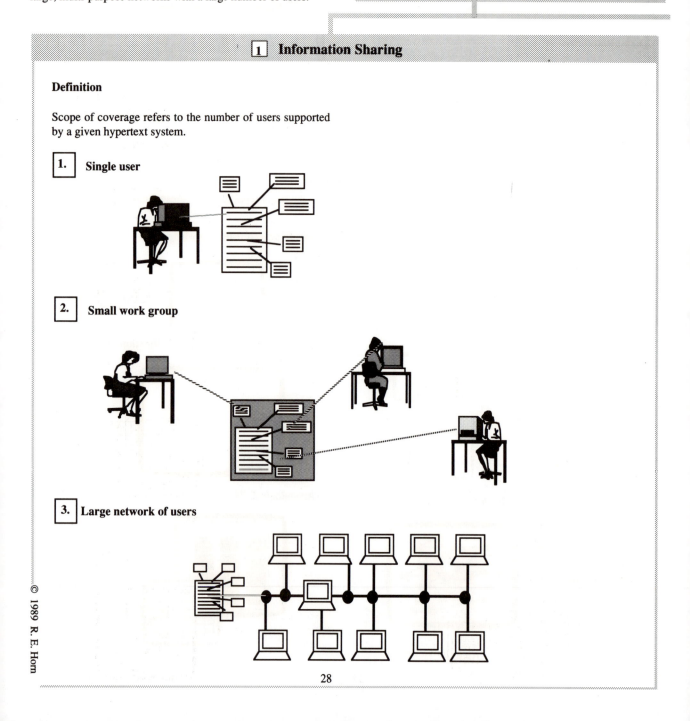

1 Information Sharing

Definition

Scope of coverage refers to the number of users supported by a given hypertext system.

1. Single user

2. Small work group

3. Large network of users

2 Modes

Definition

Modes are different ways of interacting with hypertext.

1. Using Modes   These include browsing, learning, referencing, etc.

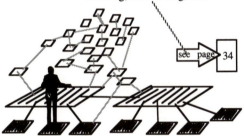

see page 34

2. Authoring Mode

3. Editing Mode

4. Administration Mode

3 Applications

Definition

Scope of software refers to the generality of the hypertext and its applicability to a very limited or larger group of tasks.

1. One specific task (e.g., argumentation analysis)

Argumentation analysis Δ is one way of arranging the sentences to support a rationale or analysis of a disputed point. Systems which handle argumentation analysis are quite task specific.

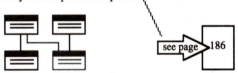

see page 186

2. General purpose hypertext

Many of the current hypertext implementations handle a variety of text and graphics with fixed or variable sized chunking.

3. All the world's literature

Theodor Nelson Δ has suggested that eventually a hypertext system should be built to connect all of the world's literature, so that you could jump from one place to literally any other place.

see page 258

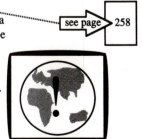

Paper Metaphors for Hypertext Linkages

Introduction

Paper metaphors identify the ideas used on paper that are implemented in different hypertext systems. Usually a specific hypertext software system has a dominant metaphor and may have facilities for other metaphors.

Eight Metaphorical Sources of Hypertext-like Linkages in Paper

---

1 Library Card Catalogs

Example

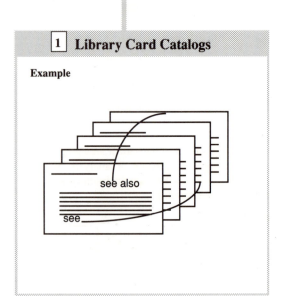

---

2 Footnotes

Explanation

Footnotes are, perhaps, one of the original link types in paper text, used to identify sources of information and to amplify or comment on topics in the main text.

Example

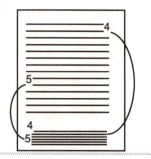

---

5 Commentaries

Definition

Commentaries are extended discussions of one text in another text, usually in parallel fashion.

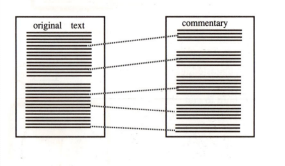

---

6 Indexes

Explanation

Indexes are a kind of linkage system because they enable the reader to go to specific places in the text.

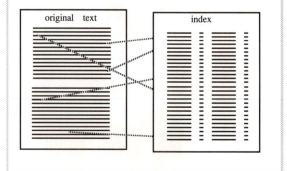

Commentary

Ever since the invention of writing, people have been trying to get their associative links onto paper. Over the ages, we've used quite a few devices to convey these associations. Note on this page how these associations have been integrated into the link and node structure of hypertext quite easily. (REH)

3 Cross - References

Example

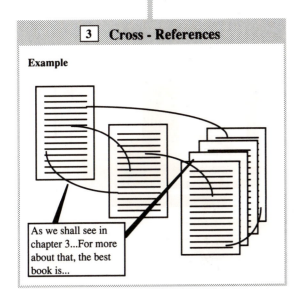

As we shall see in chapter 3...For more about that, the best book is...

4 Sticky Notes

Explanation

Those little yellow stick-ons can be found all over with new information added to original document.

Example

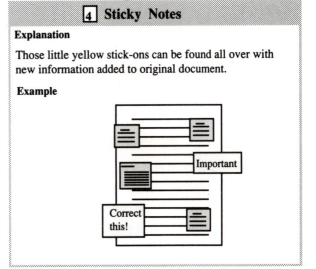

Important

Correct this!

7 Quotes

Explanation

Quoting is a basic kind of linkage in paper, where a part of one text is reproduced in another with a reference back to the original.

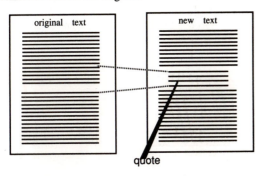

original text

new text

quote

8 Anthologies

Definition

Anthologies are books which are made up of chapters and long quotes from other books. They thus provide a kind of metaphor for hypertext of gathering parts of other books together for some purpose.

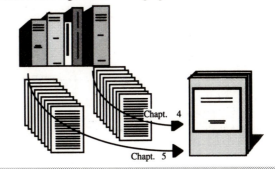

Chapt. 4

Chapt. 5

Computer Metaphors for Hypertext

Description

Computer metaphors have been used in conceptualizing several specific hypertext systems. Usually, but not always, a given hypertext software system has a dominant metaphor and may have facilities for other metaphors.

> **Eight Computer Metaphors Used as Sources for Hypertext Links**

1   Linked Note Cards

Example

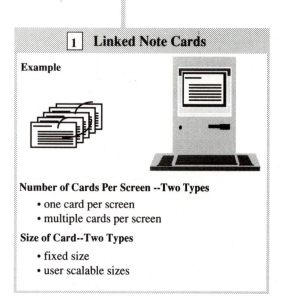

Number of Cards Per Screen --Two Types

- one card per screen
- multiple cards per screen

Size of Card--Two Types

- fixed size
- user scalable sizes

2   Popup Notes

Example

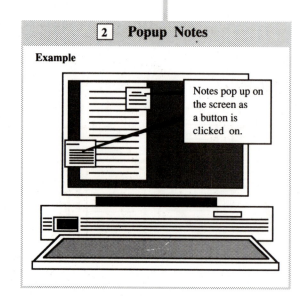

Notes pop up on the screen as a button is clicked on.

5   Semantic Nets

Definition

A semantic net is a knowledge representation method consisting of a network of nodes (which represent concepts) and links (which represent relationships between the nodes).

Example

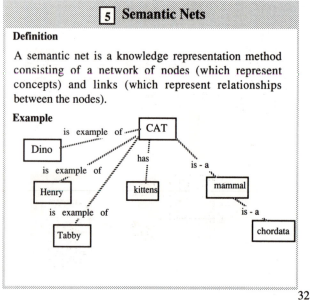

6   Branching Stories

Definition

Branching stories are a genre of fiction, normally presented on computers, that permit the reader to make key choices along the way and hence influence the outcome, plot, or action of the story. They have influenced the design of some hypertext systems.

Example

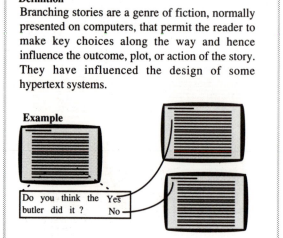

Commentary

One of the intriguing things about hypertext software is how it brings together a number of ideas that have been around quite a while and integrates them into something that has quite different dynamic properties. (REH)

3 Linked Screens or Windows

Example

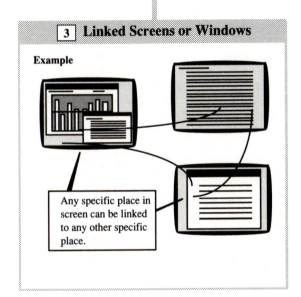

Any specific place in screen can be linked to any other specific place.

4 Stretch Text (Outline)

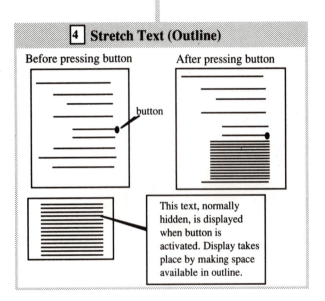

Before pressing button

After pressing button

button

This text, normally hidden, is displayed when button is activated. Display takes place by making space available in outline.

7 Relational Databases

Definition

Relational databases are databases constructed in suchaway that if any 2 files have a common field, then the data base can link these files to other files also sharing common fields, and keep track of these links so that users can find what they are looking for along many different paths.

Example

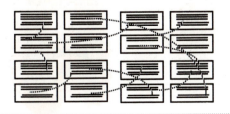

8 Simulations

Definition

Discrete state simulations have the capacity to branch in many different directions and lead to many different outcomes. This property appears in some of the hypertext simulations.

Example

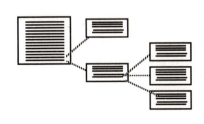

Ways of Using Hypertext

Introduction

Too often, discussions about hypertext fail to identify the purpose the user has for looking at the text. While user surveys are scarce, we can identify a small number of ways that users typically read text. Different ways of using hypertext will call forth the need for different features and produce different problems, as we shall see in the next chapter.

Six Principal Kinds of User Modes

1 Browsing Mode

Description

Browsing is skimming, usually quickly, over large amounts of text to find regions of interest. We distinguish it from referencing, which is the search for very specific information or places known to exist.

Characteristics: Speed / Highlights Only

ZAP !   ZING !   wow

Implication

Browsers need a variety of tools to enable them to see different views of subject matters and documents. They need large scale maps of the subject matter as well as very well defined routes.

Comment

Jan Walker, one of the readers of an early version of this manuscript, wrote: "Thanks to unthinking use, the word 'browse' is too vague to be useful anymore. Anyone trying to read the litrature needs to be alerted to this. The original English-language implications of the term have been drowned in drek. When most implementors say 'browse' they mean nothing more than 'use.'"

2 Training Mode

Introduction

Training covers a fairly wide variety of activities with quite different implications for the design of hypertext.

Description

Training suggests that there are organizational goals for specific accomplishment levels within a specific time.

Implication

Hypertext can be useful in training, but the most important variables will continue to be the setting of goals, the use of practice exercises, and the provision of feedback.

5 Help Mode

Description

Help mode is a special kind of referencing mode that provides (usually) brief amounts of information to aid users of computers to accomplish their current tasks.

Implication

Hypertext can be useful for linking users to glossaries and to other forms including computer-based training.

On-Line Help

Grazing as a Kind of Browsing

Some observers have also described a kind of information grazing where the user simply meanders munching on whatever is nearby. Some think of it as a sort of slow-motion browsing. (REH)

Commentary: Too Much Focus on Browsing?

It appears that sometimes hypertext discussions take place as if browsing were the only important way that human beings interact with text. We probably do browse more in this age of information overload. But hypertext must be able to support many ways of learning, not only browsing. (REH)

3 Briefing (Presentation) Mode

Description

Briefing (or Presentation) Mode is generally not a user directed mode. It is, of course, user chosen in the sense that the user chooses to ask for a briefing. The system presents an overview and summary of the subject, project, organization, sequence of events.

Characteristics: Speed / Highlights Only

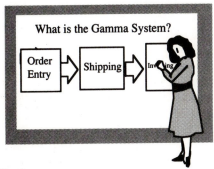

Implication

Building good briefings into each hypertext region is an important value in good hypertext production. A whole separate set of guidelines and standards applies to the design of presentation briefings.

4 Learning and Analysis Mode

Description

The learning and analysis mode is that mode in which users are solving problems or making decisions. They are typically involved in the collection, analysis, and rearranging of information.

Examples

Scholars gathering and rearranging notes for a book or paper; scientists and engineers working on problems.

Characteristics

Users in this mode often have time and inclination to explore alternatives that may be provided by hypertext.

Implication

Hypertext may be of considerable use in this mode, especially in the exploration of different viewpoints, alternatives, and data.

6 Referencing Mode

Description

In the referencing mode, users are focused on trying to retrieve information from the hypertext database in response to a specific question or a specific need. Perhaps they have seen it before. Or they have been told that it exists. Or, knowing the status of the knowledge base, they conjecture that it exists.

Characteristics

Highly focused, fact-oriented. Users are usually looking for a specific place and stop referencing when that information is found.

Implication

This mode relies on more traditional methods of information retrieval, such as indexing, tables of contents, or state-of-the-art reviews, than it does on hypertext linkages.

Chapter 2. Current Issues with Hypertext

Chapter 2
Current Issues with Hypertext

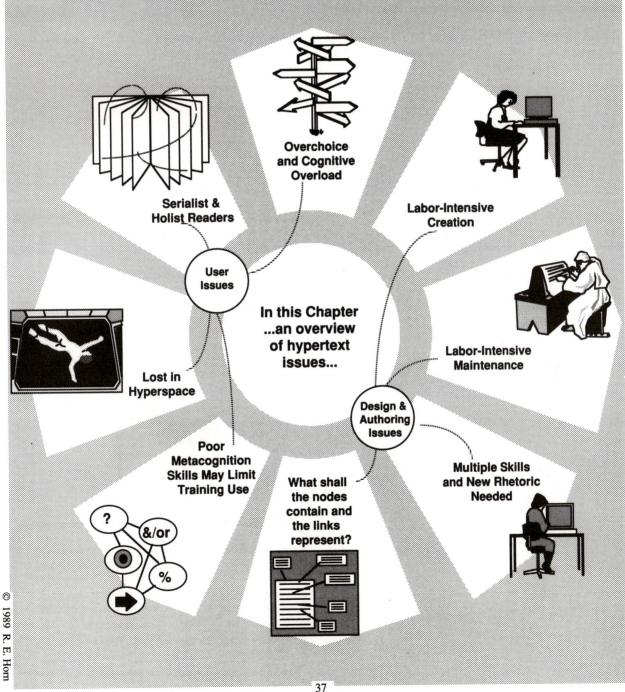

Overchoice and Cognitive Overload

Serialist & Holist Readers

User Issues

Labor-Intensive Creation

Labor-Intensive Maintenance

In this Chapter ...an overview of hypertext issues...

Lost in Hyperspace

Design & Authoring Issues

Poor Metacognition Skills May Limit Training Use

What shall the nodes contain and the links represent?

Multiple Skills and New Rhetoric Needed

? &/or %

Overview of This Chapter

Introduction

Hypertext certainly provides features and advantages that many of us can use in our work and study. But these advantages do not come without their corresponding problems. It is important to sort the big problems from the smaller ones. Many of the smaller ones will go away as hypertext software designers and authors work on upgrades and new systems. But there are some more fundamental problems, those that have to do with the limitations of human information processing capacity. These must be addressed in a more basic and more structured fashion. In this chapter we survey the major issues that have been raised in connection with various hypertext implementations. These two pages present an overview of the rest of the chapter.

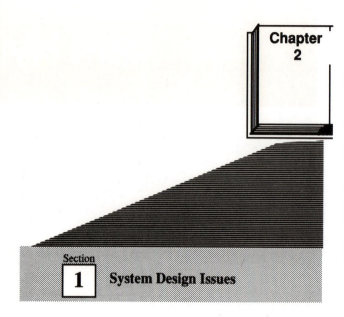

Chapter 2

Section 1 — **System Design Issues**

In this section we point out that the software designer must solve certain very basic issues about text construction:

- What size shall the nodes be and what shall they contain and why?
- What shall the links connect?
- Characteristics of links
- Where to put how many buttons of which kind?

Commentary

All hypertext authors will have to pay attention to these issues as well. We will have to understand our text better and understand better how our users will use on-line hypertext and hypermedia. It's not only a system designer's issue. Recent history is littered with software systems that have been left in the dust because the designers made the wrong decisions about the fundamentals. (REH)

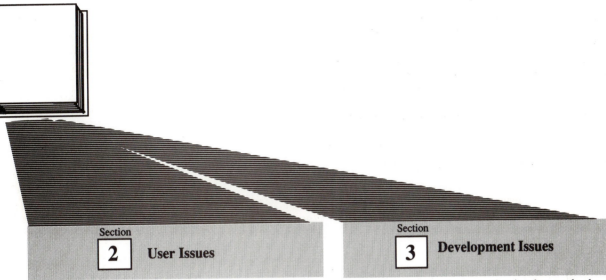

Section

2 **User Issues**

We focus in this section on some of the major problems that have been raised by researchers and users:

- Normal reading cues may be inadequate in hypertext and these are often missing
- Poor metacognition skills may hinder usefulness of hypertext in business training
- Serialist readers may have considerable difficulty when forced to branch
- Readers may become lost in hyperspace
- Users may experience overchoice and cognitive overload
- Chaos in titles for documents and their parts

Commentary

This sections says in another way "buyer beware!" as well as "know thyself." (REH)

Section

3 **Development Issues**

In this section we look at what it takes to do the intellectual work that makes hypermedia and hypertext possible and the knotty problems of organizations or groups of people trying to use hypertext systems:

- Labor-intensive creation
- Labor-intensive database maintenance
- Additional skills needed for hypertext authoring
- Relating hypertext with other on-line documentation and training
- Managing the creation of different versions
- Rewrite or convert to on-line text "as is"

Commentary

The real world uses accounting and you have to pay attention to your costs as well as the benefits you think you will derive. Another real world issue: Once you start making revisions on multiple drafts of a document you get a spaghetti-like tangle of links. "A plate of spaghetti looks the same from every angle," someone has said in the context of hypertext. (REH)

What Shall Be the Size and Contents of Nodes?

Introduction

Many of the problems that we will discuss in this chapter are related to more general questions about nodes, links, and buttons. In this opening discussion we will examine nodes.

Major Questions

The major questions about nodes include:
- What shall the nodes contain?
- What principles shall we use to determine contents of nodes?
- On what basis should size decisions be made?
- Is there any systematic way of determining "natural" divisions of a subject matter that will help us?

Definition: Granularity

Granularity refers to the amount of the information contained in a node relative to the large size of the information. Loosely, it is the "amount of information in a node."

Seven Different "Sizes" of Nodes (as they appear to a user)

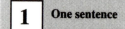 **1** | One sentence

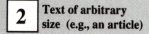 **2** | Text of arbitrary size (e.g., an article)

3 | Index card size

4 | The size of the screen

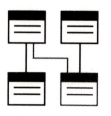

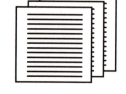

Description

Some experimental hypertext systems enable authors and users to use single sentences as nodes.

Example

In Chapter 7, we present a description of argumentation analysis which is based on sentence node size.

see page 186

Description

Some hypertext systems have been built that enable authors and users to insert nodes at any point in text. The typical size of the node follows current practice in document composition, i.e., chapters, articles, paragraphs, etc.

Description

Some hypertext systems have used the fixed index card as the size of the node.

Description

Some hypertext systems have used the entire screen as the definition of the size of the node.

> **Commentary**
>
> In many cases the fixed card size should be avoided. Far better is some form of scrolling that permits chunk sizes that can more fully cover sufficiently large thought patterns. (REH)

Commentary

While I call these system design issues, these are issues that software purchasers have to pay attention to as well, because they need to get the maximum flexibility and usefulness from their systems. (REH)

Commentary

Point of View

Each piece of hypertext software has to incorporate some way of indicating nodes - independent of other aspects such as the interface. Since the focus of this book is on how the hypertext appears to the user, we present a classification of these views below.

5 Scroll of any length	**6** Variable size	**7** Variably sized, precisely and flexibly chunked

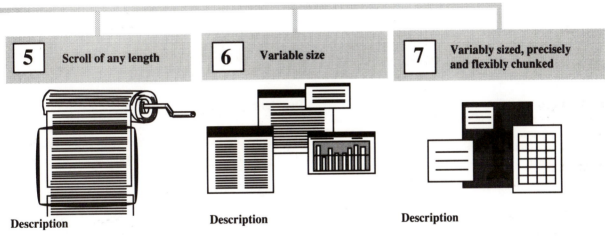

Description

Some hypertext systems permit the screen to scroll a sizable amount, sometimes up to chapter size, yet allow the insertion of buttons for links at any place in the text.

Description

Some hypertext systems have flexibly sized chunks that correspond to the individual author's view of the "size" of the subject matter. This permits virtually any size (or shape) of display.

Description

It is possible to devise a methodology to segment subject matter into variably sized chunks that also provide the user and the author with a *systematic* way of chunking the subject matter. It would then be useful to have a hypertext system that "understood" this chunking methodology and would provide such facilities for both author and user.

Commentary: Our Bias

Precise yet variably sized blocks is the bias of this book, as the reader will see in Chapter 3 when we explain Information Mapping's method of structured writing. (REH)

see page 84

What Shall the Links Connect?

Introduction

Hypertext software creates links between the nodes rapidly and conveniently. But if the author and user can link anything to anything, what is to stop them from "over-linking" or "mis-linking" to the ultimate confusion of everyone? The question about "which links?" is a significant one.

Major Questions

The major questions about links are:
- Which kinds of links to implement?
- How many links should one use?
- How can we implement different hyperlinkage networks of the same node?
- How shall the links be represented?
(This question is an interface issue which we take up under the heading of buttons. Δ)

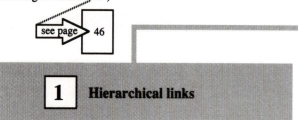

see page 46

Four Kinds of Links
(from the user's standpoint)

1 Hierarchical links

2 Keyword links

Description

Organizational links implement hierarchical tree linkages within the hypertext network. Terms are parent, child, sibling. Organizational links include tables of contents and other such hierarchical structuring.

Description

Keyword links are links created by the system and permit the users to find the location of specific words in the text. They aid in search for strings of information.

Example

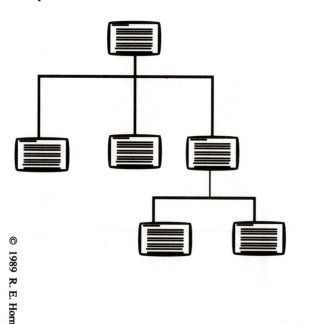

Example

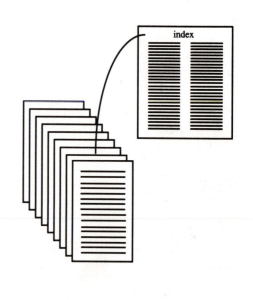

3 Referential links

Description

Referential links connect points or regions of text and are non-hierarchical. In the terminology of some in the field, referential links go from link source to link destination.

Link source is also called a *link point* or a *link icon.*

Destination is also called a *link region.*

Example

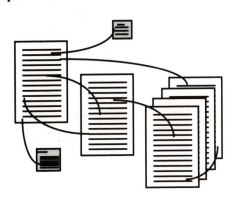

4 Cluster links

Description

Cluster links are links that enable a user to organize a group of shorter pieces of information as they proceed through the project.

They may resemble file boxes, groups of notes and the like.

Example

Characteristics of Links

Introduction

In hypertext systems, the designer of the system must consider a number of issues, such as, whether you can get back to where you jumped off from, the kinds of links permitted, the value of particular links, and the size of the node to which the links are made.

Two Fundamental Issues With Links

1 Directionality of Links

Two Types of Link Directionality

A One-way Directionality

Definition

A one-way link will take the user in one direction after pushing a button and will leave the user there. Users will not be able to return to the original button from which they came.

Example

A button which goes to another place in the text but does not return.

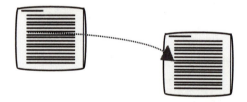

B Two-way Directionality

Definition

A two-way link enables users to go to another place and return.

Example

A button which has a comment on it and then goes back to the main text.

Problems

A major interface design issue is to show which kind of button you have.

A Category Filter

Definition

In this type of filter, the user would pick a category from a list provided and the software would follow links associated with that category.

Example

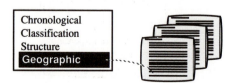

Chronological
Classification
Structure
Geographic

B Voting Filter

Definition

In this type of proposed filter, the system keeps track of user choices and asks for an evaluation after the user has used a link to establish over time some kind of priority for linking.

Most traveled links
click here △

2   Multiplicity of Links

Problem Statement

Some systems which have been proposed would conceivably have a large number of links that different people have attached to a single point in a given text. It is possible that everybody would want to comment and link. For users, this would produce a bewildering array of choices.

Proposed Solution

One proposed solution is to have a dynamic filtering system selectively displaying links.

Definition

A filter is a user controlled software feature that selects and displays some, but not all, of the links at a given node.

Four Types of Proposed Filters

C   Expert Filter

Definition

Authorities on a particular subject would examine a given area of the hypertext and provide a series of links that would give the reader a path to follow.

```
Choose your expert
trail:
Δ Nelson
Δ Sculley
Δ Atkinson
```

D   Menu of Links

Definition

Menu links would provide users with a dynamically constructed display of links available when a particular button is activated.

```
Available Links:
Δ Experts (3)
Δ Standard Hypertrails
Δ Glossary
```

Where to Put How Many Buttons of Which Kind?

Introduction

A third major question area is the button. In principle, you can sprinkle them around anywhere in the text and any place on the rest of the screen. But that raises a whole series of questions described on these pages.

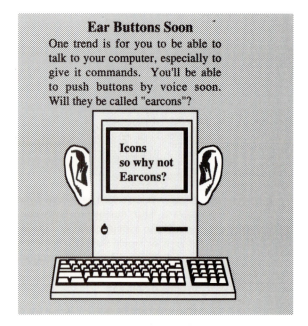

Ear Buttons Soon

One trend is for you to be able to talk to your computer, especially to give it commands. You'll be able to push buttons by voice soon. Will they be called "earcons"?

Icons
so why not
Earcons?

| **1** | **User Issue: How to Spot the Button** |

How do you tell where an "activated area" (i.e., a button) is on a screen, particularly in the graphic areas? Putting in the game of "hide and seek" for the buttons is of some limited use in playful hypertexts, but not in those for serious purposes.

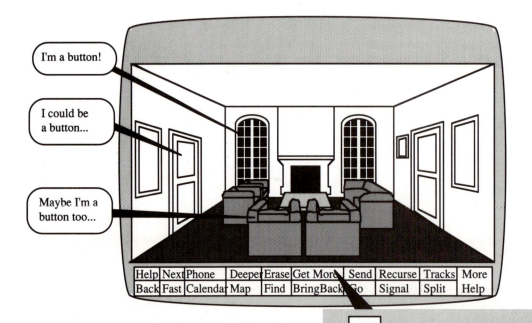

I'm a button!

I could be a button...

Maybe I'm a button too...

| Help | Next | Phone | | Deeper | Erase | Get More | | Send | Recurse | | Tracks | More |
| Back | Fast | Calendar | Map | | Find | BringBack | Go | Signal | | Split | Help |

| **2** | **User Issue: Button Clutter** |

The button clutter problem is the one of too many buttons scattered aimlessly or packed densely on a screen, forcing users to study their choices on each screen with considerable diligence. Already in some systems we see a confusing array of choices that begin to look like this.

3   The User's Question: Can I Trust This Button?

Where does it lead?   What happens when I push it?   Where will it take me?   What will be the nature of the text when I get there?   Will it meet my needs?   Will I just get lost in a mish-mash of confusing buttons and screens and links and not be able to get back here?   Another wild goose chase... another fishing expedition.   Maybe I shouldn't even push this button at all...

4   Interface Designer's Question: How Can I Possibly Know What This User (or Any User) Wants?

How can I tell what the user wants?
- The screen next in prerequisite order?
- The screen(s) previous in prerequisite order?
- A definition only?
- An example?
- Both a definition and example?
- Something opposite?
- A menu of choices?

5   User Issue: Seductive Buttons

Writers work hard at what they do. Quite naturally they want to have their words read by somebody. Designers want people to use all of their system features -- often whether the user needs them or not. Sometimes designers go beyond what is necessary to seduce the user to follow a particular path. We need some sort of "truth in button advertising" law.

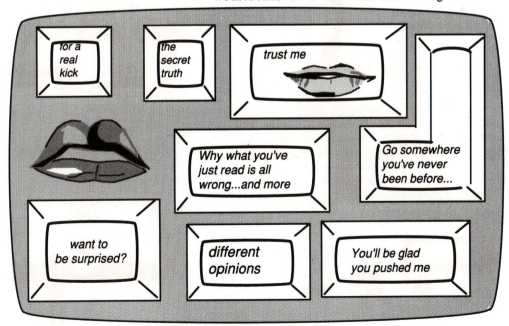

47

Inadequate (and Missing) Reading Cues

Introduction

Hypertext -- especially unstructured hypertext -- may run into difficulties by the very nature of its linking and branching facilities. These remove some of the discourse cues that provide readers -- particularly initial learners of a subject -- with information essential for making learning efficient and effective.

Definition: Discourse Cues

Discourse cues are different elements of text that give readers orientation information to guide the process of reading.

Discourse Cues That Hypertext Destroys or Disrupts

Some of the discourse cues that hypertext may destroy or disrupt are:

1   Hierarchical Text Organization

When we read, research suggests that we tend to build an hierarchical framework for ideas. Many discourse cues, such as outlines, patterns of subheadings, words such as "initially, next, finally, firstly," etc. provide cohesiveness and may also provide cues as to where in the author's hierarchy, the reader is. These aid reading and may be unused or meaningless if the reader jumps across links that leave them dangling out on the furthest limb of some hierarchical structure.

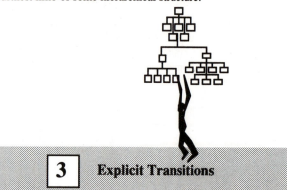

2   Overviews, Introductions, Summaries

Authors are taught to prepare readers for what is coming up in text by providing overviews and introductions that summarize or preview the content and structure of the document. Traveling across links may cause users to miss these transitional remarks or to fail to find them easily.

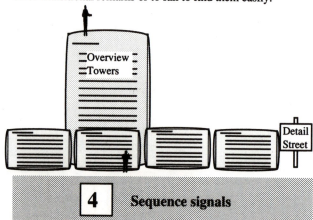

3   Explicit Transitions

Most authors alert readers to transitions. Readers expect to have transitions made explicit. These transition words such as "however, moreover, then, when, more importantly, etc." often refer back to previous text structure. When they are absent or when they refer back to someplace readers have not visited (because they arrived here by a link), they experience a jarring sense of disorientation or a feeling of being lost.

4   Sequence signals

Text contains signals about local organization such as "There are seven kinds of..." Readers arriving from links in the middle of such text structures must do extra work to take advantage of the cues they provide. It would be very helpful to have an "overview button" or some other kind of structure cues.

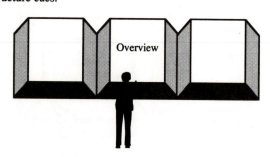

Commentary

Any author reading this will begin to draw conclusions about how to write and, perhaps most importantly, where **not** to put links.

---

5 Contrast and Similarity Cues

Introducing new concepts frequently requires the distinguishing of the current idea from other ideas. Conventional text provides cues to the reader that this is about to take place (or is taking place). Hypertext may leave the reader puzzled as to what these cues refer to if the reader has just arrived via some link.

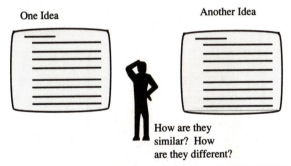

6 Metaphors

The extended metaphor running through pages of text can be a useful text organizer. It is of less use if readers arrive in the middle of the text from some other link.

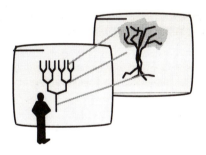

7 Pronouns as Cohesiveness Cues

One of the ways that conventional text provides cohesiveness is through the use of pronouns which refer back to material that the reader is assumed to have read because linear reading is assumed. Authors of hypertext may not be able to make that assumption.

8 Content Schemas

There are different conventional schemas for organizing text (e.g., narratives). Discourse cues such as "once upon a time..." or "she looked deeply into his eyes" tell us that a fairy story or a love story follows. These may be less meaningful in hypertext that is heavily laced with links.

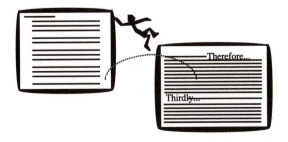

Special Provisions for Common Reader Behavior

Introduction

How do novice readers approach the task of learning from text? Are there important patterns in the behavior of average readers that may affect how hypertext is written?

Novice Readers

Some research suggests that a significant number of readers who are novices in a subject matter exhibit the following behavior:

1 Novice readers may stop reading too soon.

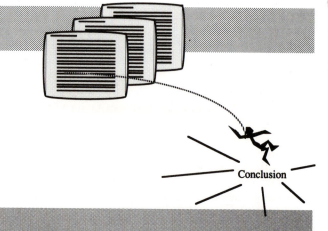

Many who are new to a subject matter may think they understand a subject before they have read all they should. They jump to premature conclusions.

2 Novice readers are often misled by superficial features of the subject matter.

Readers new to a field may be unable to tell the important from the less important, either undervaluing or overvaluing particular passages.

Nothing important here...

It all looks important to me...

3 Novice readers rarely seek non-contiguous information.

Novices to a subject matter rarely are observed to go to another page to look at the diagram when the text says "See diagram number ... "

see diagram next screen

Research on Reading Gives Insights on How Average Readers Behave

Recent research on reading suggests these generalizations about how many readers go about the task of reading:

1 **Readers usually construct hierarchical representations.**

Readers build within their minds representations that often have a hierarchical structure whether or not that structure is present in the text.

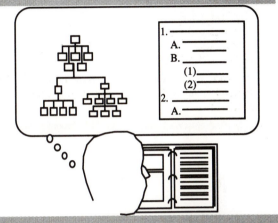

2 **Readers usually remember the top level information better.**

When tested later, readers tend to remember the information in the higher levels of the hierarchies better than lower level information.

3 **Readers depend on repetition of key words.**

Readers tend to use the words that are repeated in successive sentences to build their meanings.

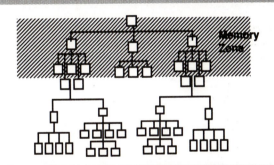

Branching Difficulties of Serialist Readers

Introduction

Research by Pask and Scott has shown some interesting results on how different kinds of people learn. They find two basic learning strategies which they designate serialist and holist. They find that serialists and holists are quite different in their characteristics and in their approach to text. Pask and Scott found that about 50% of readers fall into each of the categories of holist and serialist.

see → Notes

---

1 Serialist Learners

Definition

Serialist learners proceed through learning tasks starting from the beginning and taking each task in turn. They will fulfill all prerequisites necessary at one level in order before starting the next level.

How a Serialist Reads

Serialists almost always start a book on page one of chapter one and start reading at the upper left hand corner and proceed sentence by sentence. They often will not go to the next sentence until they have fully understood the sentence they are currently reading.

1....2....3....4....5....6....7....

---

2 Holist Learners

Definition

Holist learners like to understand the big picture before getting to the details. So they may try hard exercises before they are prepared to solve them. They skip around in learning, trying out what interests them, making their own survey and connections or they may read the author provided overviews and then decide where to dip in.

How a Holist Reads

Holists almost always open a book in the middle and jump around, scanning, forming impressions.

1. ═══
5...
6...
7
4.
2.
3.

Path of the Serialist Reader

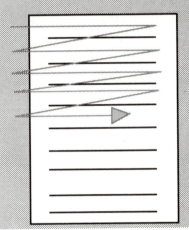

Implications for Hypertext

Serialists will have some difficulty with hypertext. They will resent the forced choices. Traveling to new links they will be thrown into confusion and disorientation much more easily than holists. They may not use links nearly as much and as a result may not be able to take full advantage of the system. They will resent the introduction of words and concepts they don't understand. They will not accept large "conceptual maps" of the subject matter because they contain terms they don't understand. They will benefit from the definition links more than holists because they will be able to satisfy their need for certainty about the meaning of unfamiliar terms.

Path of the Holist Reader

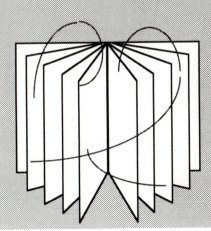

Implications for Hypertext

Holists will love hypertext. Its browsing capabilities are perfectly matched to the natural inclinations of holists.

Poor Metacognition Skills May Limit Training Uses

Definition: Metacognition

Metacognition can be defined as persons' "knowledge about their own cognitive processes and their ability to control these processes by organizing, monitoring, and modifying them as a function of learning outcomes." (Weinstein and Mayer, 1986) In other words, metacognition refers in part to those skills that have been called "study skills" and "learning how to learn."

Applying this definition to learning tasks "metacognition refers to an individual's ability to accurately determine the goal of a given task, apply appropriate strategies to reach the goal, monitor progress towards the goal, and adjust strategies as necessary." (Clark, 1988)

Implications

It is clear from looking at this model that every learner brings to the learning task a more or less complex set of metacognition behaviors. It is certainly possible to observe a wide range of variability among learners. Learners with poor metacognitive skills are unlikely to be able to make the choices involved in self-instruction that are required by hypertext and are likely to be among the chief sufferers of problems of cognitive overload and "lost in hyperspace."

It is possible that hypertext environments specifically structured in particular ways may help learners with poor metacognition skills improve these skills. This, in particular the ability of hypertext to rapidly reward such things as exploration and curiosity and the ability to put together topics of different kinds, may improve metacognition skills. On the other hand, some kinds of hypertexts and interfaces could really interfere with organization and consolidation.

Determine Learning Objectives

Ability to set realistic learning objectives.

Manage Time in Learning

Ability to realistically determine how long various tasks will take to learn.

Understand Sequence

Ability to sequence learning goals effectively.

Determine Prerequisites

Ability to determine prerequisites required to learn a specific set of task of knowledge items.

Use Learning Resources

Ability to determine when to use the instructor or other experts effectively as a resource.

Self-Monitoring Skills

Ability to monitor progress towards achieving goals with reasonable accuracy.

Kinds of Skills Generally Included in the Concept of Metacognition

General Learning Skills

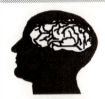 Ability to determine when, where, and how to put something into long term memory.

 Ability to read, to take notes, practice, review, take self tests, check feedback, in order to make remembering efficient and effective.

 Ability to scan rapidly to make decisions about whether to commit something to long term memory.

 Ability to determine whether outside evaluation is necessary to determine level of accomplishment.

 Ability to devise and use mnemonics and visualization to memorize.

 Ability to paraphrase, summarize, and abstract information.

Metacognitive Tactics

 Ability to organize learning tasks into manageable chunks. Ability to choose which of these tactics to use in specific situations.

Organizational Techniques

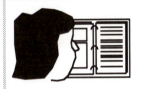 Ability to reorganize new information in integrating it with what is already known.

 Ability to draw appropriate diagrams to show relationships among concepts, processes and other ideas.

 Ability to adequately use categorization techniques to break down information and learning tasks into manageable subunits.

Memory Consolidation Techniques

 Ability to insure knowledge is integrated into current understanding of a field of study or inquiry.

 Ability to add own questions and comments of the material to integrate it with current knowledge.

 Ability to create more visual or more personal examples of purely abstract or verbal information in order to retain it in long term memory.

Ability to use metaphors and analogies to link what the reader knows to the new material as well as to move beyond the new material.

Motivational Awareness

 Ability to monitor motivation in learning so as to conduct learning under the best circumstances possible.

Lost in Hyperspace

Introduction

In some of the early hypertext systems users frequently reported that they had the problems of knowing

- Where am I?
- Where have I been?
- Where am I going?
- What are my options?

These together are also known as the "context" or "lost in hyperspace" problem. Hypertext authors and designers often responded with "solutions" that merely compounded the problems.

"Solutions" that haven't solved the fundamental problem

1	**Show them all of the connections**

If the reader is lost, some hypertext systems have been built that show all of the connections to a particular piece of text (card, window, article).

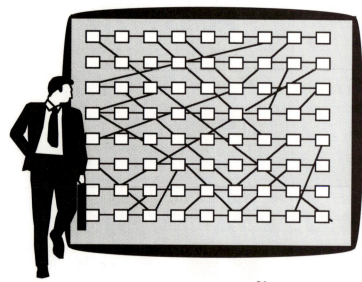

"Solutions" that haven't solved the fundamental problem

2   Go back to where they've started

If readers are lost, some hypertext systems take them back to where they've started. That works sometimes but wastes a lot of the user's time.

"Solutions" that haven't solved the fundamental problem

3   Show them where they've been

When readers are lost, some hypertext systems have facilities that show them the path they have followed or enable them to flip through the screens they've just seen. This works sometimes, but often avoids the fundamental problem of what the structure of the subject matter is.

Overchoice & Cognitive Overload

Introduction

In the experimental hypertext systems of the late 1980's, readers frequently report being overwhelmed by too much information and being constantly bombarded by overchoice. They were presented with more links than they needed for their purposes and found themselves wasting time with a great deal of extraneous information.

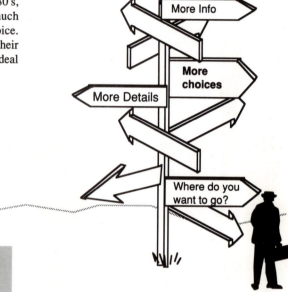

1   Overwhelmed by Windows

In some windowing systems the reader can pile up many windows until the screen looks like a messy desktop. That tends to look like this....

2   Overwhelmed by Nodes and Links

Some card-based or screen-based systems can only display one small bit of information at a time. Users have great difficulty determining just where they are in the overall context of the topic they are browsing or learning. Many users in many jobs and learning situations can't handle and shouldn't have to handle a lot of linkage choices.

3   Overwhelmed by Endless Scrolls

In some large on-line text systems, the dominant metaphor is the scroll, with few markers to tell you where you are or where you are going. It is easy to get lost and it takes considerable mental effort to keep going under these circumstances.

Chaos in Titles for Documents and TheirParts

Introduction

One of the major causes of wasted time in scanning documents is the failure of authors to consider user needs when they provide titles for documents and provide subtitles. People like to create cute, idiosyncratic, short, often cryptic names for files. This is the opposite of what is needed for rapid, easy browsing. How will we be able to prevent the building of millions of electronic Towers of Babel? To illustrate the problem, consider two simple tables of contents for a training manual below.

Compare this table of contents...

...with this table of contents...

Table of Contents for the Best Little Tool You'll Ever Use

1. Starting to Work

2. Getting It Going

3. Making It Work in the Long Run

4. Help

5. Finding Mistakes

6. When Nothing Goes Right

7. Anybody Can Run It

8. Happiness is a Tool Like This

Table of Contents for the Training Manual for the Model 501KX Network Integrator

1. Setting Up the Equipment

2. On-site Testing and Initial Operation

3. Putting the 501KX into the Network

4. Troubleshooting the 501KX

5. What to Do When Local Troubleshooting Does Not Work

6. Preventive Maintenance for the 501KX

7. Operating the Network Integrator

8. Specifications for the 501KX

From which table of contents would it be easier to locate what you are looking for?

Commentary: Multiple Representational Ecologies

Chris Dede has warned that hypertext must face and solve the problem of different people using quite different clusters of terms for roughly the same phenomena. He calls this the dilemma of "multiple representational ecologies." I call it naming chaos. Hmmm. (REH)

Commentary: Label Standards

For the reasons spelled out on these pages, guidelines and standards for labeling have been a part of Information Mapping's method from its inception. They are relevant as much to paper as hypertext. (REH)

see page 93

The major question is how will we get people to feel as obsessive about putting fully informative titles on their documents as they are about finding spelling errors?

Compare the Titles in These Two Files

File 1
Plan for the Human Resource Handbook
Handbook First Draft
Employee Task Force Comments
Specific Rebuttals to the Task Force Comments
Legal Department Comments

File 2
Plan
First Cut
Reactions
Betty's Remarks
Comments on Comments

Which is more informative?

The Seven Commandments for Titling Thy Documents and Their Parts

1. Thou shalt name thy documents neither too general nor too specific, neither too long nor too short.

2. Thou shalt use the language we all use unless thy document is only for a technical or special audience.

3. Thou shalt itemize all thy possible readers and consider whether each shall be able to understand thy titles and thine other subtitles and labels.

4. Thou shalt not surrender to the adolescent urge to label with cuteness or silliness, for the rest of us might suffer at not getting thy joke.

5. Thou shalt not put the rest of us through the hell of vague, mislabeled documents lest thou be thrown into that hell thyself for an eternity.

6. Thou shalt honor thy peers, thy boss and thy subordinates and all the sentient beings that may have to browse thy writing by providing them with well considered titles.

7. Thou shalt use the same words in the table of contents, the titles, on the pages, and in references within the text.

Labor-Intensive Creation

Introduction

Text is created by people sitting at workstations and writing. The intellectual labors of creating hypertext are no different. But in some ways, hypertext adds to the time required for creation.

| 1 | **Additional Text Preparation for Nodes** |

Description

For hypertext that is prepared in advance for learners and referencers, all of the major textual information has to be developed. This is a labor-intensive project even without any hypertext requirements. Just to write a competent training manual, good report or good technical documentation requires training, methodology, management, and a lot of effort. The requirements for such projects usually limit the effort to "need to know" information. Every jump, comment, or branch in a hypertext database must go somewhere and presumably text must be there if someone jumps or browses to that place.

Adding possible hypertext requirements of analyzing additional "nice to know" or "nice to browse" information can add a considerable cost to the information gathering, organization and writing phases of projects.

Implication

For most projects in business and industry, it is unlikely that much additional writing will be done. Efficiency and "need to know" criteria will prevail.

| 2 | **Additional Work to Create Linkages** |

Description

Hypertext software has made the creation of buttons and links rather automated, although we would say that it is not "highly automated." At present, many links must be decided upon and created by hand.

Implication

Adding links has many implications both for the user and for the maintainer of the hypertext network. Primarily, they add cost. The strategy of cost benefits decision-making is yet to be worked out in any general way. Research on automating link creation is only in its infancy. The problem may perhaps never be completely solved by wholesale or generic strategies.

3 Additional Quality Control Requirements

Description

Links and nodes must be correct and sensible, especially if large numbers of people in your organization are going to use them. If the nodes don't give users the information they want and if links don't get them there efficiently, users will stop using the hypertext system.

Implication

Quality control will become more important than ever in the construction of text.

4 Greater Need for Standards When Groups Author a Document

Description

When several people in a work group or task force work on preparing a document, editorial tasks increase. The group has to develop agreements that function as standards for style, format, organization, level of detail, and many other criteria. This is rarely easy, not only because of the requirements of a high level of cooperation and planning skills, but also because the intellectual tasks of conceptualizing a large network of writing is difficult. Somebody must understand the whole structure before writing, and the whole team must have a common language and a common understanding of the structure of the project.

Implication

Hypertext increases the demands upon these skills and will require carefully planned systems of standards that are managed in a disciplined way to provide useful publications.

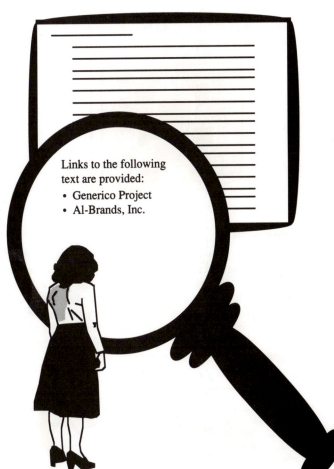

Links to the following text are provided:
- Generico Project
- Al-Brands, Inc.

Labor-Intensive Database Maintenance

Introduction

Not only does hypertext make larger demands in the text development phase, but it also increases many of the time, cost and quality requirements for the maintenance of the database after it is in operation.

| 1 | **Bigger Job of Routine Updating** |

| 2 | **Additional Editing for Quality of Updates and Comments** |

Description

Information goes out of date. New facts are discovered. Concepts are revised. Classifications are expanded to encompass new specimens. Whole views of subjects are turned on end by new technology and new ideas. All of this takes routine updating of the hypertext knowledge base. Companies specifically select projects that need constant updating for hypertext because updating is so difficult to do with paper. But putting the manual in a computer will not eliminate the cost of updating. As of now, there are only a few software aids to help in this process.

Implication

Such routine updating of hypertext files will have to be carried on. It will be a labor-intensive job.   The more branches and links that are connected to a node, the more labor it will require to keep the knowledge base current.

Description

Most print-oriented information sharing networks have institutionalized such jobs as newsletter editor that help the members of the network maintain some semblance of order and quality to the information they receive. Those networks that do not have this, exhibit the worst qualities of bulletin boards on many college campuses and corporate hallways where layer upon layer of old lecture notices compete with important announcements.

Implication

For personal networks, mild chaos will prevail.   For institutional networks, analogues from paper-based systems will be there. We will have editors, but their jobs will be more difficult because of the difficulties of overchoice. A few researchers have suggested that the job of network hygiene or network maintenance be automated or that some kind of "automated filters" be developed to help people navigate a crowded network of dubious quality.

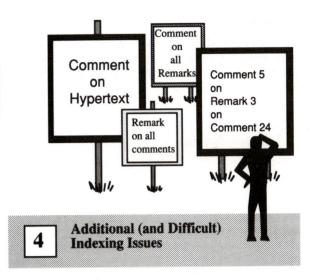

3   Additional Pruning and Filtering Links

Description

With the possibility of more links and nodes come the problems of rampant growth. One can imagine metaphors of the growth of weeds in untended lawns or of the jungle reclaiming the carefully cleared villages.

Every link will demand an answer to the question: "Shall we leave it in or take it out?" We will need to understand the value of each link (i.e., make an assessment of its costs and benefits).

Implication

The cost-benefits of links will become a minor new branch of economics, with the focus on the cost of intellectual labor in creation, maintenance, and use of links. Many have pointed out that time is becoming one of our most valuable resources. This implies that economists will have to examine the opportunity costs of actually following many branches. The cost of traveling in hyperspace is partially the cost of not being somewhere interesting. Hyperspace traveling is not free. In terms of the high cost of professional labor, we may see demands for superhighways. Toll booths will certainly follow.

4   Additional (and Difficult) Indexing Issues

Description

Indexing has taken large strides with the development of automatic indexing software. We are now able to get around quite usefully -- but by no means easily without professional help -- in large bibliographic databases such as Lexis, Nexis, and Dialog. And the indexing of large textual documents with full text searches is a routine if not really widespread facility.

The indexer's difficulty is the creative communicator's delight. You can describe the same event or thing with many different words. You can even create new terms for the same old things. But how do you find your way back to terms you were working with last year and have forgotten?

Implication

We will have to build automatic indexers that can incorporate new documents as they are created and integrate these into larger search strategies that are somehow constrained so that the search space doesn't become too large. This will not be an easy task if hypertext databases grow as rapidly as it now appears.

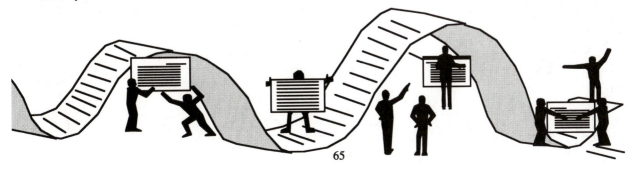

Additional Skills Needed for Hypertext Authoring

Introduction

"Authoring" in hypertext is different from ordinary writing. Developing hypertext and hypermedia will require considerable additional skills. These pages suggest some of those skills.

1	**Knowledge Base Management Skills**

2	**Hypertext Rhetoric & Analysis Skills**

Description

Knowledge base management skills include a knowledge of the theories included in this book about the organization of knowledge and a practical working knowledge of how hypertext systems work.

Description

Hypertext rhetoric and analysis skills include a working fluency in developing structured analysis and writing. It also involves understanding how to prepare special parts of hypertext knowledge bases that help readers connect widely separated and perhaps loosely connected meanings.

List of Skills and Knowledge

Some of the skills needed, in varying degrees, are:

- Planning databases
- User analysis
- Instructional design (in some applications)
- Hardware and software knowledge
- Network knowledge
- Knowledge of database construction.

List of Skills and Knowledge

Some of the skills needed are:

- Awareness of the limits that hypertext places on writing done in large chunks
- Understanding how to integrate effective visuals with text
- Understanding of most of the skills taught in the Information Mapping® seminars Δ
- Knowledge of how to create and use hypertrail structures Δ

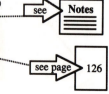

see Notes

see page 126

3 — Interface Design & Human Factors Skills

4 — Graphics Skills

Description

Hypertext implementations will provide great flexibility to the user to create and modify human interfaces. Already we have seen problems arising from the lack of knowledge about human factors in interface design.

Description

Systems will have provisions for highly graphic communication. Users will begin to expect more than just text. The writer or team that produces hypermedia will need to have considerable graphic skills.

List of Skills and Knowledge

Some of the skills needed are:

- Ability to use results of human factors research that influence effective communication to design effective screens
- Ability to apply the same research to the design of links and larger subject matter organizations.

List of Skills and Knowledge

Some of the skills needed are:

- Knowledge of aesthetic guidelines for use of color
- Recommendations for effective use of typefaces
- Ability to integrate graphics with text
- Ability to create simple visuals and specify more complex ones.

Relating to Other On-Line Documents and Training

Introduction

Who will use the knowledge base and for what purposes? That is the basic question organizations planning the conversion of large amounts of paper-based text to on-line storage have to ask. Not all software meets every need. How does hypertext relate to these different types of software products? On these pages we present a description of the four major kinds of on-line text and describe some of the problems and possibilities that hypertext will provide for each.

 Full Text Search

Definition

Full text search of computer-stored documents is software that examines every single word of a document and prepares an index either prior to the search or as part of the search. The result of using such systems is that the computer provides a list of all the places where specific words or groups of words are found in the text. The user may then examine one or more of the specific places in the text where the word appears.

Advantages

The major advantage of this kind of search is its completeness. Users who must find every appearance of a term, find this facility essential. Another major advantage is that you can transfer existing paper documentation to on-line search without extensive rework, important in some applications (such as legal cases) where you cannot justify extensive rewrite (or in paper evidence in legal cases where no rewrite is needed).

Disadvantages

Full text search also calls for relatively sophisticated search strategy skills. The disadvantage of full text search is that users may receive, very often, a larger list of places to look than they may want. Moreover, users often don't know all of the words to search for and can never feel assured that they've found everything.

Relation to Hypertext

Full text search facilities would be important in hypertext environments but are no substitute for the linking of hypertext. It is the thesis of this book that structured hypertext will be the most important form of hypertext and that, for particular purposes, full text search will be important. Indexes of most documents will continue to be essential research devices.

2 Computer-Based Training

Definition

Computer-based training software is software that is designed to give learners specific performance situations and exercises in which they can practice the new skills and knowledge presented in the course using the computer. The computer also provides feedback on the outcome of their answers to the exercises.

Advantages

An advantage to computer-based training systems is that they provide carefully designed lessons that insure that if the learners do the exercises they will be able to use and apply the new skills and knowledge rather than simply "know about" them. The computer also tracks the success of the student, provides feedback, and flexibly inserts branching for more practice or for review.

Disadvantages

Many current computer-based learning systems do not provide for rapid browsing for better prepared students.

Relation to Hypertext

 see page 126

Computer-based training software will benefit from hypertext links, particularly for glossaries of specific terms that the learner may not know or may have forgotten. In the future, hypertrails Δ, such as those described in this book, will be inserted in the computer-based training courses for more flexible learner-controlled exploration of the knowledge base. Also, on-line hypertext systems will give CBT learners a reference manual that can be used with the system they're learning about, which is one of the major problems with current CBT implementations.

3 | On-Line Help Messages

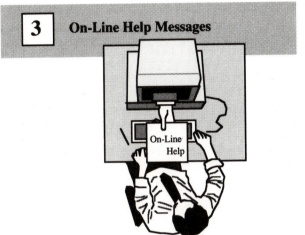

Definition

On-line help messages are components of an increasing number of software packages which provide users with instantaneous access to information that will help them in doing whatever task the software has been written for.

Advantage

On-line help messages are increasingly regarded as the primary kind of documentation supplied with computer software because they are much more frequently referred to than is the paper documentation.

Disadvantages

On-line help messages are by their nature quite short and in most systems do not link users to more extended learning situations.

Relation to Hypertext

Hypertext linkages and buttons will get users to follow a trail to on-line help to computer-based instruction courses.

```
═══════ Commentary ═══════
One of the reasons that much paper and on-line
documentation is not used is because they are
incomplete and badly written, a topic we take up in the
next chapter. (REH)
```

4 | Search Large Databases With Keywords or "Controlled Vocabulary"

Definition

On-line structured databases, such as those containing large numbers of bibliographic entries and abstracts, provide users with the ability to find up-to-date information on a variety of sources. They are called structured not only because each item is quite similar in form, but also because the index terms used to index the database are controlled by a thesaurus which generally aids search strategies.

Advantages

The advantages of the structured databases are that the reader has excellent navigational control over what to expect of the data and also has good navigational control over the vocabulary search.

Disadvantages

To find items in such massive databases requires professional skills of an on-line search specialist, although the ordinary lay person or scientist can learn these search skills.

Relation to Hypertext

These databases show the advantages of structure in writing and in search methodologies. They give greater precision and efficiency in the search.

Managing the Creation of Different Versions

Introduction

Seldom does a writer write only one draft. In fact, teachers and writers often say that good writing is produced by editing and revision, not by writing. Frequently in organizations, writing is a group project. Some new software permits groups of authors or authors and their editors to comment upon current drafts and keep track of previous versions. Some authorities -- including Ted Nelson -- have classified "versioning" as one of the problems hypertext should solve.

Definition: Versions

Versions of documents are drafts of all or parts of documents that are produced during different stages of the analysis and writing project.

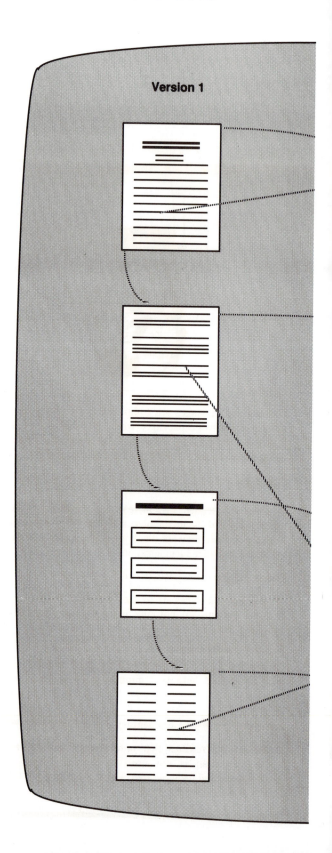

| 1 | **Issue: Linking Alternative Sections of Drafts** |

One of the important problems in hypertext is to show the links that are all connected to a draft and whether or not to carry all of these links ahead to the next draft. This set of issues is not an easy one and is illustrated on this page by a schematic that shows comments and corrections on a single draft, alternative versions, and other suggestions which are then carried over to another draft. It shows the complexity of the problem and the difficulty of solution.

| 2 | **Issue: When is a Version a Version?** |

Suppose just one little change is made on one page of a draft. Does this create a new version? If so, who names it? What is it named? How are the other people -- if any-- who are working on the draft to know that there is a new version? How are they to know where the change was made? And by whom?

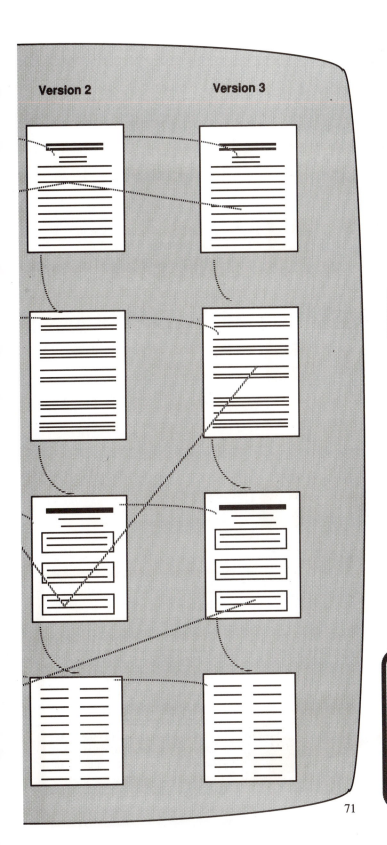

Version 2   **Version 3**

3 | Issue: Database Design

Once you've answered the basic questions about what will be permitted and what is a version, the next problem is how to represent this usefully in a database, so that the information can be tracked automatically.

4 | Issue: Interface Design

Assuming that you can keep all of the versions in the database straight, how do you display to users all of the differences in the versions and the actual changes as well as the suggested changes?

Commentary
In general, keeping track of versions is very difficult even with a good system. You don't usually want to keep a lot of old drafts around, because digging through them is excessively time consuming. There are exceptions of course. CAD documentation is one such example of needing it because of the multiple versions of drawings and their critiques. (REH)

Rewrite Text or Convert to On-Line Text "As Is"?

Introduction

Now that most people have a computer on their desks, in many companies the idea springs to many managers' minds that you just put whatever text you have into a database -- paper into electronic storage with no pain.   A number of major failures have resulted from this oversimplified idea. These failures have resulted in on-line text systems that go unused because they are so bad.

Three Options in Converting the Text

1   Keep Text "As Is" (No rewriting or revision)

 It is cheap just to scan in the text with an optical character reader.

BUT

The "keep as is" choice raises most of the user issues raised in this chapter -- lost in hypertext, cognitive overload, lack of normal reading cues, etc.

2   Superficially Chunk and Label

 Adding more labels, leaving the text "as is" but divided into more parts is less expensive than rewriting.

BUT

This choice may reduce some of the user issues but it is my claim in this book that the major costs come on the user side rather than on the costs of putting text on-line in the first place.

3   Reanalyze and Rewrite as Necessary

 This option will cost more on the "make" side than leaving as is, but it will   save money on the "use" side.

BUT

 This choice will reduce costs on the "use" side, and you may end up with a more useful paper document as well.

Commentary: The Major Cost Tradeoff

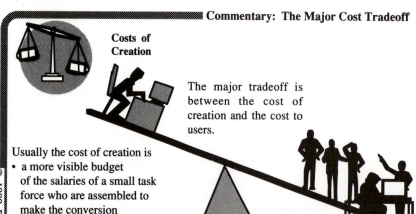

Costs of Creation

The major tradeoff is between the cost of creation and the cost to users.

Usually the cost of creation is
• a more visible budget of the salaries of a small task force who are assembled to make the conversion
• a one time cost.
The elapsed time of the project is also a major factor.

Costs of Use

Usually the costs of use are the
• costs of a large number of high priced professional users whose time is their most valuable resource being frustrated by the system
• costs of users not using a system because it is not easy enough to use
• costs of errors generated from poor analysis, organization and writing of the text database
These costs are often hidden in overhead--although some studies have revealed their magnitude. (REH)

> **Commentary: Computer Created Links Will Not Solve Many Problems**
>
> Some people believe that we will be able to write computer software that will automatically search text and make hypertext linkages between appropriate places. While this is possible to some degree, especially with Information Mapping's method, it is difficult in relatively unstructured text. (REH)

Four Major Options in Choosing the Retrieval Method

1 Use Full Text Search

This software searches the entire text and retrieves every mention of a search word. There are a variety of commercially available packages that will do this kind of search.

BUT

In very dense technical, administrative or business files, the software would present far too many "hits" on words that are frequently used. (E.g., if the search of the text in this book were on "hypertext," there would be hits on almost every page. Not very useful.) Too many synonyms is also a problem. Even with Boolean search capability, the searches would require a relatively high level of search skill and considerable time in large databases.

2 Create Keyword Index

The text is linked to specially selected keywords decided upon by a human indexer which provides a more controlled search and a likelihood of more precise retrieval.

BUT

The cost of creation is higher than for automatic full text searches.

3 Develop Hierarchical Structured Index(es)

These are one or more tables of contents or similar hierarchical lists of subjects in the text. Usually not much of a problem to create and very helpful.

BUT

Hierarchical indexes, even very good ones are not adequate for searches of very large text databases. They are best for searches of a relatively small number of pages, for example, the size of a single volume manual.

4 Develop "Applications Overviews"

These are job aids, checklists, procedures that might link to many different parts of a text. They are very helpful in task-oriented organizational situations.

BUT

They require a good structuring of the original database or they create a messy tangle for the user. Successful implementation depends on the subject judgments of a few writers.

> **Commentary: Choice Depends on User Requirements**
>
> The choice of which of these four (including the choice to use all four) depends on the analysis of user needs and the objectives of the system.
>
> All, but the full text search option, are labor intensive on the creation side, but less costly to the organization on the use side. (REH)

Chapter 3. Introduction to Information Mapping's Method of Structured Writing

Chapter 3
Introduction to Information Mapping's Method of Structured Writing

Definitions

Definition of Information Blocks

40 million pages

Results

In this Chapter ...an Overview of Information Mapping's Method

Definition of Information Maps

The Process of Analysis

What are Information Types?

Discourse Domains

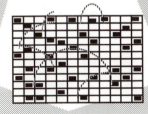

The Mapping Metaphor

Overview of This Chapter

Introduction

Chapter 3

In this chapter, we provide a description of Information Mapping's approach to the analysis, organization, and presentation of information in different kinds of documents. The reader can expect a "what is" rather than a "how to" level of detail.

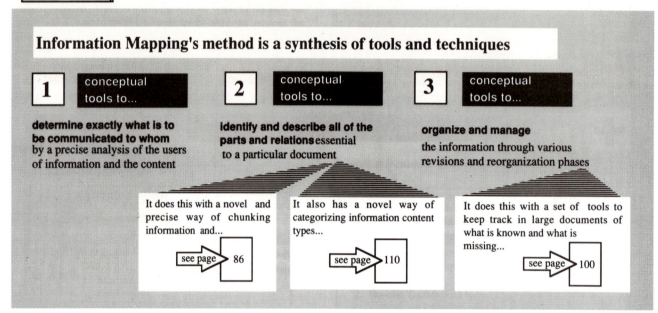

Information Mapping's method is a synthesis of tools and techniques

1 conceptual tools to...

determine exactly what is to be communicated to whom by a precise analysis of the users of information and the content

It does this with a novel and precise way of chunking information and... see page 86

2 conceptual tools to...

identify and describe all of the parts and relations essential to a particular document

It also has a novel way of categorizing information content types... see page 110

3 conceptual tools to...

organize and manage the information through various revisions and reorganization phases

It does this with a set of tools to keep track in large documents of what is known and what is missing... see page 100

Brief History of Information Mapping

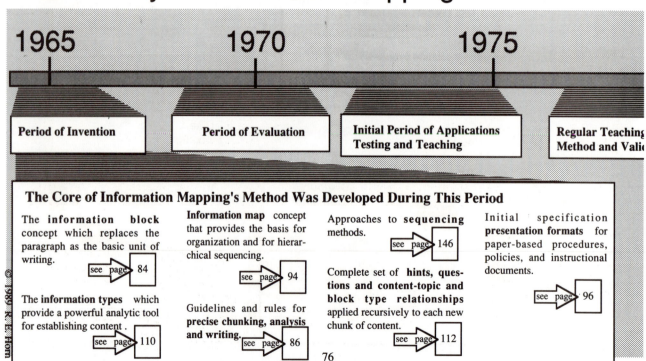

1965   1970   1975

Period of Invention

Period of Evaluation

Initial Period of Applications Testing and Teaching

Regular Teaching Method and Vali

The Core of Information Mapping's Method Was Developed During This Period

The **information block** concept which replaces the paragraph as the basic unit of writing. see page 84

The **information types** which provide a powerful analytic tool for establishing content . see page 110

Information map concept that provides the basis for organization and for hierarchical sequencing. see page 94

Guidelines and rules for **precise chunking, analysis and writing.** see page 86

Approaches to **sequencing** methods. see page 146

Complete set of **hints, questions and content-topic and block type relationships** applied recursively to each new chunk of content. see page 112

Initial specification **presentation formats** for paper-based procedures, policies, and instructional documents. see page 96

Commentary: Goal of Information Mapping 's Method

My goal in developing the method was to enable people to produce better communication documents in business, industry, government, technology and science. (REH)

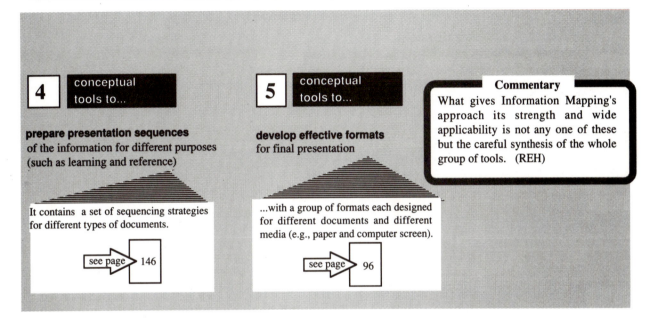

4 | conceptual tools to...

prepare presentation sequences
of the information for different purposes
(such as learning and reference)

It contains a set of sequencing strategies
for different types of documents.

see page 146

5 | conceptual tools to...

develop effective formats
for final presentation

...with a group of formats each designed
for different documents and different
media (e.g., paper and computer screen).

see page 96

Commentary
What gives Information Mapping's
approach its strength and wide
applicability is not any one of these
but the careful synthesis of the whole
group of tools. (REH)

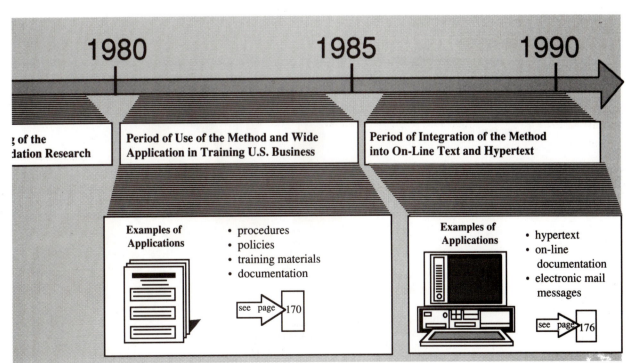

1980   1985   1990

...; of the
...dation Research

**Period of Use of the Method and Wide
Application in Training U.S. Business**

**Period of Integration of the Method
into On-Line Text and Hypertext**

**Examples of
Applications**

- procedures
- policies
- training materials
- documentation

see page 170

**Examples of
Applications**

- hypertext
- on-line
  documentation
- electronic mail
  messages

see page 176

Some Problems Addressed with the Method

Commentary: Ask People What Is Wrong With Writing

As I have travelled around the country giving speeches and workshops, I have often asked people to tell me, "What are the main problems with the documents that come across your desk?" This is what they tell me. (REH)

Reader Problems

I'm not sure what I'm supposed to do with this information.

Where are the key ideas? They're buried somewhere around here. You can't tell what's important.

These examples are too complex. And sometimes they aren't even there.

I can't tell what the organization of this document is.

Commentary: To Solve These Problems

When you compare the problems of readers and writers, you can see that there is a relationship. Many of the same things that writers complain about are exactly issues that readers have with writing that comes across their desks. As we shall see in this chapter, these problems are the ones that Information Mapping's method has addressed. (REH)

Often, all I need is one or two sentences. I wish this were set up so I could scan it. I don't have time to read it all.

The words the author uses are unnecessarily technical.

There is just too much to read!

The report is just too long. The sentences are too long. The whole thing is too long. Who can read it?

They send down these instructions that are so vague we can't figure out what they mean.

Parts of the same thing I need are scattered all over the document.

Commentary: Ask People About Their Writing Difficulties

The other side of the coin, of course, is, "what are the difficulties that writers face?" I ask people that question too. Here is what they say. (REH)

I always have trouble getting started. Sometimes that blank piece of paper can keep me from writing all morning.

Writer Problems

When it gets longer than a page, I don't know how to get it organized. It takes a long time to put it all together.

I have trouble being concise. I'm afraid someone will misconstrue what I write so I write each point into the ground.

Commentary: Connection With Hypertext

Since the mid-seventies, Information Mapping's method has been used on an increasingly wider scale. It appears that it will resolve a number of the hypertext issues that we discussed in the previous chapter. But before we can describe the solutions, we have to look at the basic structure of the method itself. (REH)

I never know how much detail to use. People tell me I overwrite.

Getting it to flow. I can't seem to tie it all together the way my English teachers kept telling me I had to.

I can't always figure out a good sequence to put things in.

I have trouble knowing when to stop.

I spend an inordinate amount of time getting my thoughts down on paper.

I can't figure out how to write for diverse audiences.

What is the Information Mapping Approach?

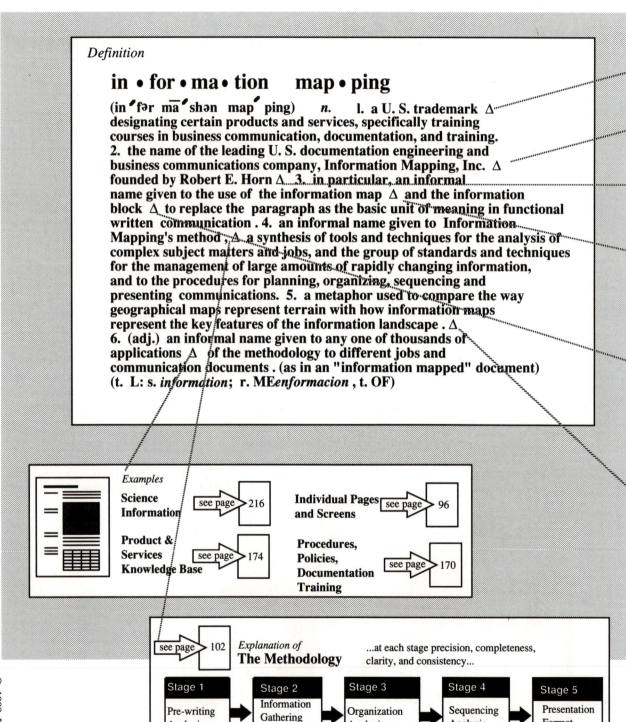

Definition

in • for • ma • tion   map • ping

(in ′fər mā′shən map′ ping)   *n.*   1. a U. S. trademark △ designating certain products and services, specifically training courses in business communication, documentation, and training. 2. the name of the leading U. S. documentation engineering and business communications company, Information Mapping, Inc. △ founded by Robert E. Horn △. 3. in particular, an informal name given to the use of the information map △ and the information block △ to replace the paragraph as the basic unit of meaning in functional written communication . 4. an informal name given to Information Mapping's method , △ a synthesis of tools and techniques for the analysis of complex subject matters and jobs, and the group of standards and techniques for the management of large amounts of rapidly changing information, and to the procedures for planning, organizing, sequencing and presenting communications. 5. a metaphor used to compare the way geographical maps represent terrain with how information maps represent the key features of the information landscape . △. 6. (adj.) an informal name given to any one of thousands of applications △ of the methodology to different jobs and communication documents . (as in an "information mapped" document) (t. L: s. *information*; r. ME*enformacion* , t. OF)

Examples

Science Information see page 216

Individual Pages and Screens see page 96

Product & Services Knowledge Base see page 174

Procedures, Policies, Documentation Training see page 170

see page 102 *Explanation of* **The Methodology**   ...at each stage precision, completeness, clarity, and consistency...

Stage 1	Stage 2	Stage 3	Stage 4	Stage 5
Pre-writing Analysis	Information Gathering Analysis	Organization Analysis	Sequencing Analysis	Presentation Format

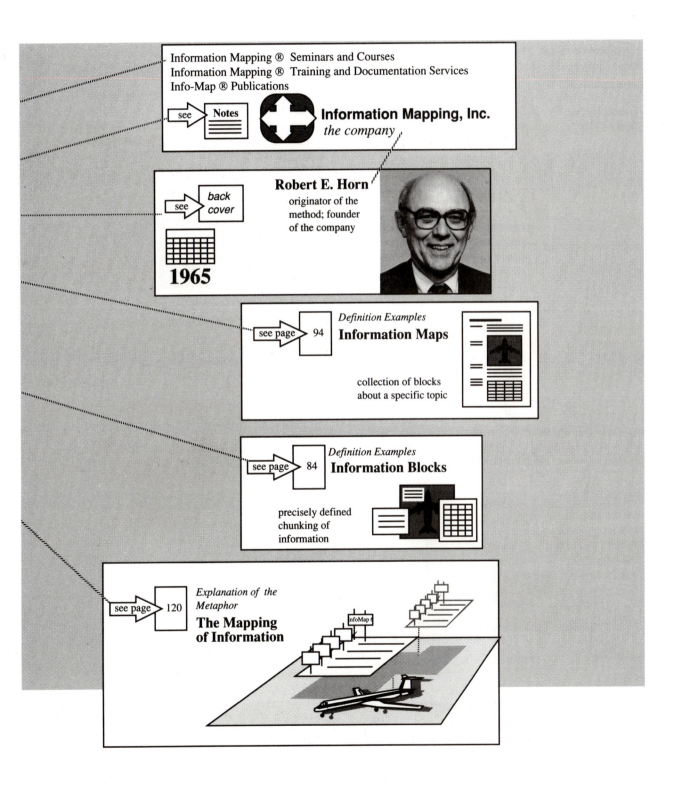

Information Mapping ® Seminars and Courses
Information Mapping ® Training and Documentation Services
Info-Map ® Publications

see → Notes

Information Mapping, Inc.
the company

see → back cover

Robert E. Horn
originator of the method; founder of the company

1965

see page → 94
Definition Examples
Information Maps
collection of blocks about a specific topic

see page → 84
Definition Examples
Information Blocks
precisely defined chunking of information

see page → 120
Explanation of the Metaphor
The Mapping of Information

InfoMap

The Problem of Human Short Term Memory

Introduction

Part of the rationale for structured writing starts with the limitations in human short term memory, limitations which every human being has. We introduce the problem with an example (first used by Herbert Simon).

Example One

While in the shower, multiply 1776 by 1492. Next remember the answer long enough to check it.

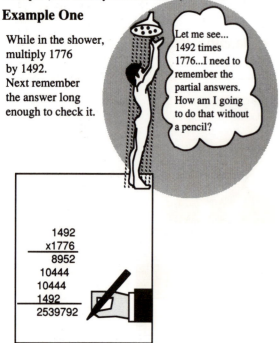

    1492
   x1776
    8952
   10444
   10444
    1492
 2539792

This situation highlights the limitations of human short term memory. It will probably take you several minutes to do the multiplication task, if you succeed at all.

Example Two

You look up a phone number.

A little interruption and you've forgotten the number...

Problem

Why do we have these memory problems?

Answer

Human short term memory capacity has severe limitations.

Two Estimates of the Size of Short Term Memory

Every thought process that requires what we call "attention" has to be held in short term memory and human beings can hold only a small number of "chunks" of information in short term memory. George Miller, △ an outstanding communications psychologist suggested in 1956 that the number of chunks you can hold in short term memory is 7 (plus or minus 2).

Research by Herbert Simon, the Nobel prize winning economist and information scientist, suggests the number is smaller -- around 4 to possibly 9 chunks. Whatever the size, all agree that the number of chunks is very small.

see page ▷ 218

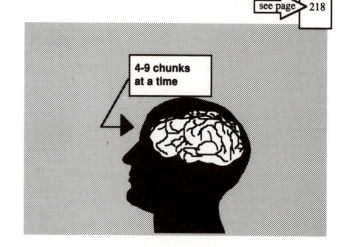

The Chunk

Definition

A chunk is any familiar pattern. Chunk size itself depends on your prior learning.

Examples

For one person for one subject matter, a chunk may be one sentence, while in another subject it may be several sentences.

For younger children, a chunk might be reading a single word; for still younger ones, simply recognizing a single letter would constitute a chunk.

Long Term Memory

In order to do the "1776 x 1492 in the shower" problem, you would have had to transfer some of the information to long-term memory (i.e., some of the intermediate products of the multiplication).

How does transfer to long term memory take place?

What does our brain do with the contents of our short term memory in order to turn it into long term memory? We don't know exactly, but somehow we have to gather these 5 to 9 chunks of information, add some sort of identifier and link them in with other previous experience. All this takes place on an unconscious or partially conscious level in every human being every day. Miller is saying that all human beings everywhere chunk information in order to transfer it to long term memory and this process has severe limits in its capacity.

How long does transfer to long term memory take?

To store 5-9 chunks of information in long term memory takes, according to Herbert Simon, △ 5 to 10 seconds per chunk.

see page 220

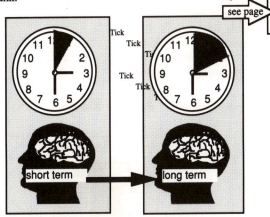

Principle: Organize thought so as to stay within memory limits

"We must," Herbert Simon says, "organize our thought processes so they do not require us to hold more information than 4 to 7 chunks in short term memory simultaneously."

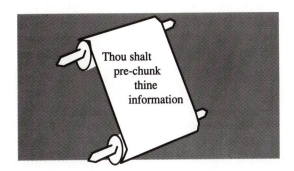

Thou shalt pre-chunk thine information

Overcoming transfer time limits

How do we overcome limits? Simon points out that we do it

- by external aids to memory (computers and calculators, paper and pencil)

- by aids to long term memory, such as books, reports, manuals

- by discovering and using strategies for accomplishing thinking tasks.

Definition: Recoding

Miller suggests that the process of grouping many chunks of information into larger chunks by conscious and unconscious processes could be called re-coding.

Example

How do we recode our experience? Miller suggests, "Probably the simplest is to group the input events, apply a new name to the group and then remember the new name rather than the individual input events."

Importance

And he says, " . . .I am convinced that this process is a very general and important one for psychology . . ." He says, "The point is that re-coding is an extremely powerful weapon for increasing the amount of information that we can deal with. In one form or another, we use re-coding constantly in our daily behavior."

Three Types of Recoding

a. verbal code (rephrasing in our own words)
b. seeing something and then making a verbal description of it. Miller says, "I suspect that imagery is a form of re-coding, too, but images seem much harder to get at operationally and to study experimentally than the more symbolic kinds of re-coding."
c. presupplied codes (such as the labeling system of Information Mapping △).

see page 92

What are Information Blocks?

Introduction

We have made it a principle that we must help the reader by "pre-chunking" the information into blocks.

This not only permits readers an easier way of taking information in, but also helps writers in their analysis of the information.

Definition

in • for • ma • tion   block

(in ˈfər mā shən ˈblŏk)ˋ   *n.*   **1. any one of 200 precisely defined kinds of information that together make up the basic subject matter of a manual, book, or course, used in the analytic method developed by Robert E. Horn and taught by Information Mapping, Inc. 2. the basic subdivision of a subject matter, replacing the paragraph as the fundamental unit of analysis and presentation in functional and task oriented text. 3. composed of one or more sentences and/or graphical structures, but not more than (usually) seven sentences, identified clearly by a label; blocks are constructed according to four principles, the chunking, relevance, consistency, and labeling principles; blocks are normally a part of a larger structure of organization (called an information map △).**

Icon for Blocks

In this book we sometimes use this icon to indicate the information block.

Examples

For example, a definition block is an example of a block.

So, in this book each of the labeled chunks of information is an information block.

| For Other Examples of Information Blocks | see page 88 |

see page 94

Information Blocks: Different Types

The large differences between these blocks introduce the concept that blocks are of quite different types, depending on the kind of document they are a part of. And each block type △ may have quite different rules and guidelines for analysis and writing.

see page 108

Four Principles for Constructing Blocks

Chunking Principle

Group all information into small, manageable units, called blocks and maps.

Relevance Principle

Include in one chunk only information that relates to one main point based on that information's purpose or function for the reader.

Consistency Principle

For similar subject matters, use similar words, labels, format, organizations, and sequences.

Labeling Principle

Label every chunk and group of chunks according to specific criteria.

Commentary: Intuitive Chunking vs. Precision Modularity

One of the reasons that Information Mapping's method is so useful and powerful in managing large amounts of information is the precision modularity provided by information blocks. Precision modularity is a term we use to distinguish information blocks from the practice of "intuitive chunking." Intuitive chunking is forced upon people by screens of limited size. Intuitive chunking is simply dividing information into small chunks without knowing exactly why you are doing that. Precision modularity means following specific principles and guidelines throughout the analysis. The four principles act as constraints Δ to the construction of blocks, and the information typology Δ we develop in forthcoming pages provides "engineering-like" guidelines for the construction of information blocks.

see page 86

see page 110

Commentary

The four-principle approach is used in all analysis at all levels in the method.

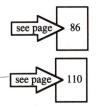

Documents Chapters & Sections Maps Blocks

How Four Principles Constrain Block Construction

Introduction

We have introduced the information block as the smallest unit of analysis in Information Mapping's method. We construct blocks by applying four basic principles to any piece of information in a subject matter. This constrains how any block is made and what it may contain. The process of using the four principles transforms mere intuitive chunking into precision modularity. The diagram on these pages depicts the four basic principles and how they perform this constraining function.

see page 110

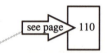

When combined with a strong system of types Δ of information, these block construction principles provide the foundation for the entire methodology.

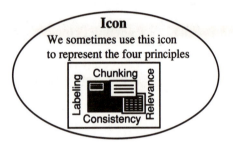

Icon

We sometimes use this icon to represent the four principles

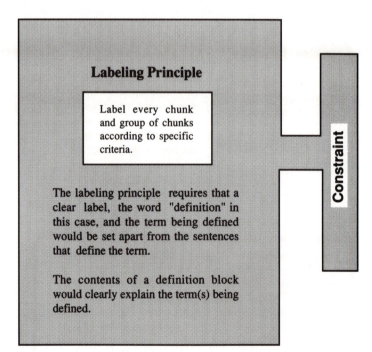

Labeling Principle

Label every chunk and group of chunks according to specific criteria.

The labeling principle requires that a clear label, the word "definition" in this case, and the term being defined would be set apart from the sentences that define the term.

The contents of a definition block would clearly explain the term(s) being defined.

Constraint

Chunking Principle

Group all information into small, manageable units, called blocks and maps.

The chunking principle suggests that all of our text will be divided into relatively small units of information, about the amount that humans can handle with their short term memory limitations.

Constraint

Definition: Cash Value

Cash value is the amount of money a life insurance policy is worth at a specified time.

Constraint

Relevance Principle

Include in one chunk only information that relates to one main point based on that information's purpose or function for the reader.

The relevance principle is interpreted in this instance to say "don't put anything other than definitional sentences into the block."

If you have information that is nice to know, or contains examples or commentary, the relevance and consistency principles demand that you put it some place else and label it appropriately, but do not put it in the definition block.

Constraint

Consistency Principle

For similar subject matters, use similar words, labels, format, organizations, and sequences.

The consistency principle says "Do this same thing for every other definition in your report, manual, book, hypertext." In other words, it would be interpreted in this example as "Treat all definitions alike, i.e., put them in blocks by themselves labeled 'definition.'"

▶ *put in a different block*

(e.g., this sentence, "Cash value is only one of the kinds of value an insurance policy has," would go in some other block, not in the definition block because the sentence is not definitional.)

Examples of Information Blocks

Size and Content

An information block may be one or more sentences long. It may also be a list, a fairly complicated table, or other kinds of graphic structure. On these pages, we present examples of each kind.

Information Block: Smallest Meaningful Chunk

What do all of these blocks have in common? All three represent the smallest meaningful chunk for most readers. So, to repeat, a block may have one to seven sentences (very occasionally more). It may also contain a table or simple graphics so long as it meets the criterion of meaningfulness, relevance, and consistency.

Three Kinds of Information Block Contents

---

1 Example of a One-sentence Information Block

Definition: Cash Value

Cash value is the amount of money a life insurance policy is worth at a specified time.

---

2 Example of a Block that Contains a Table

IF the book is . . .	THEN send the patron . . .	AND send . . .
available	the book	an invoice to the Billing Unit.
not available • never owned • lost	Form 25	--
checked out with no waiting list	Form 66	a copy of Form 66 to Circulation Desk.
checked out with a waiting list	Form 66 and Waiting List Notice	a copy of Form 66 to Circulation Desk.

3   Example of an Information Block Using Graphics

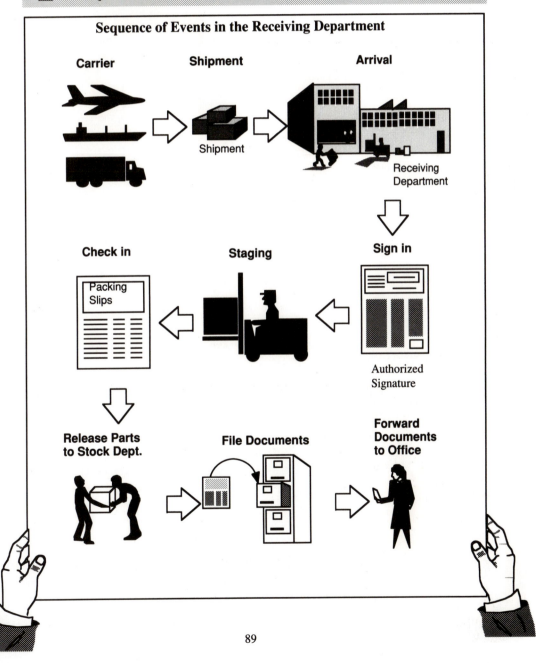

Sequence of Events in the Receiving Department

Block Replaces Traditional Definition of Paragraph

Definition: Paragraph

The Random House Dictionary defines "paragraph" as: "a distinct portion of written or printed matter dealing with a particular idea, usually beginning with an indentation on a new line . . ."

Usual Definition Too Vague

The usual definition of a paragraph is much too vague. All you need is an idea and an indentation, and you have a paragraph. And a paragraph is supposed to be one of our basic units of thought! This, of course, contributes to the difficulty in teaching about paragraphs. If they are too vaguely defined, you have difficulty agreeing on what one is with your teacher or your students (or your editor).

In addition, paragraphs generally do not show the basic organization of writing very well. They all appear as the same almost endless gray rectangles.

Types Not Carefully Defined

Although in English class we are taught a variety of different kinds of paragraphs, the types are not very clearly delineated. And as frequently as not, we find that we are writing ones never mentioned in school and rarely writing the kinds we were taught.

Boundaries Fuzzy

Nobody can tell when a paragraph is supposed to stop. That's another problem with traditional definitions of paragraphs. Many writers simply scribble until they get the uneasy feeling that they should start a new paragraph. So they pull out their little bag of "dents" and start in a new paragraph. And all this passes for "organization!"

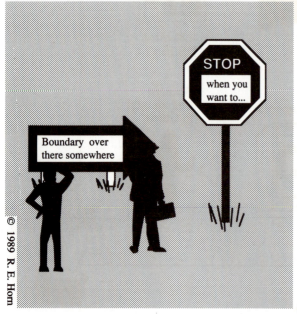

Topic Sentences Often Not Used

You may remember being taught that every paragraph should have a topic sentence. The topic sentence is supposed to be the first sentence in the paragraph (at least most of the time, or a lot of the time, or some of the time), depending on what your teacher said you should do. And all the other sentences are supposed to "support" the topic sentence. Rules like this don't work, not in the quality control situations we find ourselves in our usual day-to-day writing. Many, if not most, of the paragraphs that the average business person dictates in a letter do not have topic sentences.

While it is a good idea to use topic sentences in certain kinds of literary essays, they simply aren't relevant in technical or business writing.

Like "unity and coherence," the topic sentence turns out to be a concept that makes you anxious and guilty when you can't tell if you've done it -- which is most of the time.

Implied Topic Sentences Are Not Even There

Perhaps the most maddening thing of all is that when English teachers observe that there are *no* topic sentences in many paragraphs, they simply declare that every paragraph has an "implied" topic sentence.

Poor Writers Just Compound These Difficulties

How do you teach writing to young persons telling them they are supposed to write an "implied" topic sentence for every paragraph and then leave them out? Certainly, the topic sentence is a concept that must be significantly modified or dropped.

It isn't so bad for good writers. They will find some way to accomplish their purposes. They will analyze and organize and come up with usable text. But inexperienced writers, trying to follow impossible rules, simply compound the problem in most business and technical situations.

Information Mapping Replaces Paragraph With Precision Modularity

As we have described a few pages back Δ, see page 86 Information Mapping's method carefully defines chunks of writing that are larger than sentence size. It has identified different types of documents and the specific types of "blocks" and can teach people to write them well enough to meet stringent quality control checks.

We have developed a set of guidelines and standards for the contents of these blocks that are very easily followed.

How Did We Get Stuck With Paragraphs as a Way of Organizing Writing?

Aristotle Invented Rhetoric

In Ancient Greece, a young scholar named Aristotle, the teacher of Alexander the Great, set out to write down all that was known about philosophy, natural history, logic Δ, and just about everything else. One of his lesser known, but most influential, books was on rhetoric -- the rules of written and spoken argument. see page 188

Modified by Philosophers & Literary Critics

Of course, over the years some of these rules were modified and refined. New rules were added to the study of rhetoric. The ideas of the originators of many of these ideas were formalized by philosophers of the Middle Ages where rhetoric was one of the Big Three core subjects -- called the Trivium -- at universities. Literary essayists of the seventeenth and eighteenth centuries in Western Europe also contributed to the subject.

Passed Along To Us By Habit

Most of these rules were then automatically taught by your teacher and mine. We started learning them in the first grade and we've kept getting the same Aristotelian rules right on through college.

Anxiety About "Unified" Paragraphs

Most of us have forgotten the precise formulation of rhetorical rules. But they still operate on us in an unconscious way. When we sit down to write, we still ask ourselves, "Is my paragraph unified?" "Do I have 'coherence' in my writing?" And we ask ourselves even more vaguely, "Does my writing show 'unity?'" These criteria only produce anxiety and guilt, because they are not precise enough. We cannot define them in any way that we can get the kind of agreement we can with information blocks.

Habit Keeps Us Using It

Habit keeps human beings using what they have done in the past even if it barely works. If it gets us by, we don't bother to learn a new skill.

You Wouldn't Use Aristotle's Science in your R & D Program, So...

As wise as he was for his time, you wouldn't use Aristotle's natural history for your biochemical research planning. Too much science has developed.

But, we are still using Aristotle to do our hypertext and our communication. And we are hampering ourselves, just as if we were using him as a consultant for our research and development.

Developing Guidelines and Standards for Blocks

Introduction

As we have noted, Information Mapping's method does not have vague, fuzzy rules for writing paragraphs. Information must be part of a precision-developed information block for it to fit into a larger document and to be managed in an efficient manner.

So, for each domain (and often for a specific document type) it has been important to specify the most frequent types of blocks.

After the blocks have been identified, we then need to develop the guidelines that will make the consistency principle operational for both the contents and the labeling of all blocks of a similar type. On these pages, we present an overview of how we approach this task of developing guidelines that enables us to ensure that basic communication functions are accomplished on a consistent basis. Note that these are samples of the guidelines and apply only to the labeling. Space in this book does not permit reproducing all of the specifics of block development.

Two Basic Kinds of Block Labels

1 Analytic Labels

Definition

Analytic labels are those block labels that are used in the content analysis phase of document or training development to manage completeness and (often) share the bulk of information.

Where to Find Examples

Lists of analytic labels (but not the criteria for sorting information to identify them) are provided in this book for

- documents in the relatively stable subject matter domain see page 168

- scientific papers, reports, abstracts and presentations. see page 216

2 Display Labels

Definition

Display labels are those block labels that are used, depending upon document type, to make it easier for the user to understand what the block contains than if it had analytic labels. Sometimes, and in some cases even frequently, the analytic labels are used as display labels. But often, words must be added to analytic labels to make contents readily accessible.

Example

A definition block would have the analytic label "Definition" as a part of it. If a display label were called for, the writer would use "Definition" (followed by the term being defined) as in "Definition: Cash Value."

Three Kinds Display Labels

1 Subject Matter Independent Labels

Definition

A subject matter independent label is a label that identifies the purpose or function of the information in the block for the reader. A subject matter independent label is independent of the content of the block. It could appear on many different documents regardless of the subject.

2 Subject Matter Labels

Definition

A subject matter label is a label that describes the content of the information in the block.

3 Combination Labels

Definition

A combination label is a label made up of two parts:
- a subject matter independent label that indicates the purpose or function of the information, and
- a subject matter label that identifies the content.

Implication of the Principles of Relevance and Consistency

Insofar as possible, block labels should be consistent and relevant not only for a single block but across **all blocks of a similar type.**

And there may be guidelines for labeling that apply to all blocks.

Constraint

Constraint

Constraint

Definition

Definition

Definition

Definition: Cash Value

Cash value is the amount of money a life insurance policy is worth at a specified time.

Constraint

Guidelines for Managing the Size of the Message Growing Out of the Principle of Chunking

Insofar as possible, blocks should be no more than 7 plus or minus 2 sentences.

Insofar as possible, information maps should be no more than 7 plus or minus 2 blocks.

Insofar as possible, parts of chapters or short chapters should be no more than 7 plus or minus 2 maps.

Here we follow the suggestions of the short term memory research.

see page ▶ 82

Usefulness of Block Labels

For the reader, block labels perform three functions:

- to act as "advance organizers" about the contents of the block for learners
- to act as "access tools" for persons who are scanning or browsing
- (in some very limited discourse domains) to act as a tool to attract the reader's attention.

For the writer, block labels facilitate and constrain analysis and organization of the subject matter.

Some Guidelines That Apply to All Block Labels

Clear: Use labels that clearly describe the function or the content of the Block.

Brief: Make labels brief. Shorter labels are better than longer ones as long as they don't introduce ambiguity. In general, use no more than 3-5 words. The label should not be so brief as to be meaningless.

Consistent: Use the same vocabulary in the label that you use in the Block.

Familiar: Use vocabulary that is generally familiar to anyone in the audience. Avoid technical jargon unless you are certain all readers will know the jargon.

Appropriate: Make sure that the label reflects the significance of what you want to say. "Comment" may work well as a label for optional information. However, if the Block contains crucial information, "Important" or "Caution" would be a better choice.

Independent: Make each label stand alone and act as an advance organizer for a single Block. Avoid labels that act as transitional devices.

Other guidelines have been developed for specific types of blocks and for the three types of labels described on the facing page.

Other Conventional Quality Control Factors Used in Blocks

- Grammar
- Sentence length & complexity (i.e., readability index)
- Syntax
- Spelling
- Word usage
- Style (formal, informal)

Hierarchy of Chunking and Labeling Principle

Introduction

When we begin to deal with several blocks about a similar topic, we apply another principle, the hierarchy principle. And, of course, we continue to apply religiously the other four principles of chunking, labeling, relevance and consistency Δ

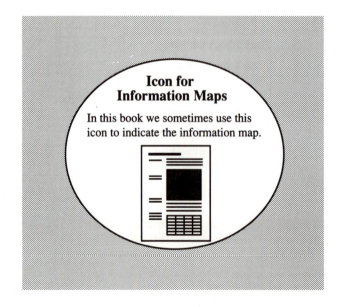

For Definitions and Examples of the Four Principles

see page 86

- chunking
- labeling
- relevance
- consistency

Principle: Hierarchy of Chunking and Labeling

Organize small, relevant units of information into a hierarchy and provide the larger group(s) with labels.

Rationale

As the number of groups of subject matter chunks grows beyond the seven plus or minus two limits of short term memory, readers have difficulty comprehending or remembering the information.

Information Map

Introduction

These clusters of seven plus or minus two blocks of information are as different from other forms of organization of writing as the blocks are different from paragraphs.

Definition: Information Map

An information map is a collection of two or more, and usually no more than nine, information blocks about a limited topic.

Approximate Page Size

In general, we can think of an information map as approximately one to two pages in length, but some maps of certain well specified types run several pages in length.

Icon for Information Maps

In this book we sometimes use this icon to indicate the information map.

Apply The Hierarchy of Chunking and Labeling Principle to Larger Aggregates

Introduction

Size is always important. We must keep applying the hierarchy principle and the other four principles for grouping larger and larger aggregates.

Guidelines

We have said that if you get more than 5 to 9 sentences in a block, it is time to chunk them into two blocks (or, in certain circumstances, into two or more sub-blocks).

Group all Blocks into Maps

If we get more than 5 to 9 blocks in a map, make two, give them an overview and call it a "section."

Chunk every 5 to 9 sections into chapters and every 5 to 9 chapters into "parts" and so on until a document is complete.

Sequencing Blocks When Presenting Maps

The definition of a map only requires clustering of similar blocks together. It does not specify their sequence. This permits us to display them in different order for, say, initial learning by novices in a subject matter, and from the order used for reference. And it encourages the temporary formation of map-like clusters during the early stages of information gathering and subject matter analysis. There is no demand for strict sequencing at these early stages.

We can always think of two distinct levels of blocks (or collections of blocks, maps, parts, etc.):

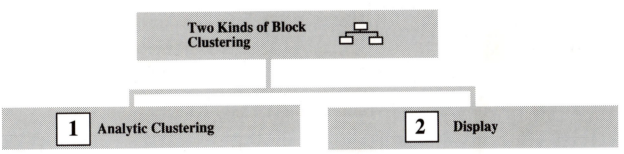

Two Kinds of Block Clustering

1 Analytic Clustering

Description

The most elementary analytic task is to cluster blocks of information around the concept of the map. We assert that "this block belongs to this map."

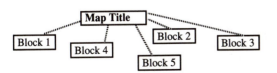

2 Display

Description

When actually presented to a user, blocks need some kind of order and sequence. This is a separate set of decisions from those used to cluster blocks into maps.

...for reference	...for initial learning...
Map Title	**Map Title**
Block 1	Block 1
Block 4	Block 2
Block 2	Block 3
Block 5	Block 4
Block 3	Block 5

Examples of Maps Displayed on Paper

Introduction

Information Mapping's method works equally well on paper as on computer screens. We have presented many examples of the method in computer screens in this book.

The reader may be wondering about some of the ways that examples of this method look when displayed on the printed page. We present two typical pages.

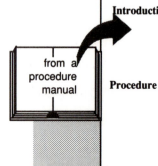

from a procedure manual

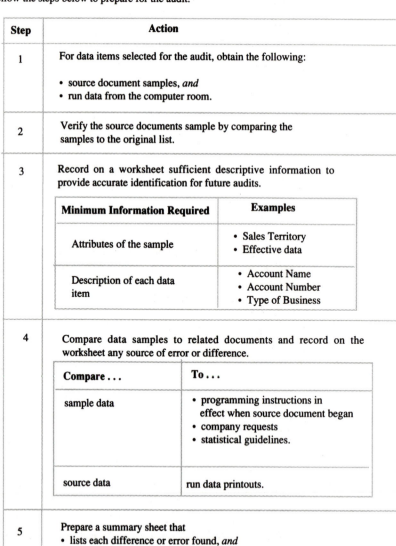

How to Prepare Data for an Audit

Introduction

One of the most important procedures in an audit is preparing the data.

Careful preparation ensures that the data is correct and that each step of preparation has been carried out.

Procedure

Follow the steps below to prepare for the audit.

Step	Action
1	For data items selected for the audit, obtain the following: • source document samples, *and* • run data from the computer room.
2	Verify the source documents sample by comparing the samples to the original list.
3	Record on a worksheet sufficient descriptive information to provide accurate identification for future audits. | Minimum Information Required	Examples
---	---
Attributes of the sample	• Sales Territory • Effective data
Description of each data item	• Account Name • Account Number • Type of Business	
4	Compare data samples to related documents and record on the worksheet any source of error or difference. | Compare . . .	To . . .
---	---
sample data	• programming instructions in effect when source document began • company requests • statistical guidelines.
source data	run data printouts.	
5	Prepare a summary sheet that • lists each difference or error found, *and* • analyzes each data item to compute accuracy ratios for the audit sample data items.

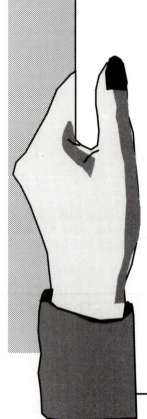

While this book emphasizes the display of structured hypertext, most of the work today with the methodology -- millions of pages -- has been done on paper and paper will probably continue to outrank electronic display for some time.

Rules for Defining Audit Accuracy Ratios

from a procedure manual

Introduction	In order to compare the statistics of one audit to the next, the accuracy ratios must be defined and presented consistently.
Terms and Definitions	Each audit must contain the following ratios.

Ratio	Definition
Data Field Verifying Ratio	The number of times a given data field is correct, divided by the total number of transactions reviewed
Transaction Accuracy Ratio	The number of times all data fields reviewed on a transaction are correct, divided by the total number of transactions reviewed
Account Accuracy Ratio	The number of times all data fields audited are correct on all transactions relating to a single account, divided by the total number of accounts reviewed

Rule 1: state data items	In your audit report, you must clearly state in the accuracy ratios which data items are included in the Data Field Verifying Ratio.
Rule 2: note any changes	When the company requests changes or additions to the Data Field Verifying Ratio list, you must note these changes in your Audit Report.

Rationale

- Any changes will affect the results of the transaction and account accuracy ratios. The more data fields reviewed per transaction, the lower the accuracy ratios.

- Comparison of audits would be impossible unless the changes were listed.

Rule 3: use consistent definitions	When you are comparing transaction accuracy ratios over a specific time period, you must use the same transaction definition for all audits going on within the time frame.

Example: If the Cash Receivable transactions included international receivables as part of the transaction during the first audit, then you must include international receivables in the next audit.

Change Traditional Document Structure

Introduction

We have made the case that hypertext requires a re-examination of writing. And in this chapter we have introduced Information Mapping's method as a research-based thoroughly tested and proven way of analysis and organization and presentation of writing. It may have occurred to the reader that we are introducing nothing less than a complete overhaul of the traditional rules of rhetoric. We are doing just that.

Definition: Rhetorics

Rhetorics are rules for writing particular documents for particular purposes.

Comment

We use the classical definition for "rhetoric." The reader should note that this meaning is quite different from the more common meaning of the term, i.e., "tricky special pleading."

Kinds of Rhetoric

Usually, rhetoric has been thought of as a single unitary subject. However, it is clear that we use different sets of rules for different kinds of writing situations. Think of how different the rules for writing for newspapers and popular magazines are from those for technical writing. We can't go into a complete analysis of all of the different kinds of rhetorics in this book. That isn't our purpose. But we do want to contrast the approaches taken in hypertext and in Information Mapping to the traditional approaches. We have done this with regard to the paragraph Δ and below we spell out some of the major rules for organization of prose in newspapers and magazines so the reader can contrast them with what we are saying about Information Mapping in this chapter. Obviously, we do not usually use the rhetorics for newspapers and magazines for books, training manuals, and business letters. The point of the contrast is that there are very clear rules for rhetoric in each document domain and we must be very clear about these guidelines.

see page 90

Summary of Rules for Organizing Newspaper Articles

As usually taught, the rules of rhetoric for newspapers are as follows:

1. Grab the reader in the headline by

   a. summarizing the important point in the headline
   b. an unusual human interest angle.

2. Use any kind of cute, attractive, possibly informative, subheads to attract the reader. Occasionally, subheads can be an informative summary of what is coming up. The rule for insertion of subheads is break up the gray space.

3. Organize the entire story by decreasing importance. That means that the most important elements of the story are first and the less important elements and details of the story are last. (The reason for this is so that a newspaper editor can cut it at any place to put more ads in the newspaper.)

4. Summarize everything in the lead paragraph with answers to the questions who, what, where, when, why, and how.

© 1989 R. E. Horn

The New Tim

Economy Contin

Drug War Accelerates

Experts Puzzled by New Changes in U.S.S.R.

Business Needs are Different

Business has special needs.

There is *no* need to have everybody read every word of a technical or administrative report, so we don't want to use journalistic gimmicks to attract readers.

Business documents are often much longer than newspaper stories, and require much more sophisticated methods of organization. They, in fact, require the kind of systematic approach we have used in Information Mapping's method.

Our Conclusion: Informed Access Is Better Than Tantalizing Hints

In magazines, as we pointed out below, the whole idea is to hint at fascinating material coming up later and hide it in the back pages.

In business, we assert the absolutely opposite principle. The reader should be able to locate quickly any key information and make decisions appropriately. Moreover, we would recommend that the piece be organized, not by a continual series of hints, but by very clear chunks clearly designated by subheads.

In newspapers and some magazines, editors do provide informative headlines and readers are able to scan and skip to what they want to read.

es Times

ues to Boom

Deficits Pile Up But People Keep Buying

Terrorists Bomb Restaurant

Summary of Rules for Organizing Magazine Articles

Magazine rhetoric is much like newspaper rhetoric with a few exceptions.

1. Grab them in the title.
2. Grab them again in the first paragraph with a human interest angle. Do not give away all of the information in the first paragraph.
3. Write to keep the reader by
   a. not revealing everything right away
   b. hinting at fascinating stuff coming up.
4. Use cute, not very informative subheads to break up the gray.

Purpose is to Keep Reader Turning Pages to See Advertising

The purpose of magazine rhetoric is to suck readers into the article and keep them reading so they will "like the magazine" and continue to buy it. A secondary purpose is to make sure that the reader flips through the magazine, continuing to read the story to the end, increasing the probability that the reader will look at some of the advertising on the back pages.

Managing Completeness by Key Block and Topic

Introduction

An important factor in managing information is the analysis of subject matter into precise blocks. This enables us to develop a comprehensive analytic structure in which the subject matter is divided according to specific criteria and principles into small labeled chunks by which complex information can be managed in all stages of the communication process.

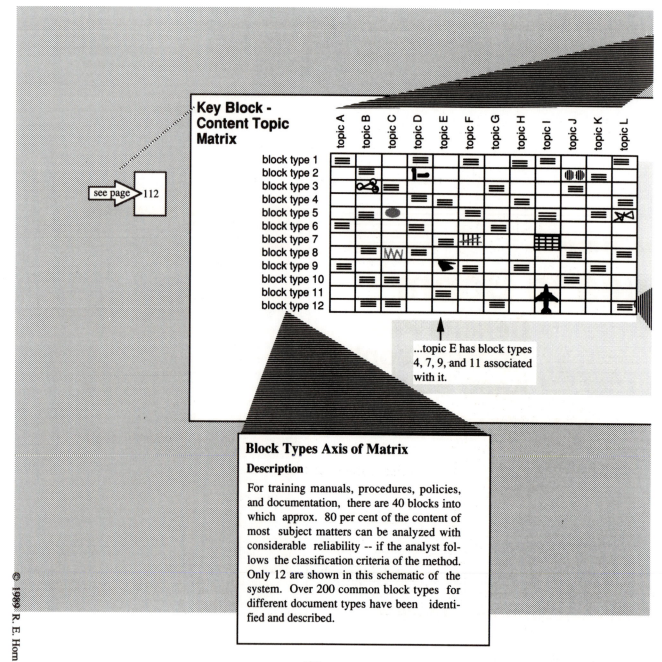

Key Block - Content Topic Matrix

see page 112

...topic E has block types 4, 7, 9, and 11 associated with it.

Block Types Axis of Matrix

Description

For training manuals, procedures, policies, and documentation, there are 40 blocks into which approx. 80 per cent of the content of most subject matters can be analyzed with considerable reliability -- if the analyst follows the classification criteria of the method. Only 12 are shown in this schematic of the system. Over 200 common block types for different document types have been identified and described.

How to Determine What the Topics Should Be

Topics are identified by specific criteria for specific document type.

Advantage

The advantage to systematic analysis of a subject matter is obvious: it is much better to know precisely when you are missing information from your analysis.

How to Understand This Diagram

.if block type 1 is "definition" then topics A, D, F, H, I, and L have definitions

When does a blank space on the matrix indicate missing information? Δ

Description

Specific key block templates for specific information types have been developed which permit the analyst to know when a blank space in the Block Type-Content Topic matrix indicates missing information that the analysis has not produced as yet.

Example

A template of key information blocks for concepts in the "relatively stable subject matter" discourse domain would include these blocks:

- Definition
- Example
- (optional) Non-Example.

Guidelines, Rules, and Standards

Guidelines indicate which terms are to be regarded as concepts for a particular audience for a particular type of document. Additional guidelines indicate how many examples and non-examples would need to be provided in the analysis. Other guidelines indicate the kind of examples and other standards.

Note:

This matrix is a conceptual rather than a physical tool. If actually put on a wall the matrix for a 100 page book would measure 4 feet by 50 feet.

Improves Efficiency Throughout Analysis Process

Introduction

The fundamental change in the basic unit of rhetorical analysis (i.e., the information block) produces many beneficial effects throughout the document development process. We use the term precision modularity to distinguish the information block from "intuitive" chunking where the criteria for chunking are not clearly formulated or where chunk size may be forced upon the writer by the fixed size of a computer screen. The precision modularity of blocks facilitates technical and administrative communication, improving its clarity and efficiency.

The stages of the process of developing a document

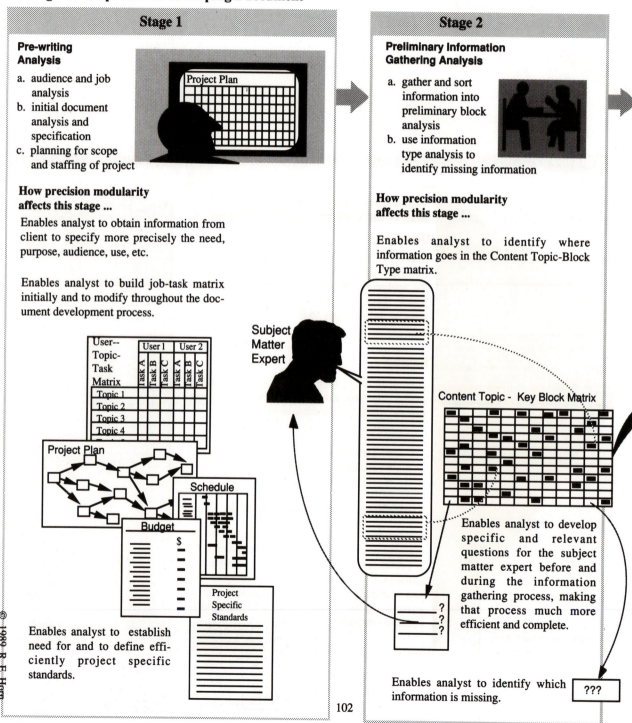

Stage 1

Pre-writing Analysis

a. audience and job analysis
b. initial document analysis and specification
c. planning for scope and staffing of project

How precision modularity affects this stage ...

Enables analyst to obtain information from client to specify more precisely the need, purpose, audience, use, etc.

Enables analyst to build job-task matrix initially and to modify throughout the document development process.

Project Plan

User-- Topic- Task Matrix

Project Plan

Schedule

Budget

Project Specific Standards

Enables analyst to establish need for and to define efficiently project specific standards.

Stage 2

Preliminary Information Gathering Analysis

a. gather and sort information into preliminary block analysis
b. use information type analysis to identify missing information

How precision modularity affects this stage ...

Enables analyst to identify where information goes in the Content Topic-Block Type matrix.

Subject Matter Expert

Content Topic - Key Block Matrix

Enables analyst to develop specific and relevant questions for the subject matter expert before and during the information gathering process, making that process much more efficient and complete.

Enables analyst to identify which information is missing. ???

102

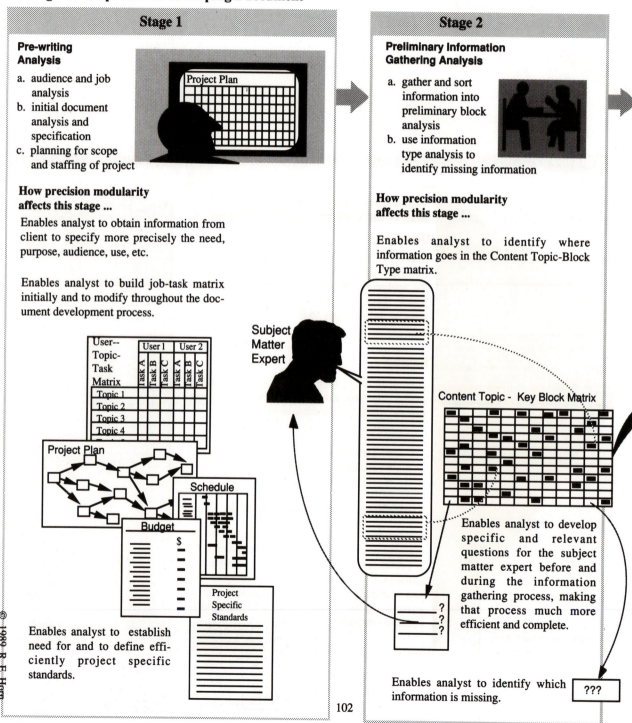© 1989 R. E. Horn

Stage 3

Organization Analysis

a. determine what information is needed for each task and for each job
b. do quality control check for completeness on entire information gathering process

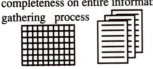

How precision modularity affects this stage ...

Enables analyst to do a completeness check on all information.

User--	User 1			User 2		
Topic- Task Matrix	Task A	Task B	Task C	Task A	Task B	Task C
Topic 1						
Topic 2						
Topic 3						
Topic 4						
Topic 5						

Enables analyst to filter information blocks through User Topic-Task Matrix to determine precise information needs of each job task.

Enables analyst to identify and manage all information in a complex project, and to track changes.

Stage 4

Sequencing Analysis

a. based on different types of documents and user types, determine sequence requirements
b. complete sequencing analysis

How precision modularity affects this stage ...

Enables analyst

A. to select sequencing templates

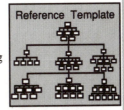
Reference Template

Prerequisite Template

B. to consistently and effectively sequence information blocks within maps

C. to sequence information maps into larger units, sections, chapters and documents.

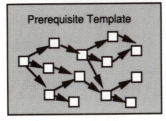

103

Stage 5

Presentation Analysis

a. use research-based principles to determine presentation format for paper-based delivery
b. develop computer screens for computer-based delivery
c. develop audio visual delivery

How precision modularity affects this stage ...

Enables analyst to determine delivery of information through appropriate media...

| IF Audience / Goals |
| AND Cost / Efficiency |
| THEN delivery media |

Standup Training

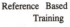

Policies, Procedures Reports, Proposals Documentation

Reference Based Training

Quick Reference

Video Training

Computer-Based Training Programs

On - Line Documentation

Hypertext Hypermedia

Discourse Domains

Introduction

How does a report of a scientific experiment differ from a sales presentation or a policy manual? In many ways: who the authors are, how they have come to know the subject matter, what they assume about their audience, what level of detail is used, what content is communicated. These are some of the ways. And how are all reports of scientific experiments alike? How are all sales presentations alike? The analysis of these similarities and differences is what we call domain analysis in Information Mapping's method. It involves examining the relationships between author and reader of different kinds of documents and the "stances" and points of view that can be seen as a result.

Definition: Domains of Discourse

A domain of discourse is the specification of information blocks of a particular class of documents, all of which share the same type of author-reader assumptions and the same stance or point of view towards subject matter.

Examples

A training manual differs quite radically from a sales presentation. Both differ significantly from scientific documents. The chart on these pages spells out some of these distinctions which provide the basis for identifying different discourse domains.

Domain of Discourse	Topic and Stance of the Discourse	Examples	Typical Documents
Relatively stable subject matter	We think we know enough to teach it.	• Well established subject matters (e.g. algebra) • How equipment functions	• Training and orientation • Documentation • Procedures • Policy manuals
Experimental knowledge	We have conducted scientific experiments to confirm and we would like to present our results and how we came by them to you.	• New results in physical, biological, and social sciences	• Reports of scientific experiments • Abstracts of reports
Part of subject matter under debate or consideration	We know enough about it to chart disagreements.	• Rhetoric of debate • Propaganda analysis • Analysis of systems • Argumentation analysis	• Systems analysis reports • Analysis of arguments • Legal briefs

Note:

The three discourse domains in the table below are *not* the only possible domains of discourse, nor is this a complete and exhaustive analysis of the domain.

Importance of Identification of Domains

An analysis of domains usually finds that there are similar clusters of information block types across many documents of the same domain. This enables us to clarify the similarities of each of the information block types in the new domain and thus to write and to teach the writing of these documents much more precisely and easily. (REH)

Reader's Understanding of the Subject Matter	For detailed examples of discourse domains look in this book at...
Does not know (most of) the subject matter.	Running through the chapter is a partial analysis of this domain. For more examples — see chapter 6
Knows a lot about the subject matter but not about this particular experiment.	An extended example of domain analysis on scientific abstracts — see chapter 8
May know a fair amount about the subject matter but perhaps not the subtleties. May be looking to change mind about something (e.g., to buy a new product, a new plan or concept).	An extended example of argumentation analysis — see chapter 7

Brief Discourse Analysis (Stable Subjects)

Introduction

We introduced the concept of discourse analysis as an examination of the components of documents all of which share the same type of author-reader characteristics and the same stance or point of view toward the subject matter of the document. Here we examine briefly one such domain, that of relatively stable subject matter. It is the domain that we have been using as an example frequently throughout this chapter.

Definition: Relatively Stable Subject Matters

A relatively stable subject matter is one which

- has been arbitrarily decided upon by an organization (e.g., administrative policies or procedures),
  or
- results from a design process (e.g., technical information about manufactured products),
  or
- has been agreed upon by a particular scholarly or scientific field and which is taught as the established information in that field.

Comment

This is the domain of discourse that has been most deeply studied and most widely applied by using Information Mapping's approach. It covers the broad range of high volume "information transfer" documents in administrative, technical and scientific subject matters that are regarded to be known well enough to teach.

Block Types for Document Types

Most documents in this domain are served by approximately 40 well understood information block types.

see page 109

Typical Document Types

- Procedures Manuals
- User Guides
- Job Aids
- Policy Manuals
- Operations Manuals
- Desktop Procedures
- Equipment Manuals
- Troubleshooting Manuals
- Screen Design Standards and Manuals
- Tutorials
- Instructor's Guides
- Course Administration Guides
- Training Manuals
- Textbooks
- System Manuals
- Installation Guides
- Systems Documentation
- Systems Standards & Functional Specifications
- Computer Language Manuals
- Applications Manuals
- Product Specifications and Descriptions

Different Document Types Have Different Proportions of Block Types

If you got together a hundred procedure manuals or a hundred policy manuals, you would see a great similarity of the pattern of the kinds of information block types appearing in them.

The Data

The two documents described in the charts below have different purposes and hence have quite different clusters of information blocks. One is a procedure manual and the other a mathematics textbook.

Commentary

What is the value of this kind of data? We can compare content types across subject matters. We can have some idea of what kind of writing tasks to look forward to and plan for. (REH)

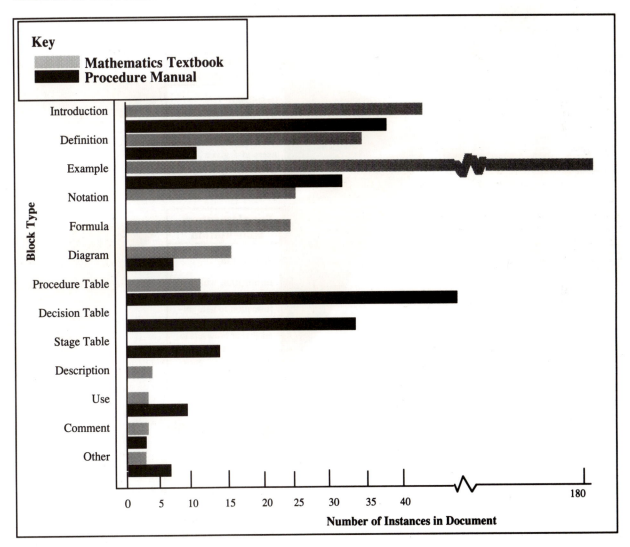

Information Type and Block Type Analysis

Application: Relatively Stable Subject Matters

Another principle that Information Mapping's methodology uses with consistency is to chunk at various levels. We have already introduced the information map as the next level of hierarchy larger than a block. The diagram below shows the general approach to chunking information at different levels.

The sentences in these kinds of documents (all relatively stable subjects)...

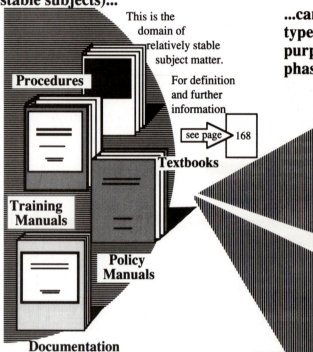

This is the domain of relatively stable subject matter.

For definition and further information

see page ➤ 168

Procedures

Textbooks

Training Manuals

Policy Manuals

Documentation

...can be divided into two types of information for purposes of early analysis phase...

Basic Information
Definition Information which can be regarded as being "new" to most of the users in a given user group description.

Supplementary Information
Definition Information which is added to the basic information to help initial learners, referencers, or browsers to find, understand or learn the basic information.

▲**What about other types of documents?**

Research has found that broad classes of documents have quite different types of information blocks, so it is important to analyze them separately into clusters that have similar blocks.

▲**Why make this distinction?**

Because during analysis of a subject matter, analysts should concern themselves only with the basic information, identifying it, refining it, and making sure they have all of it. Other information gets in the way of that process.

...and the sentences (and diagrams and illustrations) of basic information can be sorted into seven information types which can in turn be sorted into block types...

Information Types

- Structure
- Concept
- Procedure
- Process
- Classification
- Principle
- Fact

 see page 110

Information Added for Initial Learning

Definition	**Types**
Initial learning information aids learners in their first pass through the subject matter when their goal is to be able to apply or recall.	• Overview • Compare and Contrast • Course Objectives • Prerequisites to Course, Chapter, Map, Block • Learning Advice • Review and Summary • Test Questions, Practice Exercises & Performance Situations

Information Added for Reference

Definition	**Types**
Information added for reference aids users to review or look up forgotten material or to find information.	• Tables of Contents • Indexes • Lists of Notation • Lists of Formulae • Special Purpose Tables • Menus

Most Frequently Used Block Types

(in domain of relatively stable subject matter)

Analogy
Block Diagram
Checklist
Classification List
Classification Table

Classification Tree
Comment
Cycle Chart
Decision Table
Definition

Description
Diagram
Example
Expanded Procedure Table
Fact

Flow Chart
Flow Diagram
Formula
Input-Procedure-Output
Non-example

Notation
Objectives
Outlines
Parts-Function Table
Parts Table

Prerequisites to Course
Principle
Procedure Table
Purpose
Rule

Specified Action Table
Stage Table
Synonym
Theorem
When to Use

WHIF Chart
Who Does What
Worksheet

 ## Further Types and Distinctions

There are obviously finer distinctions, criteria, and standards for each of these information blocks that must be mastered to obtain the advantages of the methodology.

What are the Information Types?

procedure

process

structure

concept

fact

classification

principle

Definition

in ● for ● ma ● tion   types

(in′fər mā′shən tips)   *n.*   **1. the seven basic classifications into which sentences and/or diagrams of basic blocks of information in a subject matter associated with training or educational textbooks, procedure or policy books, manuals, and other similar forms of documentation may be sorted, namely, concepts, procedures, processes, classifications, facts, structures, and principles; each type has certain key information block types associated with it. 2. a classification system into which the information blocks in Information Mapping's method may be sorted so as to ensure completeness and efficiency in the analysis of subject matter. 3. the seven types are sometimes used, in their pure form, to refer to information maps by the same name, e.g., procedure map, process map, etc.**

Use

The information types theory is used to help the analyst identify specific information that is needed for each topic. These information type templates specify the key infor- mation blocks that are needed to ensure completeness and accuracy of the analysis. The templates also ensure a *reader* - rather than a writer-based document. The information type analysis also guides the specification of feedback and practice questions for training materials.

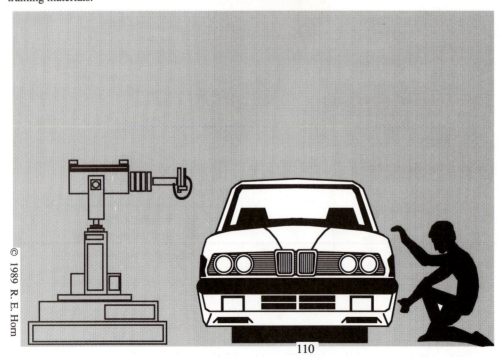

Definition	**Example**	**When to Use...**
a set of sequential steps that one person or entity performs to obtain a specified outcome. This includes the decisions that need to be made and the action that must be carried out as a result of those decisions.	...first, place the trim piece on the jig, second, take your power tool in your right hand...	When the reader needs to know "how to do it"
a series of events or phases which take place over time and usually have an identifiable purpose or result.	...when the transmission shifts from neutral to first, the following events occur...	When the reader needs to know "what happens"
a physical object or something that can be divided into parts or has boundaries.	...the spark plug is composed of the following main components...	When the reader needs to know • what something looks like • what its parts are
a group or class of objects, conditions, events, ideas, responses or relations that • all have one or more attributes in common • are different from one another in some other respect, and • are all designated by a common name.	...acceleration can be defined as...	When the reader needs to understand a term, idea or abstraction
a statement of data without supporting information that is asserted with certainty.	...the wheel base of this car is 5 feet 3 inches...	When the reader needs statements of data without supporting information
the division of specimens or things into categories using one or more sorting factors.	...we can divide this repair manual into the following parts...	When the reader wants to organize and qualify a large group into kinds or types based on some aspect of the group
a statement that 1. tells what should or should not be done such as • rules • policies or guidelines • warnings or cautions 2. seems to be true in light of the evidence such as • generalization • theorems 3. is unprovable but implied by other statements, such as • assumptions • axioms • postulates.	...the principle of road safety can be stated...	When the reader needs to know about what should or should not be done

Key Blocks Provide "Completeness Templates"

Introduction

To ensure a more complete capture of the subject matter, we have identified certain key chunks of information that go with each of the information types.

Definition

Key blocks are information blocks which help the writer capture and analyze critical content and present it in the best way for the reader.

One or more key blocks are associated with each of the seven information types.

Example

For those content topics identified as concepts, the key blocks are:

- Definition
- Example
- Non-Example

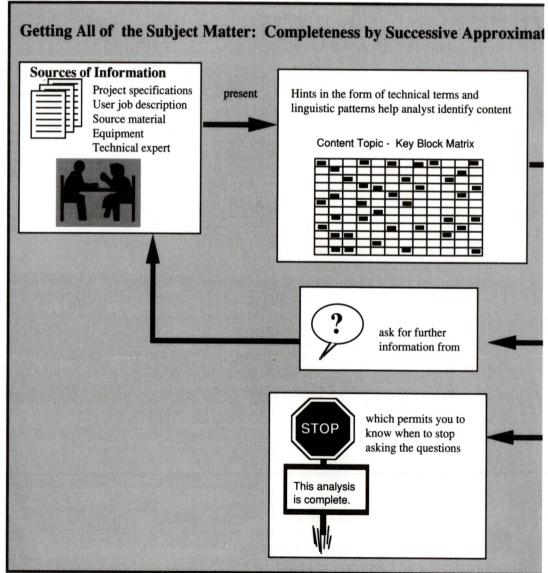

Getting All of the Subject Matter: Completeness by Successive Approximat

Sources of Information
Project specifications
User job description
Source material
Equipment
Technical expert

present

Hints in the form of technical terms and linguistic patterns help analyst identify content

Content Topic - Key Block Matrix

? ask for further information from

STOP which permits you to know when to stop asking the questions

This analysis is complete.

Myth of Completeness

All of the subject matter is in the source documents, or, if not, then the technical expert will tell you what you need to know.

Our clients tell us that we have all of the information long before that is so. A survey done in Information Mapping's consulting division showed that we never got more than 45 to 50% of the subject matter from the source documents. The technical experts have a different point of view than the user. They look at the subject matter differently. Therefore, they never tell you all of what the user needs. In fact, our surveys show they will only tell you about half of what you need to put in your written communication -- if unassisted by analysts using the Information Mapping method. And the half that is in the technical material and the half the expert tells you do not add up to 100%. Often they add up to the same 50%. So the corollary to the myth of completeness is that "Half of what they tell you is irrelevant."

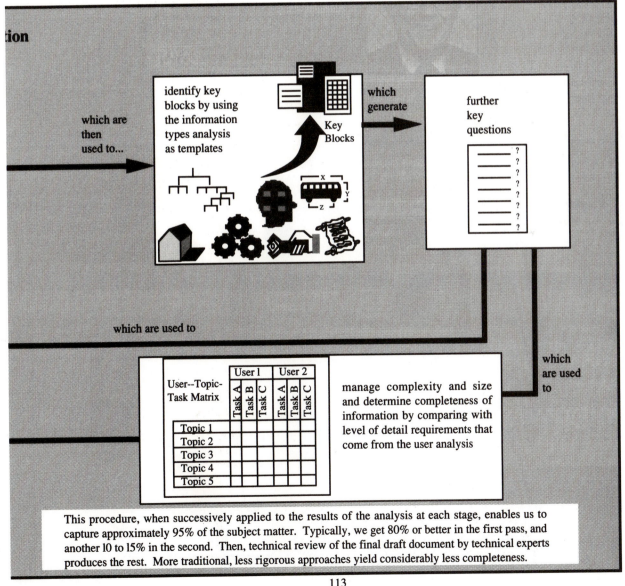

ion

which are
then
used to...

identify key
blocks by using
the information
types analysis
as templates

Key
Blocks

which
generate

further
key
questions

?
?
?
?
?
?
?

which are used to

User--Topic-Task Matrix	User 1			User 2		
	Task A	Task B	Task C	Task A	Task B	Task C
Topic 1						
Topic 2						
Topic 3						
Topic 4						
Topic 5						

manage complexity and size and determine completeness of information by comparing with level of detail requirements that come from the user analysis

which
are used
to

This procedure, when successively applied to the results of the analysis at each stage, enables us to capture approximately 95% of the subject matter. Typically, we get 80% or better in the first pass, and another 10 to 15% in the second. Then, technical review of the final draft document by technical experts produces the rest. More traditional, less rigorous approaches yield considerably less completeness.

Greater Ability to Specify Rule Domains

Introduction

If you are a writer or an editor, you want to know just when to apply a particular writing guideline. Traditional teaching of paragraphs is often too general to provide precise domains in which to apply a particular guideline. Establishing precise principles for constructing information blocks together with the specific block types for different types of documents has resulted in an increased ability to identify just where and when a guideline applies.

How this is different from most conventional approaches to writing and analysis

Note how different this approach is from the conventional approaches to writing paragraphs, which have rather vaguely specified guidelines and rules (e.g., have unity and coherence, or have topic sentences). Diagrammatically, we can express conventional writing analysis as a kind of cloudy set of constraints that literally permit almost anything...

Blocks do not necessarily have to have "topic sentences." Blocks can be one sentence long if that is what does the job. They can contain tables if that does the job.

The ability to specify the subcomponents of the document (e.g., maps, blocks, specific types of information) gives us the ability to avoid sweeping generalizations and make each standard, guideline, or rule count.

Documents

Chapters & Sections

Maps

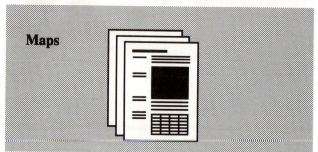

Blocks

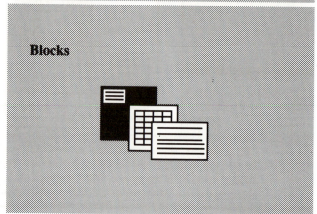

114

Examples of Quality Control Domains

Here are some examples of the domains which we have found to be the most useful in specifying standards, guidelines, and rules for analysis and writing:

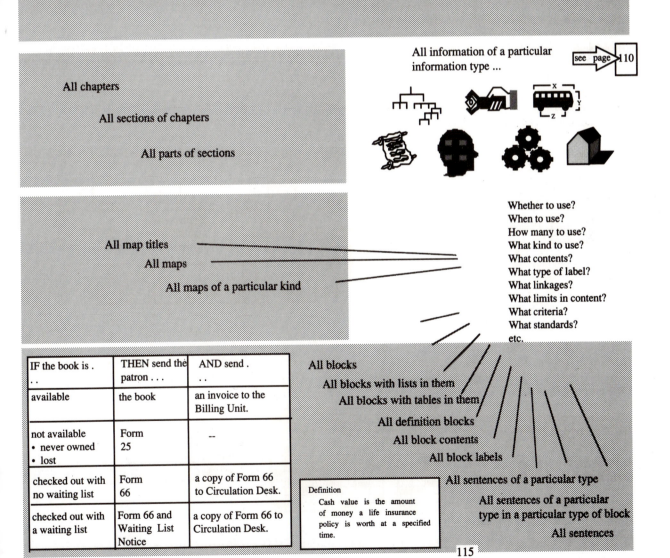

All documents of a specific type (e.g. , all policy books, all procedure manuals, all reference-based instruction manuals)

All chapters

All sections of chapters

All parts of sections

All information of a particular information type ...

see page 110

All map titles

All maps

All maps of a particular kind

Whether to use?
When to use?
How many to use?
What kind to use?
What contents?
What type of label?
What linkages?
What limits in content?
What criteria?
What standards?
etc.

IF the book is . . .	THEN send the patron . . .	AND send . . .
available	the book	an invoice to the Billing Unit.
not available • never owned • lost	Form 25	--
checked out with no waiting list	Form 66	a copy of Form 66 to Circulation Desk.
checked out with a waiting list	Form 66 and Waiting List Notice	a copy of Form 66 to Circulation Desk.

All blocks
All blocks with lists in them
All blocks with tables in them
All definition blocks
All block contents
All block labels

Definition
Cash value is the amount of money a life insurance policy is worth at a specified time.

All sentences of a particular type

All sentences of a particular type in a particular type of block

All sentences

Top Down and Bottom Up Analysis

Introduction

Most writing projects in the domain of relatively stable subject matter have as their source of subject matter either a subject matter expert or a pile of documents. The analyst/writer can proceed in two distinct ways to begin to develop an analysis of the subject matter.

Two Ways of Analyzing Subject Matter

---

1 Top Down Analysis

Definition

Top down analysis of a subject matter proceeds from the top of a hierarchy of information breaking the subject matter into parts hierarchically.

Example

To prepare a new procedure book on accounting, an analyst might look at the project from the point of view of what has to be accomplished by the people following the procedure and then continue to subdivide a task into more and more detail.

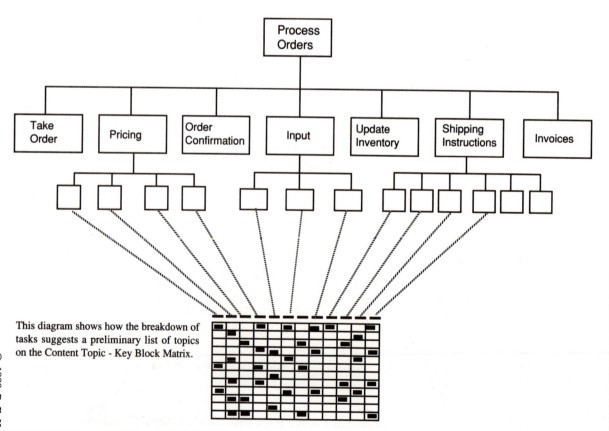

This diagram shows how the breakdown of tasks suggests a preliminary list of topics on the Content Topic - Key Block Matrix.

2 Bottom Up Analysis

Definition

Bottom up analysis of a subject matter proceeds by doing an information block analysis of pieces of the subject matter as they become available either from the subject matter expert or from documents.

Example One

An analyst may interview a subject matter expert (SME) who is the only source of information (e.g., the design engineer on a product or the manager in charge of a new service). The SME may ramble from one topic to another in the interview. The analyst can nevertheless "track" the subject matter acquisition by immediately putting the information into provisional information block assignments which assume that other maps and blocks of information will be obtained later. Thus the experienced Information Mapping analyst always has a dynamically changing framework to attach the subject matter chunks they obtain one by one.

Content Topic - Key Block Matrix

Example Two

Content Topic - Key Block Matrix

The analyst can approach a stack of source documents with a "fishing net" of block type and content topics, leaving for later the task of initially organizing and identifying what is missing. This enables the analyst to move rapidly and quickly through a subject matter without great repetition and with great efficiency.

Reference-Based Training

Definition -- Reference-Based Training

Reference-based training is a way of arranging training that relies on reference manuals, on-line documentation, and on-line help messages, rather than on instructors or other media, to provide information needed to perform skills. The method recognizes that many tasks do not need to be or cannot be efficiently learned ahead of the time they are needed for use. Rather, users need good reference manuals and the confidence in their skills of finding the information when they need it.

A key element of the training design is that the practice exercises during training require the user to look up information in the user guides, reference manuals, and on-line help so that the user gets accustomed to using them and finds them helpful, thereby making it more likely that they will use them on the job after the training.

Reference-based training may be self-instructional and used at the work-site or may be partially used in the classroom with instructors

---

Factors That Can Trigger Consideration of Reference-Based Training

☑ information that is not used frequently

☑ lack of trained staff of instructors

☑ geographically diverse group of trainees

☑ large number of trainees to be trained in small amount of time

☑ training costs must be kept to a minimum

☑ replacement training important

☑ computer-based system (can use on-line and in paper-based reference)

Typical Components of Reference-Based Training Systems

Reference Manuals
provide all of the information needed to operate the system in readily accessible form

On-line Help for Systems

provides quick information and training for shorter, low-prerequisite skills

Training Exercises
provide a sequence of practice situations that ensure that the trainee will come away with skills

Exercises

Tutorials
provide careful initial sequence of training familiarization with the job and with the reference materials

Tutorials

Simulation Exercises

provide practice situations that are similar or identical to those done on the job

Simulations

Why is Reference-Based Training emerging as an important alternative?

- Software is proliferating -- nobody can learn every function of the products they use.

- Excellent reference-based training can cut user reliance on hot lines, personal handholding, need for trained instructors.

- Contemporary documentation engineering makes it possible to create excellent reference manuals efficiently and consistently.

Why is Information Mapping's method important for Reference-Based Training?

Reference-based training only works if the reference manuals are complete, accurate, easy to use, easy to access, task-based, and easy to maintain.

The Information Mapping's methodology is the only complete documentation engineering methodology that will deliver this.

Benefits of Reference-Based Training

To the Trainee

- Greater confidence in the system...sooner

- Less frustration in using the new system

- Shorter formal training time (if any)

- Greater confidence in user's ability to retrieve and learn

To the Training Development Group

- Cost savings in preparation of training materials

- Cost savings in training delivery

- Can use supervisors (or other non-instructors) as trainers

For the Organization

- Better use of sophisticated software/hardware
- Cost savings for the hotline
- Increased productivity
- Less supervisory time spent correcting errors and answering questions
- Increased customer satisfaction
- Fewer errors in system use
- Lower technical support requirement
- Improved morale

Important Conditions for Success...

Reference manual must be task-oriented and written from user point of view

Reference manual must be complete, easy to access, easy to learn from

Exercises must be close in level of simulation to on-the-job tasks

On-line help messages must be extraordinarily clear, provide access to more detail and more context

Tutorials must take beginner through only the main path, not the detailed exceptions

The Mapping Metaphor: Subject Matter Structure

Introduction

One of the important things about Information Mapping's analysis method is that it follows the underlying structure of the subject matter, much like a geographical map follows the exact contours of the terrain.

Geographical Maps Show Point-to-Point Correspondence

On geographical maps, the most important places have the most prominent graphic features such as the heaviest type. Major superhighways and airports are easy to spot. The smaller roads are indicated by smaller lines and the smaller towns are in smaller type sizes. We can follow the larger structure of the territory without getting confused by the detail.

On a geographical map, the shape of the territory is shown by a similar shape on the map. If the city streets or the airport runways are laid out in a rectangular fashion, then that regularity is represented on the map in a point for point correspondence.

Information Maps

How do information maps and their components, information blocks, follow the terrain? What is the terrain? The contours of a subject matter are individual concepts, structures, organizations, processes, procedures, etc. To have a correct "map" of such a territory, you have to have (metaphorically) the right viewpoint and the right way of representing the subject matter.

And you must follow the contours of the subject matter. If it is a very regular one, then the result of an analysis is straightforward. If the contours are uneven, then the information maps must follow this structure.

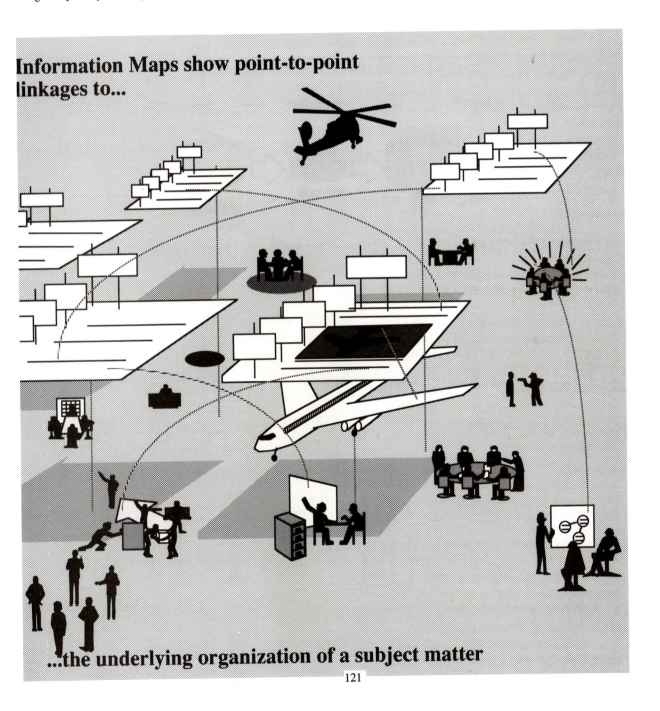

Information Maps show point-to-point linkages to...

...the underlying organization of a subject matter

Meeting the Criteria for Better Communication

Commentary:

The individual user and the organization have different criteria for a method of writing. On these pages, we present some of the most important criteria that have come out of our research on Information Mapping's method. For discussion see Notes

Criteria of the Individual User / Reader / Learner

Relevance to Purpose of Communication

 Does the document contain the right information for what I need to know or do?

Completeness

 Does the document contain all of the information I need?

Accuracy

 Is the information in the document correct?

Comprehensibility

 Is the document written so that I can comprehend the information easily and quickly?

Learnability

 Is the document written so that I can learn what I need optimally when I am completely new to the subject?

Accessibility and Easier Scannability

 Is the document organized and formatted so that I can easily and quickly find what I am looking for without having to read everything?

Improved Decision Making

 Is the document structured so that I can make better decisions? Particularly, are the recommendations, supporting data, and evaluations immediately available?

Improved Analysis

 Does the document help me analyze my problems and help me to spot easily what is not there?

Fewer Errors

Does this document help me to make fewer performance errors?

Improved Electronic Filing and Retrievability

Does the document help me retrieve what I'm looking for more quickly and easily?

Improved Creativity by Reducing Routine Work

 Does the document help me think more creatively by reducing the amount of brain work I have to do to figure out what is there and how to structure it?

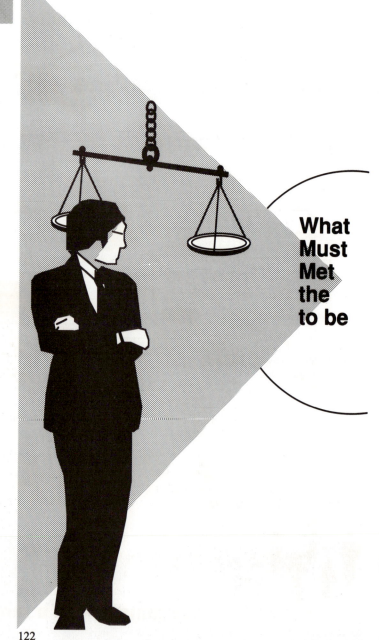

What Must Met the to be

122

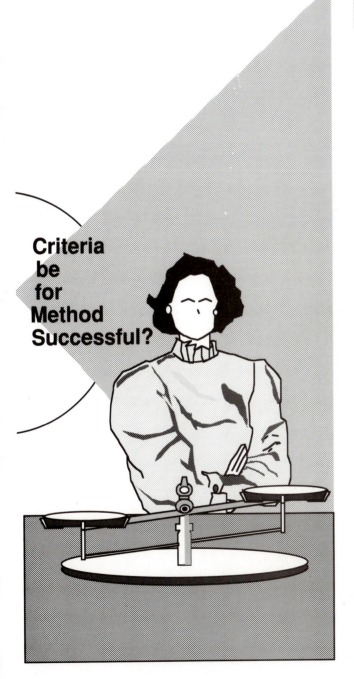

Criteria be for Method Successful?

The Organization's Criteria for a Communications Method

Increased Revenues and Profits

 Does it contribute to our sales and profits, and lower our overhead?

Lower Product Support Costs

 Does it help us lower what it costs us to provide good maintenance and excellent customer support?

Optimally Effective and Efficient Communication and Training

 Does the method help us be more effective in the human side of business -- communication -- and does it do so efficiently?

Lower Training Costs

 Since our products and services are changing so much more rapidly, does the method help us keep training and retraining costs in line?

Maintainability

 Are the documents developed such that, if information needs to be added, deleted, or changed, this can be done efficiently and effectively?

Teachability for Group Use

 Can the method be taught quickly to a level that different members of a group can work together to compose a document?

Comprehensiveness

 Is the methodology appropriate for a large number of different kinds of documents?

Chapter 4. Navigating Structured Hypertrails

Navigating
Structured Hypertrails

**Prerequisite
Hypertrails**

**Geographic
Hypertrails**

**Structural
Hypertrails**

**In this Chapter
...we ask:
"What are some
kinds of generally
useful
linkage structures
in hypertext?**

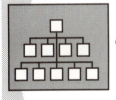

**Classification
Hypertrails**

**Definition
Hypertrails**

(__) is a
(__) with a
(__)

**Decision
Hypertrails**

**Project
Hypertrails**

**Example
Hypertrails**

polygon

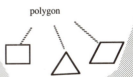

Overview of This Chapter

Definition: Hypertrails

A hypertrail is a set of links between chunks of information, such as units, chapters, articles, books, or courses (and in the context of Information Mapping's method, blocks and maps), that organize and sequence information about a particular function or characteristic of subject matters.

Use

Hypertrails enable users to take different, yet structured, paths through hypertext knowledge bases. Usually, there is a dominant trail for use of particular kinds of users such as initial learners or referencers. Multiple hypertrails have the advantage of providing both structure and the free-browsing modes of knowledge base use.

Making Hypertrail Networks Linear: Definition

Linearizing hypertrails is a process of selecting from the networks of links a series that makes sense as the primary hypertrail for the user who selects a command to be guided through the detail of the hypertrail.

see page 146

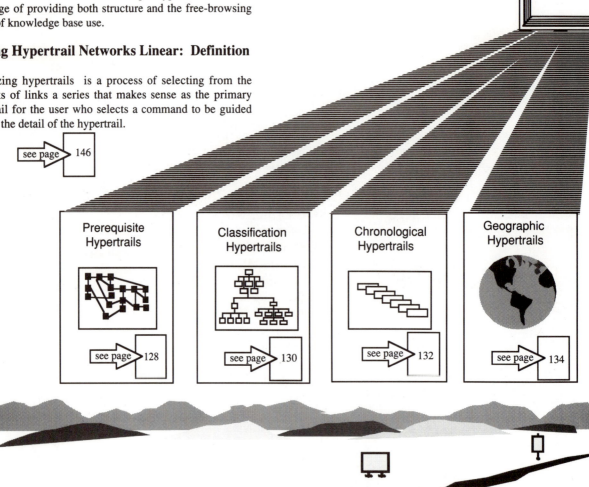

Chapter 4

Prerequisite Hypertrails

see page 128

Classification Hypertrails

see page 130

Chronological Hypertrails

see page 132

Geographic Hypertrails

see page 134

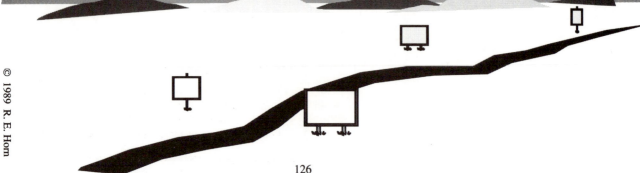

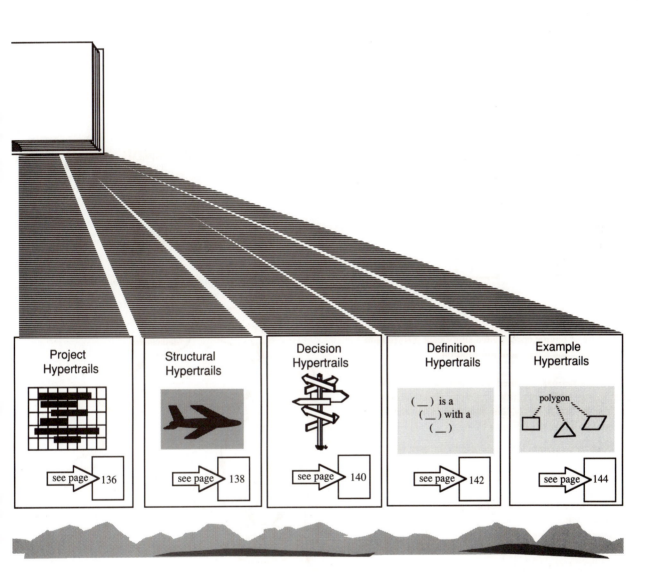

Project Hypertrails	Structural Hypertrails	Decision Hypertrails	Definition Hypertrails	Example Hypertrails
see page 136	see page 138	see page 140	see page 142	see page 144

Commentary

Other hypertrails have been identified. But these will serve to provide a good overview of the functioning of hypertrails when used with information blocks and maps. (REH)

Prerequisite Hypertrails

Introduction

Prerequisites are one of the basic ways of organizing information for users of hypertext learning systems.

Definition

A prerequisite hypertrail provides a set of linkages between information maps, information blocks (or other larger chunks of information, such as units, chapters, articles, books, or courses). These connections specify which maps learners must understand (or which tasks they must be able to do) in order to understand more advanced topics or accomplish more advanced skills.

Example

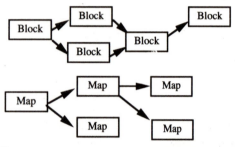

Use

The prerequisite hypertrail is typically used to sequence chunks of text in a linear way so that the learner may always be sure of having encountered significant information needed to understand the present information.

Thus, if the learner has informed the system that he or she is an initial learner and knows little or nothing about the subject matter, then the text in the system should be linearized using the prerequisite hypertrail linkages.

The prerequisite hypertrail is of most use to the user who:

1. is interested in the prerequisite structure of a subject matter, OR
2. has never studied the subject before, and is a serialist learner Δ OR
3. has never studied a similar subject before, OR
4. is interested in the most efficient (i.e., straightest) path through the material.

see page 52

Two Levels of Prerequisite Analysis

Course Level Prerequisites

Example

Here is an example of a prerequisite hypertrail at the level of courses in math and physics:

```
Calculus I                    Finite Mathematics
    │                             │
    ▼                             ▼
Calculus II                  Elementary Statistics
    │   │                         │
    ▼   ▼                         ▼
Calculus III  Elementary     Advanced Statistics
    │         Physics
    ▼             │
Advanced     Advanced
Calculus     Physics
    │   │        │
    ▼   ▼        ▼
    Mathematical
    Physics
    │
    ▼
Complex      Real
Variables →  Variables
```

Concept Level Prerequisites

Example

In analyzing the beginning concepts in the topic vector mathematics, we find these prerequisite relationships:

This ASPECT	has these concepts as PREREQUISITES
Displacement	• Distance • Direction
Vector	• Direction from a point • Magnitude
Magnitude	• Number • Unit of measurement

Fairness to Learners Principle

Synonym

The Principle of Guaranteed Access to Prerequisites

Introduction

"If ya'da told me that first, I woulda understood what you were talkin' about." Almost everybody has an intuitive notion that you have to learn some things before you can learn others. Too often in textbooks and training manuals, readers are stranded at mid-text by the introduction of concepts they are expected to be able to understand without ever having previously encountered the concepts, the words or experience.

Principle

We take as a basic principle for sequencing initial learning materials the principle, called "Fairness to Learners Principle." It says:

Learners should have previously encountered the prerequisites to all concepts they are presented with in learning materials, or should have immediate access to that prerequisite information.

Implementation

Access to all major prerequisites is provided by

1. developing a prerequisite hypertrails that can be activated by learners if they want that kind of sequence through the text, and

2. providing hypertext linkages from the currently displayed text to prerequisite information such as where terms are introduced.

Classification Hypertrails

Introduction

Classification is one of the basic ways of organizing information. It uses the basic principle of grouping similar things together into classes and distinguishing these classes from other classes by differences.

The ability to follow and display large classifications is an important characteristic of efficient hypertext systems.

Definition

A classification hypertrail is a set of linkages in a hypertext database that enables a user to

- find any linkages higher or lower on a classification tree for a particular subject

- display a classification structure of a given hypertext region.

Example of a Classification Hypertrail

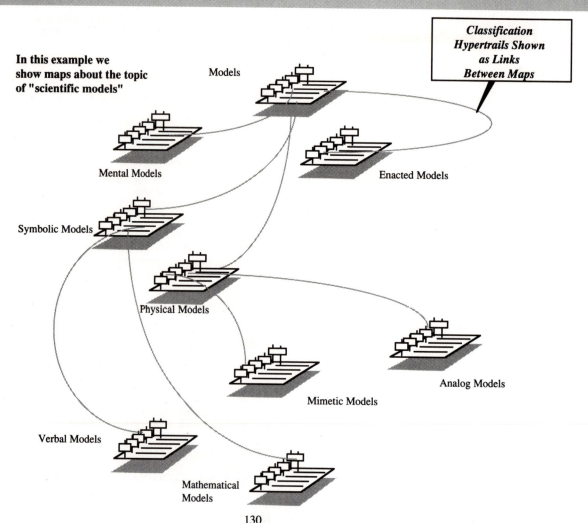

In this example we show maps about the topic of "scientific models"

Models

Mental Models

Enacted Models

Classification Hypertrails Shown as Links Between Maps

Symbolic Models

Physical Models

Analog Models

Mimetic Models

Verbal Models

Mathematical Models

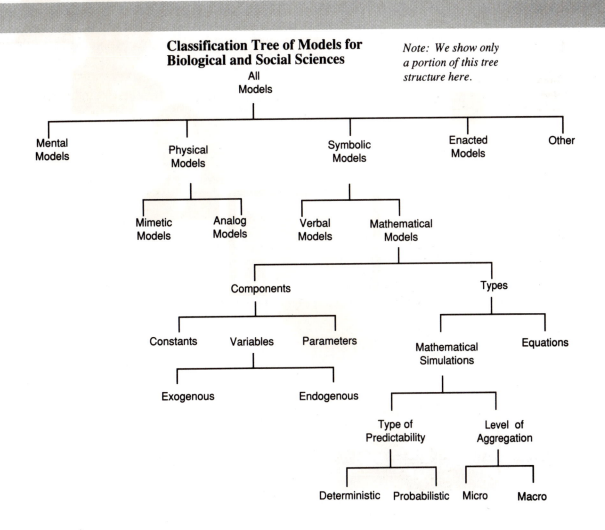

Classification Tree of Models for Biological and Social Sciences

Note: We show only a portion of this tree structure here.

Chronological Hypertrails

Introduction

Chronological hypertrails resemble the familiar time lines.
But they go beyond these graphical tools in organizing large
amounts of data.

Definition

Chronological hypertrails are linkages of nodes that organize
information with time.

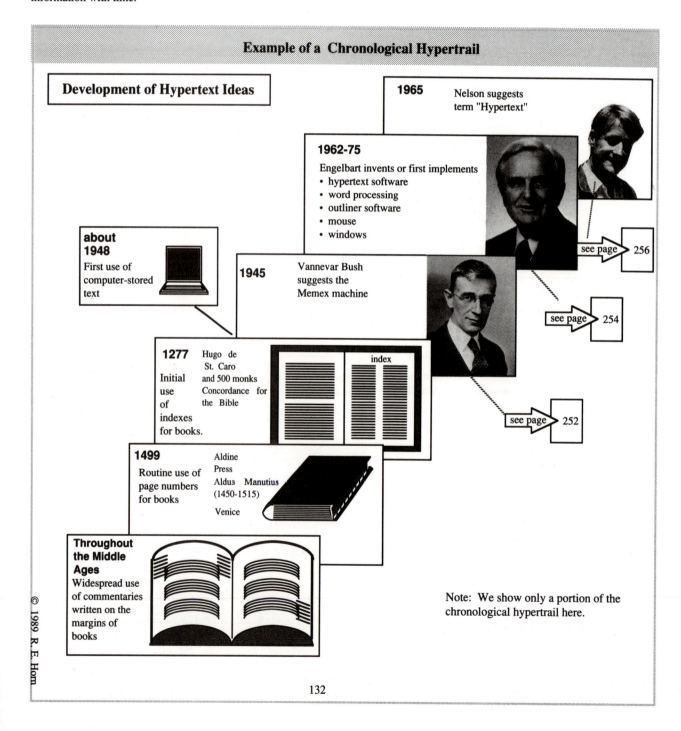

Example of a Chronological Hypertrail

Development of Hypertext Ideas

1965 Nelson suggests term "Hypertext"

1962-75

Engelbart invents or first implements
- hypertext software
- word processing
- outliner software
- mouse
- windows

see page 256

about 1948

First use of computer-stored text

1945 Vannevar Bush suggests the Memex machine

see page 254

1277 Hugo de St. Caro and 500 monks Concordance for the Bible

Initial use of indexes for books.

index

see page 252

1499

Routine use of page numbers for books

Aldine Press Aldus Manutius (1450-1515)

Venice

Throughout the Middle Ages
Widespread use of commentaries written on the margins of books

Note: We show only a portion of the chronological hypertrail here.

© 1989 R. E. Horn

132

Three Kinds of Chronological Hypertrails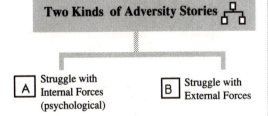

1 Sequence of Events Hypertrail

Description

A sequence of events hypertrail follows some time measurement, such as

daily

weekly

monthly

annually.

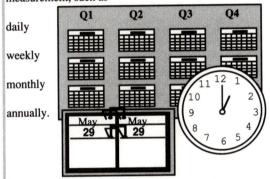

Example
- Time line of events in a Presidential campaign
- Sequence of events in a complicated industrial manufacturing process

3 Natural Development Hypertrail

Description

A natural development hypertrail follows the sequence of development of a particular process or system.

Example

- Evolution
- Development of an organization

2 Storyline Hypertrail

Description

A storyline hypertrail tells a sequence of occurrences in the life of a particular person or group of persons.

Examples
- scenarios
- stories
- docudramas

Narrative has been classified by literary critics in many ways. Here is just one such classification:

Three Kinds of Stories

1. Adventure   2. Discovery or Exploration   3. Struggle with Adversity

Two Kinds of Adversity Stories

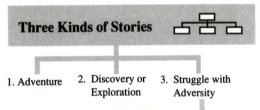

A Struggle with Internal Forces (psychological)

B Struggle with External Forces

Comment

In hypertext, branching can produce stories with different trails.

Geographic Hypertrails

Introduction

One of the major ways that we organize information is spatially. We draw maps to help us get around in space. We use word descriptions of how to get from one place to another and to describe the contents of geographical space. Geographic hypertrails link these information blocks.

Definition

Geographic hypertrails link together descriptions and maps of geographical information.

Contrast with Structure Hypertrails

Note that one of the other hypertrails, structure hypertrails, is closely related to geographic hypertrails. The major difference is that in geographic hypertrails we are linking spatial relationships between different structures. In structure hypertrails we are linking the subparts to the larger structure.

Example of a Geographic Hypertrail

Here is an example of a geographic hypertrail that zooms in on the White House starting from a look at the earth from space.

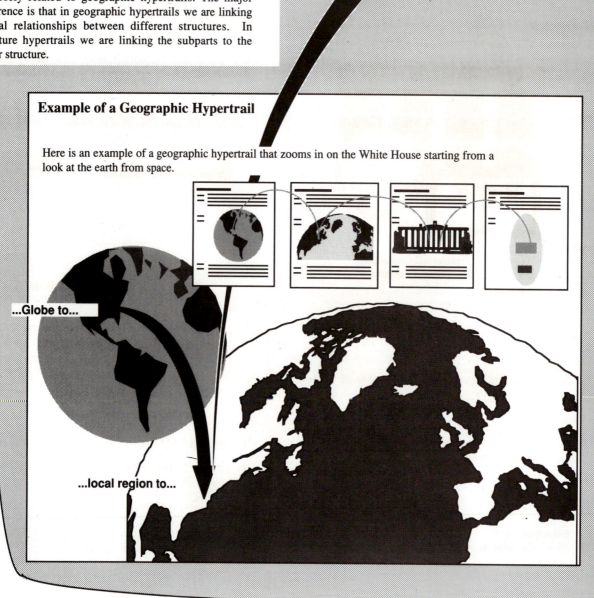

...Globe to...

...local region to...

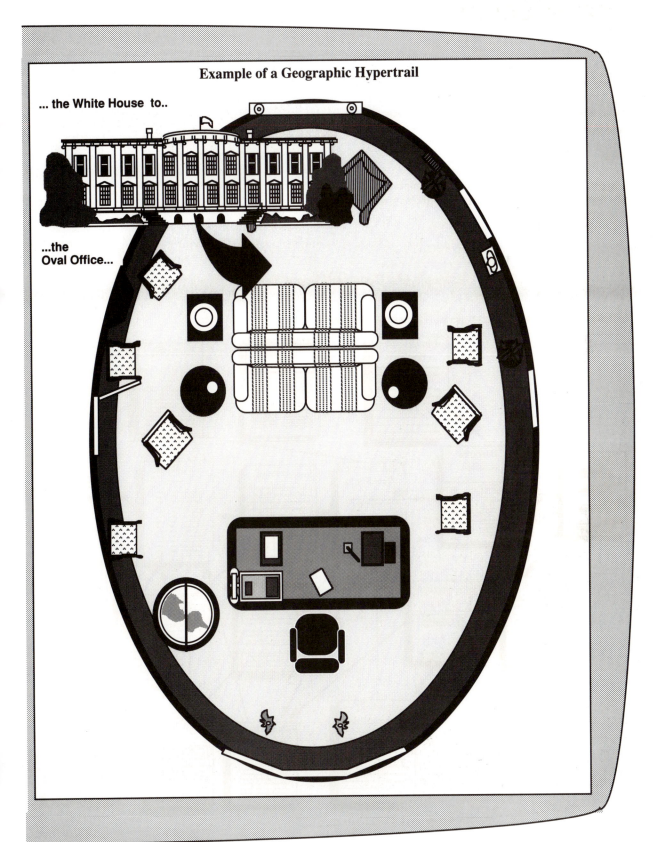

Example of a Geographic Hypertrail

... the White House to..

...the
Oval Office...

Project Hypertrails

Introduction

One of the ways we frequently organize our work is by projects. We think of projects as work organized around a specific goal that will take a period of time longer than a simple task. Hypertrails should follow natural work linkages, so a project hypertrail becomes a necessity.

Definition

Project hypertrails are specific kinds of chronological hypertrails that link planned and past events all focused on a personal or group project.

Two Kinds of Display Metaphors for Project Hypertrails

---

1 **Example of a Document Event Network Hypertrail**

In this example we show project hypertrails for a survey research project :

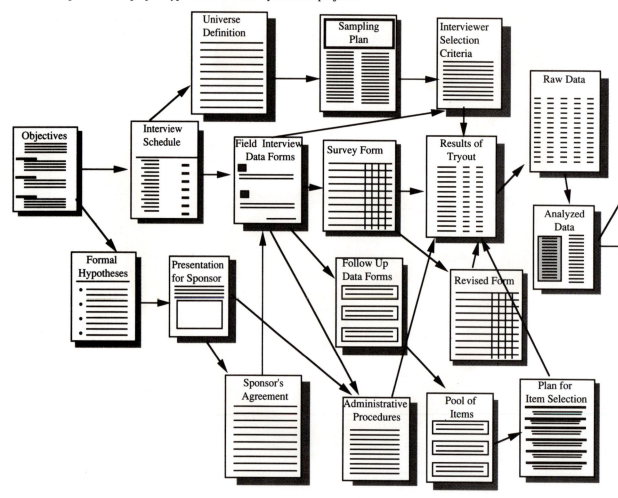

2 | Example of a Document Event Network Hypertrail

In this example we show project hypertrails for a survey research project :

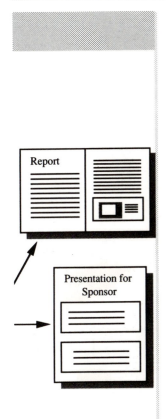

Report

Presentation for Sponsor

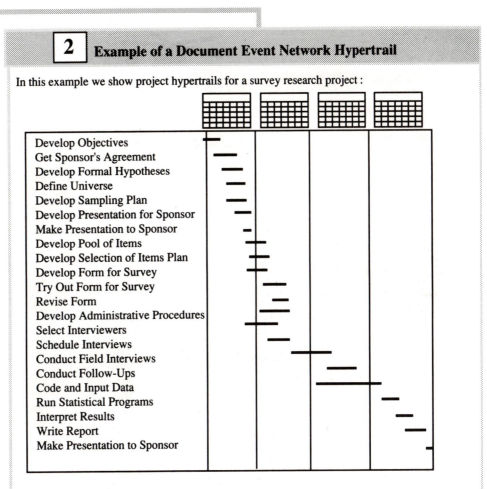

Develop Objectives
Get Sponsor's Agreement
Develop Formal Hypotheses
Define Universe
Develop Sampling Plan
Develop Presentation for Sponsor
Make Presentation to Sponsor
Develop Pool of Items
Develop Selection of Items Plan
Develop Form for Survey
Try Out Form for Survey
Revise Form
Develop Administrative Procedures
Select Interviewers
Schedule Interviews
Conduct Field Interviews
Conduct Follow-Ups
Code and Input Data
Run Statistical Programs
Interpret Results
Write Report
Make Presentation to Sponsor

Structure Hypertrails

Definition: Structures

Structures are physical objects. They have boundaries and occupy physical space. They have parts. A useful hypertrail links the parts to the large structures.

Definition: Structure Hypertrails

Structure hypertrails link specific substructures described in information blocks to the larger structure. A user can begin searching a structure hypertrail from any part of the structure or substructure in the hypertrail.

Boundaries: Alternative Way of Defining Structure Hypertrails

A variation on the standard structural hypertrail is a structural hypertrail that links a structure by its physical boundaries, i.e., by the name of the boundary lines or by the boundary itself (where the two structures or substructures meet).

Example of a Structure Hypertrail

Here is a structure hypertrail of a wind tunnel arranged by names of the subassemblies:

Here is a structure hypertrail of a wind tunnel by picture of the equipment subassemblies:

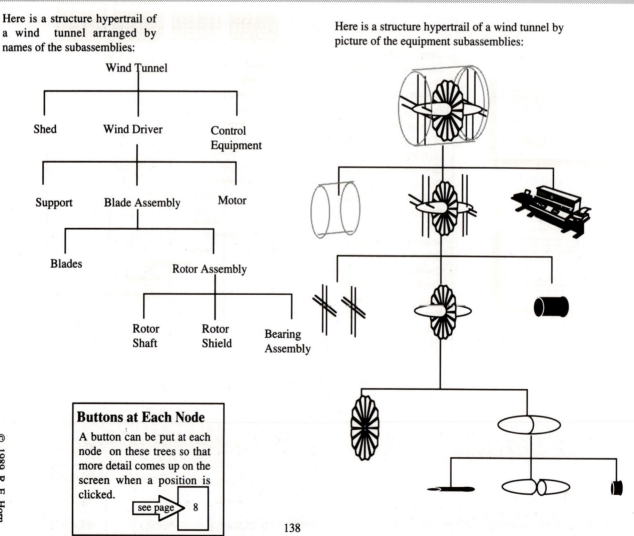

Buttons at Each Node

A button can be put at each node on these trees so that more detail comes up on the screen when a position is clicked.

see page 8

Here is a structure hypertrail of the maps describing a wind tunnel divided into subassemblies:

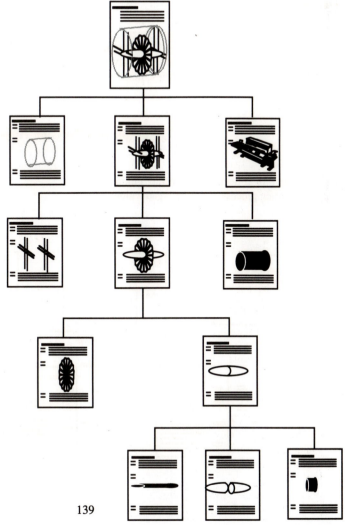

Popup Menus

When clicked, the button might bring up a popup menu which contains these options:

- Description
- Specifications
- Source
- Manufacturer
- Maintenance Information
- Troubleshooting Guides

139

Decision Hypertrails

Introduction

Organizations are shaped around processes for making decisions. They must have orderly ways to prepare for, make, implement, and document decisions. In the framework of hypertext systems using Information Mapping, decision hypertrails help track all information about a given decision.

Definition: Decision Hypertrails

Decision hypertrails link all of the information (blocks, maps, or documents) about a particular decision that a person (or organization) has made (or is in the process of making).

Layering and Structuring Required

To make a reader's job manageable, decision hypertrails need to be layered and structured. That is, they require the specification information blocks and maps to provide the components of the trail.

Types of Decisions

There are many kinds of decisions and many "sizes" of decisions. The approach to assembling and displaying information for each type of decision must follow an analysis of these kinds of decisions. We do not go into these details in this book.

Example of a Decision Hypertrail

Following is an example of a decision hypertrail linking documents in the purchasing process of a large organization:

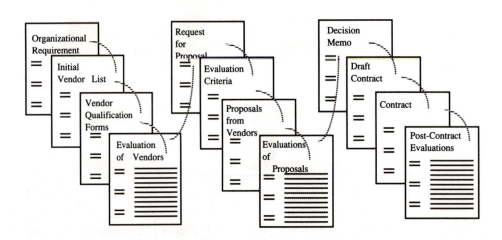

Example of a Decision Hypertrail

A policy decision hypertrail could display links between relevant documents at different "layers" of information about that decision.

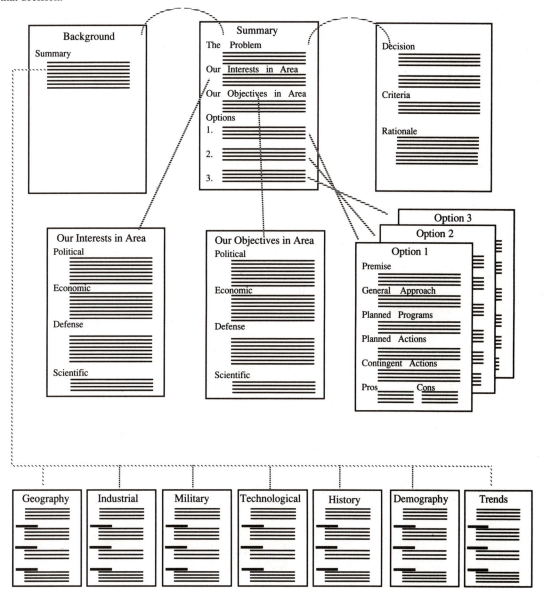

Definition Hypertrails

Introduction

Most words are ambiguous. They have more than one meaning. For the 500 most-used words in the English language, the Oxford dictionary lists 14,070 meanings. Thus, each has an average of almost 30 meanings.

So, dictionaries have proven their worth over the centuries. Using definition hypertrails within the context of an Information Mapping hypertext knowledge base will prove to be a significant advance for dictionary users.

Definition: Definition Hypertrails

A definition hypertrail provides links between the different meanings of a single term in a hypertext document, or between related terms in one or more documents.

Context designators for each of the meanings are provided, as well as examples of the use of such words in context.

Comment

The process of creating definition hypertrails is quite easy since all definitions in Information Mapping are segregated into separate information blocks and are distinctively labeled. The dictionary hypertrail approach makes a particularly useful form of dictionary since the other links (such as example blocks) are readily available.

Obviously, it may be useful to load a large conventional dictionary into the knowledge base as well, and link it to the growing definition hypertrail.

Example of a Definition Hypertrail

In Chapter One of this book, for example, you can find these definitions that comprise a definition hypertrail:

- hypertext
- links (hypertext)
- nodes (hypertext)
- buttons (hypertext)
- system-supplied links
- user-created links
- author-created links
- semantic nets
- branching stories
- relational databases
- simulations
- commentaries
- anthologies
- hypermedia

Example of a Definition Hypertrail

The blocks below illustrate taking definitions from several
related information maps to form a definition hypertrail:

Models

Definition   Models are abstract ways of representing the experience of our inner
and outer worlds enabling us to manipulate and sometimes predict
from the representations rather than from the systems they represent.

Mental Models

Definition   Mental models are representations consisting of ideas and concepts in
the human mind.

Physical Models

Definition   Physical models are models constructed from tangible material.

Mimetic Models

Definition   A mimetic physical model resembles in physical characteristics a
system it represents, but does not necessarily behave like the system.

Analog Physical Model

Definition   Analog physical models are made of concrete, tangible materials that
are built to act like a real system even though they may not resemble
one.

Simulations (Using Models)

Definition   A simulation consists of the construction of a history of the changes in
state of a previously defined model.

Enacted Models

Definition   Enacted models are processes in which people perform the roles and
actions of systems by making decisions and taking actions through time
with a particular outcome.

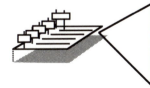

Simulation Game Models

Definition   Simulations are simplified models of reality so that reality can be better
understood. Games are competitive interactions among participants to
achieve pre-specified goals. Simulation games are simulations in
which participants act out roles and make decisions as if they were
making them in the actual or real world situation. Cooperation among
participants and teams as well as within groups may also be properties
of such simulation games.

Example Hypertrails

Introduction

Some text is organized so that there are one or more running examples throughout. Different topics are introduced and defined, then examples are presented. Some examples are "extended," i.e., they exemplify many of the topics made.

Definition: Example Hypertrails

An Example Hypertrail is a linking of

- all of the different appearances of a single extended example that appears in a single document

- all of the specific appearances where the same example is used in different places in different documents.

This permits the user to request of the system: "Show me all of the places where this example is used."

Example One

In a book on dream theory and dream interpretation, specific dreams are the examples. Each dream has a name (e.g., Grandma on the Ceiling, My Boat Sinks, etc.). The full dreams are described the first time they are introduced. Parts of the dreams may be requoted in specific sections (e.g., in sections on "symbols," or on "different ways of interpreting dreams"). The dreams may also be referred to by name in other discussions.

Clearly a useful hypertrail would be to link all of the appearances of a given dream on a single trail and to be able to link all of these individual example hypertrails into a large master example hypertrail.

Hypertrails like this were used by Walter Bonime in his book, *The Clinical Use of Dreams*. In the book there is a "dream index" so that you can go look at all of the places where the dream occurs.

Example Two

In many business procedure manuals, we use the same example in a procedure that runs several pages. These individual examples linked together in an example hypertrail form a case study of the use of this procedure.

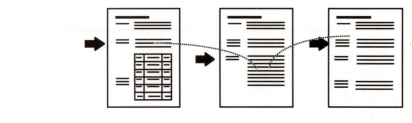

The arrows identify the appearance of the same example hypertrail in a sequence of different Information Maps.

Example of an Example Hypertrail

Here, we show how the description of a single simulation game about political process at the local level can be used as an example on several different information maps. All of these maps together provide the procedure for making an educational simulation game. Note that only the map title and an example block are presented in this example, not the whole map.

1. Define the Problem Area to Be Simulated

Example   The educational simulation selected is a local political process.

2. Define the Objective and Scope of the Simulation

Example   Objectives: To understand how the mayor and city council get elected in our city.

Scope: Our major interest is in examining the electoral process at the local city level and to see the other influences of other local organizations on the selection of city officials.

3. Define the People and Organizations Involved

Example   Organizations: Political parties, government departments, the local newspapers, television, radio stations, community action organizations, etc. Roles: Incumbent mayor, other mayoral candidates, president of city council, powerful local police chief, state political party chairman, heads of local political clubs.

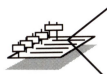

4. Define the Motives and Purposes of the Players

Example   In the local political elections game, the first goal of the incumbent mayor is to get reelected. The motive of the state political chairman is to see that the candidates loyal to the party and who have a good chance of winning are nominated.

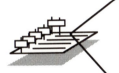

5. Define the Resources Available to the Players

example not used for this map

6. Determine the Transactions to be Simulated and the Decision Rules to Be Followed

Example   "In the local elections game, the first playing period might cover a pre-nomination period of a few months, where potential candidates for two parties lobby for the nomination. In the second playing period, players gather at conventions to nominate candidates (or perhaps primary elections are held). In the third playing period, players organize and hold a campaign, which is followed by the fourth and shorter period in which the election is held and the winner determined."

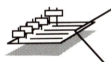

7. Formulate the Evaluation Method

example not used for this map

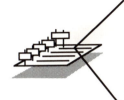

8. Develop Simulation Games Prototype

example not used for this map

9. Try Out and Modify the Prototype

example not used for this map

Hypertrail Webs into Linearized Sequences

Introduction

Because human beings live in a linear, time-sequenced world, we must always have some "next" event in our lives. In hypertext that means whatever the button is called, it is always in some sense a "next" button.

If the structure of the subject matter is a two-dimensional or multi-dimensional network or web, we must nevertheless follow some next link in the net. We must go to some next node. This raises the question of how we shall linearize the nodes of hypertrails, because there is always some limit to the size of the web that can be displayed on a single screen.

Definition: Linearized Sequences for Hypertrails

A linearized sequence for a hypertrail puts each of the elements of a hypertrail into a sequence in such a way that the user can be shown some next information. As an automatic facility of a hypertext system, it must also provide organizing elements of a document for the user, such as a table of contents, index and other "maps" of the structure of the subject.

Example of a Linearized Sequence

Here we show a structure hypertrail of a series of information maps about a wind tunnel. The linearization of this network is shown to the right.

Note: For a more complete example of structure hypertrails

see page ▷ 138

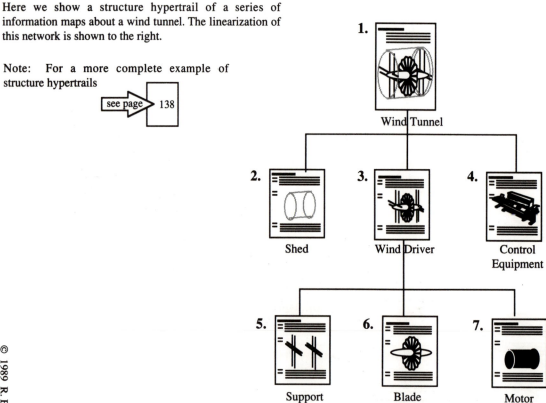

1. Wind Tunnel

2. Shed   3. Wind Driver   4. Control Equipment

5. Support   6. Blade Assembly   7. Motor

The software linearized the pages putting 5, 6, and 7 after 3. Then it places 4 next.

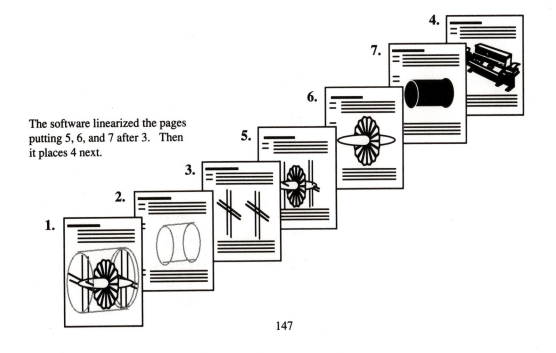

Chapter 5. Resolving Some Hypertext Problems

Resolving Some Hypertext Problems

Group Writing Issues

Reading Cues Issues

Clustering Maps into Documents

In this Chapter ...an overview of How Information Mapping's Method Resolves Some of the Hypertext Issues

Information Maps as Nodes

Lost in Hyperspace Issue

Linking Information Blocks

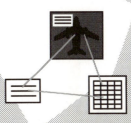

Cognitive Overload Issue

Interface Issues

Overview of This Chapter

How Information Mapping's Method Addresses the Major Hypertext Design Issues

The three major system design issue areas we introduced in Chapter 2 can now be looked at from the perspective of Information Mapping. We will look at nodes, links, and buttons and ask how Information Mapping's method would deal with each.

The Three Major Categories of Design Issues Outlined in Chapter Two

Nodes

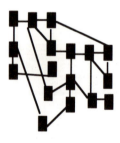

The fundamental questions about nodes we suggested in Chapter 2 were:

see page 40

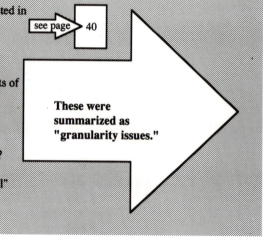

- What shall the nodes contain?

- What principle shall we use to determine contents of nodes?

- On what basis should size decisions be made?

- What size specifically should various chunks be?

- Is there any systematic way to determine "natural" divisions of a subject matter that will help us?

These were summarized as "granularity issues."

Links

The fundamental questions about links we suggested in Chapter 2 were:

see page 42

- Which kinds of links to implement?

- How many links should one use?

- How can we implement different hyperlinkage networks of the same node?

- How shall the links be represented?

These were summarized as fundamental organization of documents to provide context and meaning questions.

Buttons

The fundamental questions about buttons we suggested in Chapter 2 were:

see page 46

- What kinds of buttons should be used?

- Where do good interface design principles suggest that buttons should and should not be put?

- How do we prevent users from being overwhelmed by the number of buttons?

- How to distinguish different kinds of buttons?

- What should be the role of graphic icons and words for a particular kind of button?

These were summarized as human interface issues.

How Information Mapping's Method Addresses these Issues:

Nodes

Information Mapping 's method suggests that information blocks Δ are to be defined as the fundamental nodes in the Hypertext network. The information block is the best way of defining the node because of its properties of providing meaningful precision chunking of relationships between sentences. The rhetorical guidelines and standards for constructing blocks and larger units called maps provide the detailed, well-tested approach to analysis and writing hypertext. The block as the smallest node level is probably sufficiently fine-grained for user commentary even if the comment is about a specific single word in the block.

see page 84

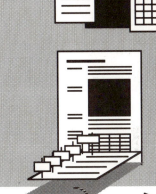

Information maps Δ form a second layer of fundamental nodes. These maps are a clusters of blocks about a related topic that (in general) should be displayed together.

see page 94

Links

Links are connections between map nam[   ] blocks with which they are associated. Blocks can be linked together to form larger nodes called information maps and these nodes are linked together in hierarchical order to form chapters and larger documents such as reports, textbooks, manuals, etc. Other links connect maps to chapters, chapters to larger documents.

see page 8

Discourse domains Δ provide the framework for specifying types of blocks needed for different messages and documents in business, science, and technology. We show a full example in Chapter 8.

see page 104

In addition, structured sets of hypertrail linkages Δ such as prerequisite and classificatory linkages provide important connections that give a meaningful point of view to the subject matter. These Information Mapping and hypertrail linkages are regarded as fundamental. Other links such as comments, critiques and rebuttals are provided under the rubric of argumentation structures.

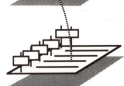

see page 126

Buttons

Within the structured writing context, specific types of buttons Δ will provide an orderly, familiar, useful, and general way of navigating different discourse domains.

At the Nodes, Blocks and Maps Structure Hypertext

Introduction

Information Mapping's method provides a powerful and well-tested method for precision modularity that is suitable for defining the size and content of the information at the nodes of hypermedia. On these two pages we show how the blocks and maps appear in hypertext. Examples of this abound in this book--in fact the whole book is an illustration of this concept.

Definition: Structured Hypertext

Structured hypertext is text that is written according to the methods and criteria of Information Mapping's method. The term is intended to distinguish the text from various forms of partially structured or relatively unstructured free association writing.

Example

Here is a schematic
of the map on
the opposite
page

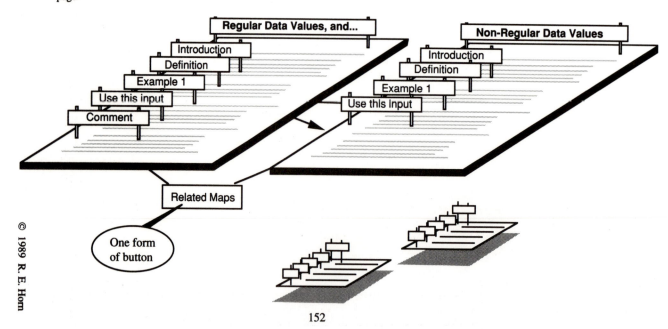

Comparing 17.1.0	Regular Data Values, and . . .	Non-Regular Data Values
Introduction	Some data have patterns. They progress by fixed increments.	Some data do not show any pattern of intervals between the values.
Definition	Data are called regular when the values of a data vector progress from some initial value with some fixed interval to another value, and then optionally from that to still other values by even increments.	Data are called "non-regular" data when they have no systematic pattern of intervals between them.
Example One	Time data show frequent regularities. Samples of blood collected from a laboratory animal every hour on the hour might be called SAMPLEHRS and might look this way: SAMPLEHRS = 6, 7, 8, 9, 10	Most measurement data do not exhibit systematic regularities that are fixed intervals between values, so they are usually non-regular data. Here is an example: LABMEAS - .01, .09, .04, .3
Use This Input Statement	Input with Computed Clause Statement	Standard Input Statement
Comment	This statement permits you to input regular data in a very compact form and is much quicker to type than a normal input statement.	This statement should be used for normal data entry.
Related Pages	Input with Computed Input Statements, 22 Standard Input Statement, 21 Variables, 19	

Clustering Documents From Different Domains

Introduction

With information blocks and maps at the nodes structured hypertext has a form that is considerably more useful than many other possibilities. On this page we show how different forms of blocks, maps, and documents link together to form documents from different domains. On this page, we show schematics of documents from three such domains.

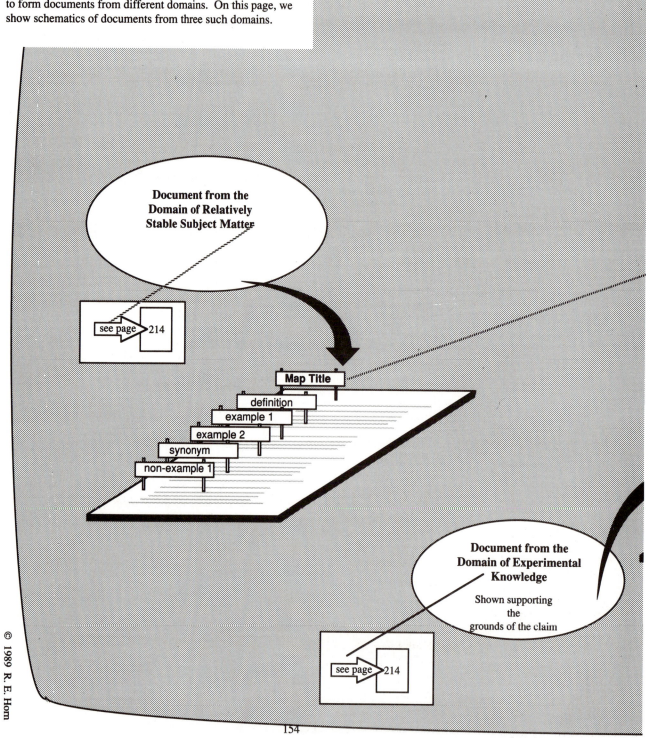

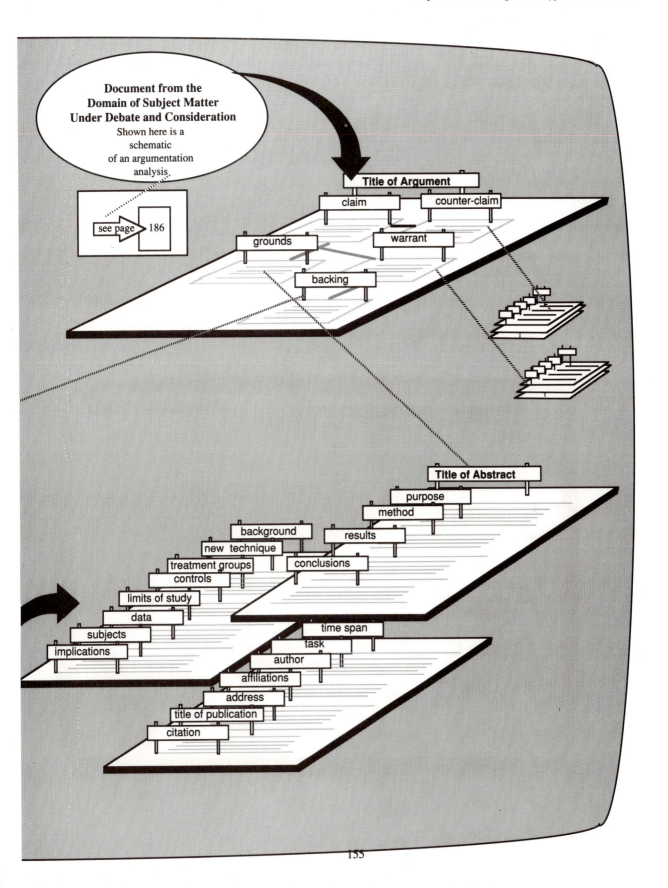

Addressing Lost In Hyperspace and Overload

Introduction

We noted in Chapter 2 Δ that two of the major user issues in the current use of hypertext were problems of knowing

- Where am I?
- Where have I been?
- Where am I going?
- What are my options?

see page 56

These questions have been generally known as the "lost in hyperspace" problems. In addition, readers have been overwhelmed by too much information and constantly bombarded by overchoice. Information Mapping's approach significantly reduces these two problems. On these pages we will describe how Information Mapping's approach reduces these two problems to manageable proportions.

Problems of Being Lost

Problems of being lost are both local (that is they have to do with the page or screen one is currently looking at) and more general (having to do with what chapter or what document I am looking at).

Overchoice

Some users have been overwhelmed by the inability to track tiny chunks of information.

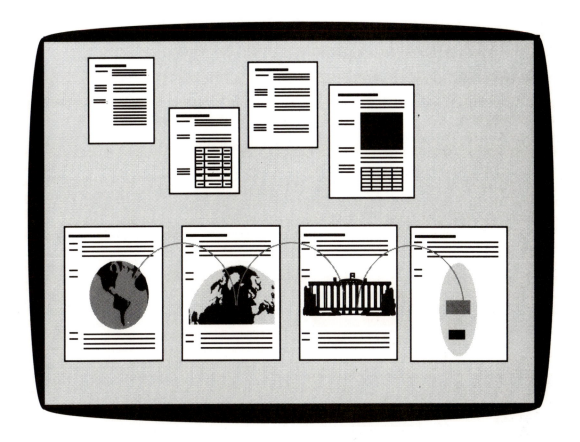

How Information Mapping Prevents Many of the Overload and Lost in Hyperspace Problems

The standards and guidelines of Information Mapping's structured hypertext method introduced such items as
- uniform careful chunking
- uniform careful labeling of each component
- hierarchical structuring and titling of larger structures
- explicit hypertrails of different kinds
- regularly provided overviews, introductions and summaries
- consistency and relevance in all titling and labeling
- table of contents that are created from the labeling and structuring

- important limits as to the kinds of linkages permitted (although readers may -- in some software implementations -- insert any kinds of linkages that are not exhibited to new users unless the new user asks for them)
- similarity of structures across subject matters for different kinds of discourse domains.

The method, while explicitly requiring chunks of information, also provides at all times an explicit context for linking them and a presentation method for assuring that the reader understands the context of the chunks.

Addressing the Major Reading Cues Problem

Introduction see page 48

We have already noted that the very nature of hypertext, its links and buttons and the ability to jump from one place to another, may provide many readers, especially poor readers, with more difficulty than they have with ordinary text. Hence, their ability to learn from hypertext may be diminished. Because we want to be able to use the advantages of hypertext without losing the coherence and discourse cues of normal text, we have suggested Information Mapping's approach. On these pages we show specifically how Information Mapping's method provides solutions to many of the problems that hypertext raises by destroying or disrupting normal discourse cues.

Discourse Cues That Hypertext Destroys or Disrupts

How Information Mapping's Method Deals With These Difficulties

Hierarchical Text Organization

Some research suggests that readers build hierarchical frameworks in their minds as they read. Discourse cues, such as outlines, patterns for subheadings, and tip-off words such as "initially, next, finally," etc. which provide clues to the structure of the text, are disrupted by readers following hypertext linkages.

...thus, next...

The Information Mapping's method introduces systematic ways of outlining, precise guidelines for providing headings and subheadings, and in general provides significantly more chunking and hierarchical structure to the presentation of text. Moreover, since Information Mapping's method is similar across subject matters, the reader is familiar with what to expect when moving to new content.

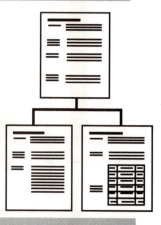

Explicit Transitions

Readers traversing hypertext networks run into transitions which link back to structures which may be difficult to find.

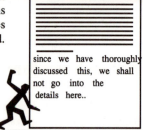

since we have thoroughly discussed this, we shall not go into the details here..

Transitions in Information Mapping's method are placed explicitly in highly visible places such as in introduction blocks and overviews. These transition locations are governed by specific guidelines as to how frequently they must appear.

Overview

Introduction

Sequence Signals

Normal relatively unstructured text may contain signals about organization, such as "there are four types of . . .," but readers traversing hypertext webs may find themselves in the middle of a text which says "fourthly . . ."

fourthly...

Information Mapping's method highlights every sequencing signal by explicitly making visible the structure of the document through a carefully designed framework of labels for all major portions of the subject and by making visible sequencing signals such as "types of, kinds of," etc. The reader can see in this book many of the ways Information Mapping's method accomplishes this.

Example

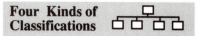

Four Kinds of Classifications

Discourse Cues That Hypertext Destroys or Disrupts

How Information Mapping's Method Deals With These Difficulties

Contrast and Similarity Cues

Discussions of similarities and differences may be scattered over large areas in conventional text. Comparisons may cover several pages and the reader may jump into the middle of such a comparison.

Compare and contrast is done with a tabular arrangement. Either the table is put within a block, or if the compare and contrast is extensive, a complete map Δ will be used to do the comparison.

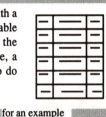

see page 153 for an example

Pronouns as Cohesiveness Cues

Conventional text uses pronouns (they, he, she, we) to refer the reader back to the material the reader is assumed to have read because linear reading is assumed. Readers in hypertext may arrive in such a sequence and not know to what the pronouns are referring.

The structured nature of Information Mapping's method and the requirements of its guidelines for constructing blocks to be as self-contained as possible reduces the reference of pronouns outside of, usually, the block which is currently on display and never outside the information map. Therefore Information Mapping's method avoids this problem.

Metaphors

Conventional text sometimes has an extended metaphor running through many pages of text. It provides a useful organization through text but provides difficulty for readers who arrive via hypertext link into the middle of such a text.

Precise analogy blocks permit the use of extended metaphors because they can be linked by an extended example or hypertrail.

Content Schemas

Conventional text generally has an organization which is not entirely evident to the reader. So a reader arriving in the middle of such conventionally written material does not have sufficient cues to orient to the overall structure of the subject matter.

Information Mapping's method, because of its always explicit structure, enables the reader to see the major hypertrail which is organizing the content. And with appropriate facilities in the software, the reader may also be able to see other hypertrails that are available.

Addressing Creation and Maintenance Issues

Introduction

We have already noted Δ that hypertext generally increases the amount of intellectual labor needed to create and update knowledge bases. On these pages we make the case that, just as Information Mapping's method has reduced the cost of producing text on paper, it will vastly outdistance less structured approaches in the creation of hypertext knowledge bases.

 see page 62

Careful Limits to Text Preparation

Information Mapping's methodology limits the amount of additional text that needs to be done to only that which is absolutely essential and specifiable by the well tested guidelines of the methodology.

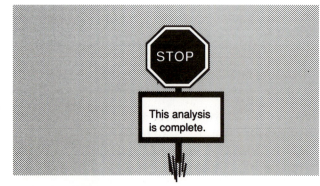

Specify Necessary Links

Information Mapping's methodology specifies the particular places and facilitates the creation of specific links .

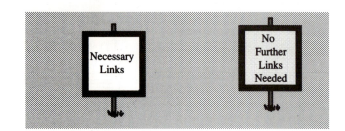

Rational Boundaries on Linkage Creation

While we have indicated that there is considerable cost from proliferating linkages, the specifications developed for Information Mapping's method limits these in commercial situations and will provide hierarchical document structures for hypertrail linkages. This puts required boundaries around the problem of overlinkage.

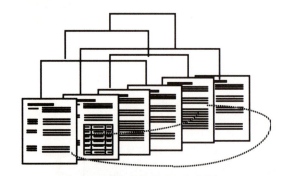

Permits Greater Automation of Link Creation

The careful definition of the information blocks and information maps will permit higher automation of linkages than would otherwise be provided in automating less structured text.

Additional Quality Control Requirements

Information Mapping's method, because of its specification of quality control guidelines, makes the quality control process of creating text much more manageable.

We have noted that the precise definition of components of the text permits establishment of readily determinable standards.

As the reader has noted in previous chapters, the method places a very strong value on managing the size of the message using the "seven plus or minus two" rule of thumb to limit the size of chunks. The method also recommends using strict hierarchies so that every block in a document has an identifiable place.

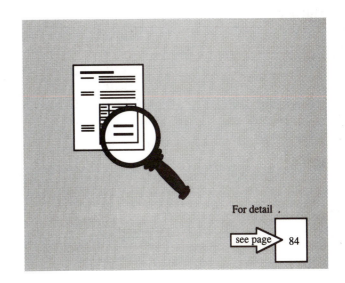

For detail .

see page 84

Rapid Cost-Effective Indexing

Information Mapping's method will provide the opportunity to do "quick and dirty" indexing of titles and labels, rather than full text. When these have been written according to the guidelines of the methodology, the indexing provides almost the level of quality of a professional indexer. The additional discipline of labeling and titling blocks and maps, thus, produces significant advantages in the indexing process.

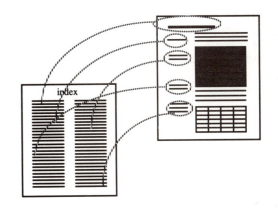

Modularity and Rationality Aids Data Base Maintenance

Because of the careful specification of types of information that belong to specific discourse domains, and because of the modularity of all material written with Information Mapping's method, the updating and revision task becomes much more manageable, efficient, and effective.

It also makes following branches and links that are connected to particular nodes rational.

161

Addressing Group Analysis and Writing Issues

Introduction

Managers have begun to recognize the importance of the many situations where many people have to contribute ideas and actually write portions of a single document. Proposals, plans put together jointly by several departments, task force reports, and documentation systems written by different design groups all share this requirement. As a byproduct advantage, Information Mapping's method provides a framework at the right level of detail for addressing many of the major problems of groups working together.

Major Issue

A major difficulty in group writing projects is that members of the group do not share meanings of key concepts. The method offers assistance in this area.

How the Information Mapping Method Helps Groups to Work Together

Stage 1 ➡	Stage 2 ➡	Stage 3 ➡
Prewriting Stage	**Preliminary Information Gathering**	**Organization Analysis**
Enables all in a group to agree on goals, scope, etc. in advance. Provides a framework for discussion of the implications of these decisions for the document.	• Different assignments are easily made for different information gathering and preliminary information block writing. • Enables different team members to work on different parts with little overlap. • Greater assurance of completeness.	• Can more easily identify quality control issues. • Can see what is missing, what needs to be done.

Commentary: Problem Analysis

Groups generally don't have so much difficulty with agreeing on the subject matter or with agreeing at the sentence level (i.e., we can generally agree on grammar, syntax, and spelling). They have problems with style. But even more difficult are the problems of context and point of view in the early phases of group analysis projects. Then, dividing the project into parts and giving assignments with little or no overlap becomes the issue. More problems arise when the organization, sequencing and presentation stages arrive. It is here that the Information Mapping method helps the most as we illustrate below. In fact, the Information Mapping method gives the group a common way of looking at the information to be communicated and a common language to discuss that information. Therefore, the process is smoother, and the end product more consistent.

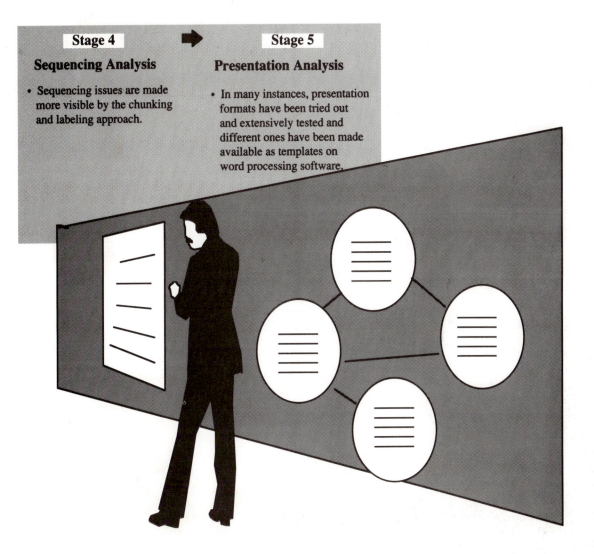

Stage 4

Sequencing Analysis

- Sequencing issues are made more visible by the chunking and labeling approach.

Stage 5

Presentation Analysis

- In many instances, presentation formats have been tried out and extensively tested and different ones have been made available as templates on word processing software.

Some Navigational Options

Introduction

Depending upon the needs of the situation and the hypertext software available, the user can access information blocks and maps with many different access paths. Some or all of the access methods described on these two pages could be used in a hypertext system based on Information Mapping's method.

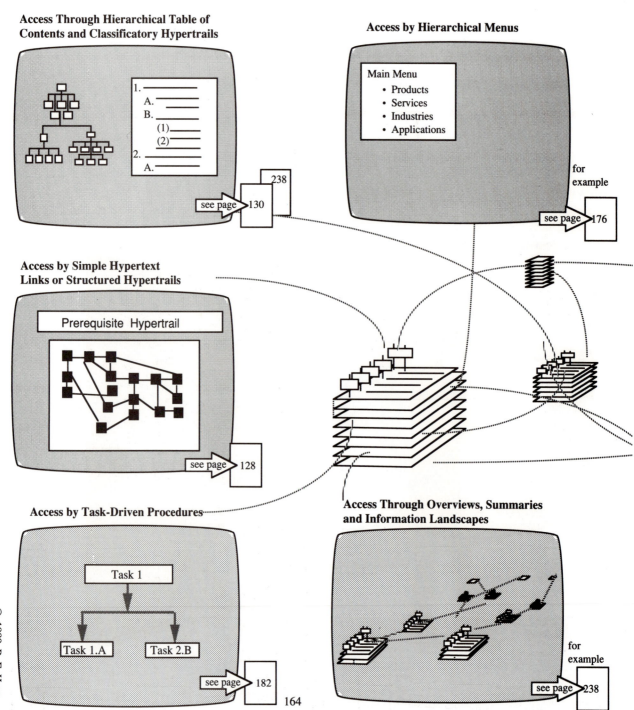

Access Through Hierarchical Table of Contents and Classificatory Hypertrails

see page 130

238

Access by Hierarchical Menus

Main Menu
- Products
- Services
- Industries
- Applications

for example

see page 176

Access by Simple Hypertext Links or Structured Hypertrails

Prerequisite Hypertrail

see page 128

Access by Task-Driven Procedures

Task 1

Task 1.A   Task 2.B

see page 182

Access Through Overviews, Summaries and Information Landscapes

for example

see page 238

Commentary -- Summary of Chapter

The ability of Information Mapping's method to address so many of the problems and issues raised by hypertext makes it a key tool in every developer's and user's tool kit. The multiple methods of access shown on these pages show how the method facilitates access because of its systematic approach.

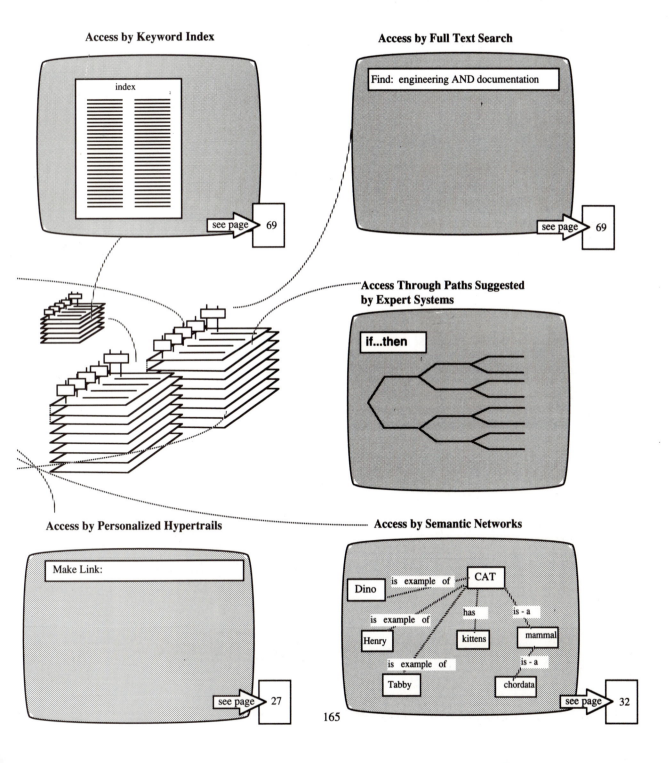

Access by Keyword Index

index

see page 69

Access by Full Text Search

Find: engineering AND documentation

see page 69

Access Through Paths Suggested by Expert Systems

if...then

Access by Personalized Hypertrails

Make Link:

see page 27

Access by Semantic Networks

Dino · is example of · CAT

is example of · has · is - a

Henry · kittens · mammal

is example of · is - a

Tabby · chordata

see page 32

Chapter 6. Relatively Stable Discourse: Documentation and Training

Chapter 6
Relatively Stable Discourse: Documentation & Training

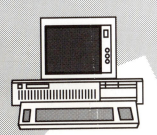

On-Line
Reference
Based Training

On-Line
Product
Knowledge

On-Line
Procedures

On-Line
Documentation

In this Chapter ...a Series of Applications to Relatively Stable Subject Matters...

On-Line
Personnel
Policies

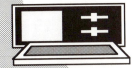

Computer-Based
Training

Corporate
Applications

Computer-Based
Marketing
Tools

Overview of This Chapter

Introduction

We defined one of the major discourse domains as that of relatively stable subject matter. In business this is where we find procedures, policies, documentation and training materials. When writing about these areas we take the stance that the subject matter is stable -- not changeless forever, but not going to change every day. In this chapter our primary aim is to present some case studies and examples of different applications of Information Mapping's method to on-line hypertext information retrieval situations. This will give the reader a more concrete idea of the method and its applications to on-line text.

Contrast With Paper

To see examples of paper-based display of the Information Mapping method

 see page 96

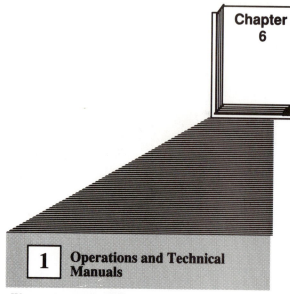

1 **Operations and Technical Manuals**

We present two examples of pages from operations and technical manuals:

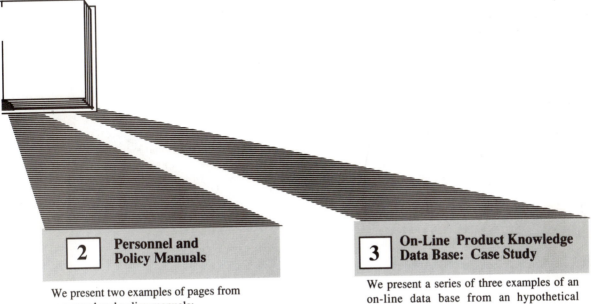

2	**Personnel and Policy Manuals**

We present two examples of pages from personnel and policy manuals:

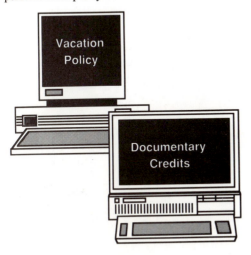

3	**On-Line Product Knowledge Data Base: Case Study**

We present a series of three examples of an on-line data base from an hypothetical company:

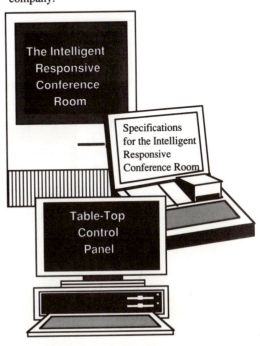

Operations and Technical Manuals

Introduction

On the following four pages we present examples of screens from manuals that fall under the classification of relatively stable subject matter. The manuals from which they are extracted have been prepared with Information Mapping's approach.

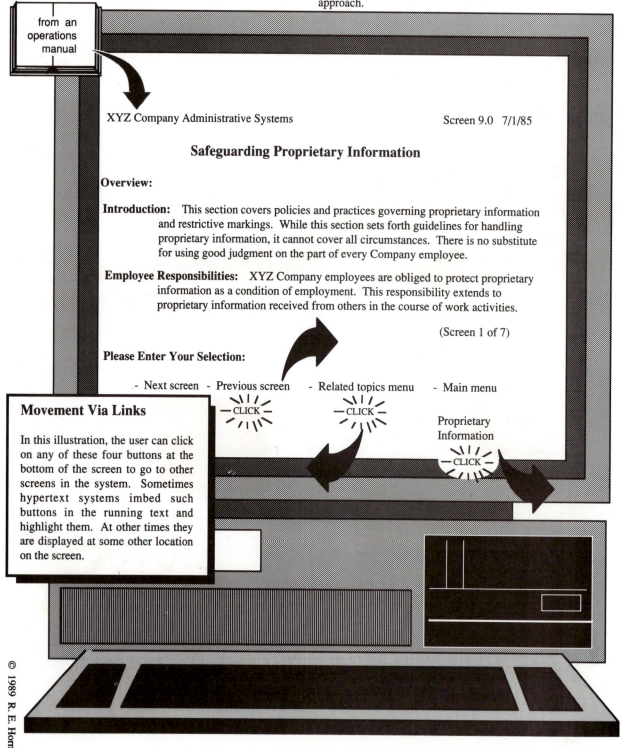

from an operations manual

XYZ Company Administrative Systems   Screen 9.0 7/1/85

Safeguarding Proprietary Information

Overview:

Introduction: This section covers policies and practices governing proprietary information and restrictive markings. While this section sets forth guidelines for handling proprietary information, it cannot cover all circumstances. There is no substitute for using good judgment on the part of every Company employee.

Employee Responsibilities: XYZ Company employees are obliged to protect proprietary information as a condition of employment. This responsibility extends to proprietary information received from others in the course of work activities.

(Screen 1 of 7)

Please Enter Your Selection:

- Next screen - Previous screen   - Related topics menu   - Main menu

CLICK   CLICK

Proprietary
Information

CLICK

Movement Via Links

In this illustration, the user can click on any of these four buttons at the bottom of the screen to go to other screens in the system. Sometimes hypertext systems imbed such buttons in the running text and highlight them. At other times they are displayed at some other location on the screen.

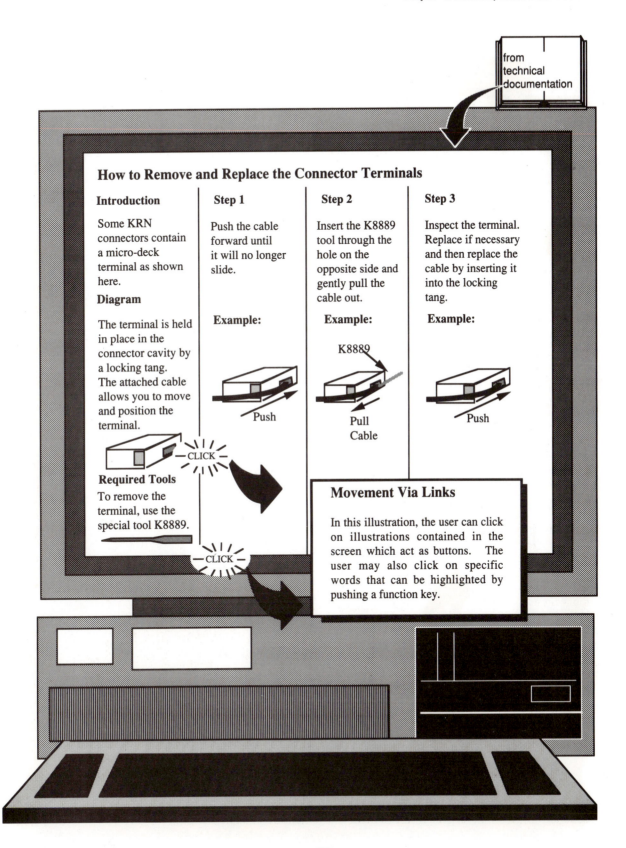

from technical documentation

How to Remove and Replace the Connector Terminals

Introduction

Some KRN connectors contain a micro-deck terminal as shown here.

Diagram

The terminal is held in place in the connector cavity by a locking tang. The attached cable allows you to move and position the terminal.

Required Tools

To remove the terminal, use the special tool K8889.

Step 1

Push the cable forward until it will no longer slide.

Example:

Push

Step 2

Insert the K8889 tool through the hole on the opposite side and gently pull the cable out.

Example:

K8889

Pull Cable

Step 3

Inspect the terminal. Replace if necessary and then replace the cable by inserting it into the locking tang.

Example:

Push

CLICK

CLICK

Movement Via Links

In this illustration, the user can click on illustrations contained in the screen which act as buttons. The user may also click on specific words that can be highlighted by pushing a function key.

Personnel Manuals and Policy Manuals

from a personnel manual

Movement Via Hypertext Links

On this screen we illustrate how different words or phrases can be highlighted to indicate where buttons are located. Buttons are indicated by boldface type.

Vacation Policy and Schedule for Exe...

Company policy	Employees may take their vac... **...niversary date of hire**.
— CLICK —	
Example	An employee hired on June 1, 1979 would be eligible for vacation after June 1, 1980.
Rule one	No vacation days will be accumulated from one anniversary to the next.
Rule two	No payment will be made for vacation days not taken.
Amount of vacation	

Years	Exempt Employees	Nonexempt Employees
1-2	2 weeks	1 week
3-9	3 weeks	2 weeks
10-14	4 weeks	3 weeks
15-19	5 weeks	4 weeks
20 +	6 weeks	5 weeks

— CLICK —

Holidays during vacation	If company **paid holidays** occur during a vacation period
	• nonexempt employees are eligible for an additional vacation day, but
	• exempt employees forfeit the holiday.

— CLICK —

Example	A **nonexempt employee** schedules his vacation during the first two weeks of July. The Fourth of July is a company paid holiday. The employee receives an additional day of vacation.

from a policy manual

Documentary Credits

Definition

A documentary credit is a conditional bank undertaking of payment for settling international commercial transactions.

How transactions work

Briefly stated, in a documentary credit transaction
- the buyer (synonym: applicant) asks
- the bank (synonym: issuing bank) to give a written undertaking to effect a payment
  - up to stated sum of money
  - within a prescribed time limit
  - against stipulated documents, to
- the seller (synonym: beneficiary).

The system of documentary credits provides security for both the buyer and the seller by assuring that

- all documents are in order (certificate of origin, commercial invoice, insurance policy, bill of lading, etc.)

- the seller will receive payment.

Important

Payment against a documentary credit does not necessarily ensure that the shipment's contents are in order, only that the papers are in order.

Conditions: buyer

Payment is made on behalf of the buyer against documents which give the buyer the rights to the goods.

However, according to arrangements between the buyer and the bank, and/or local laws or regulations, the buyer may have to
- make an advance deposit when it requests the issuance of the credit, or
- place the issuing bank in funds at the time that the documents are presented to the overseas banking correspondent of the issuing bank.

Conditions: seller

The issuing bank pays the seller who does not have to rely on the buyer and the buyer's ability and/or willingness to pay.

However, the seller can demand payment only if he/she meets all the requirements of the credit.

Therefore, the seller should not proceed with the shipment until he/she is
- aware of the requirements, and
- satisfied that the requirements can be met.

Introduction to Product Knowledge Case Study

Background

We have introduced the concept of relatively stable discourses Δ elsewhere. It is the province of training manuals, documentation, and reference manuals. It would be well to look at this discourse to see how it is different from other kinds of discourse. The best way to do this is to examine a structured hypertext knowledge base in detail. We will do that in this chapter.

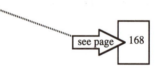
see page 168

 Case Study Situation: Need for Product and Services Knowledge

Needs of Users

Salespeople

Sales people need to have information on all of a company's products and services at their fingertips so that they can work with customers to plan installations and make sales.

Customer Service

The customer service people need to have all the information of a company's products and services to be able to answer questions and take orders and to provide other services in the implementation phase.

Instructors

Instructors receive a lot of questions from their trainees about how the training affects various aspects of the company's products and services. They need to be able to answer them.

Managers in All Parts of the Company

Managers in other parts of the company need information on all the company's products and services for planning and coordinating. They need to have the biggest picture possible as well as correct detail.

174

Solution: Hypertext of Company Products and Services

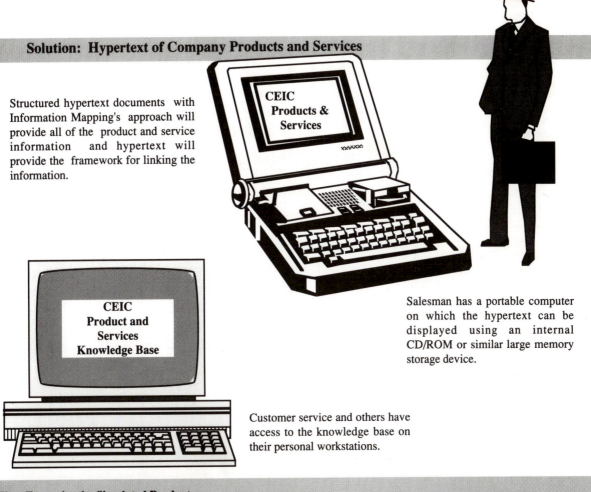

Structured hypertext documents with Information Mapping's approach will provide all of the product and service information and hypertext will provide the framework for linking the information.

CEIC Products & Services

CEIC Product and Services Knowledge Base

Salesman has a portable computer on which the hypertext can be displayed using an internal CD/ROM or similar large memory storage device.

Customer service and others have access to the knowledge base on their personal workstations.

Time Frame in the Simulated Product Knowledge Base Scenario in this Chapter

June

1989

and beyond

Case Study in This Chapter

We will provide a simulation in the next few pages. It is a simulation of a few hypertext screens for the hypothetical company, CEIC, salesman working on a sales problem.

...next few pages...

The Company in the Simulated Knowledge Base

CEIC --- Computer Environment Interfaces Corporation

Product Knowledge Case Study: Main Menu

Introduction

Here we begin the case study which we described on the previous page. The salesperson is searching for specific pieces of data requested by the client.

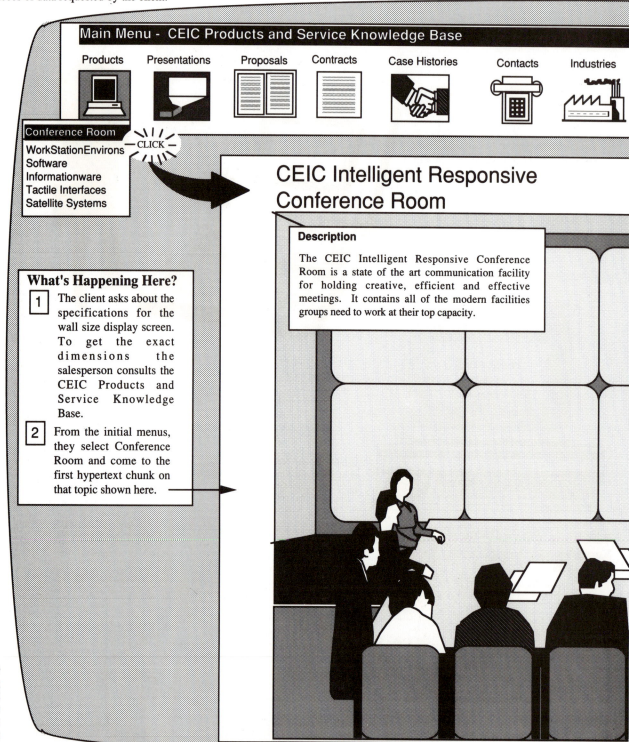

Main Menu - CEIC Products and Service Knowledge Base

Products   Presentations   Proposals   Contracts   Case Histories   Contacts   Industries

Conference Room
WorkStationEnvirons
Software
Informationware
Tactile Interfaces
Satellite Systems

CLICK

CEIC Intelligent Responsive Conference Room

Description

The CEIC Intelligent Responsive Conference Room is a state of the art communication facility for holding creative, efficient and effective meetings. It contains all of the modern facilities groups need to work at their top capacity.

What's Happening Here?

1 The client asks about the specifications for the wall size display screen. To get the exact dimensions the salesperson consults the CEIC Products and Service Knowledge Base.

2 From the initial menus, they select Conference Room and come to the first hypertext chunk on that topic shown here.

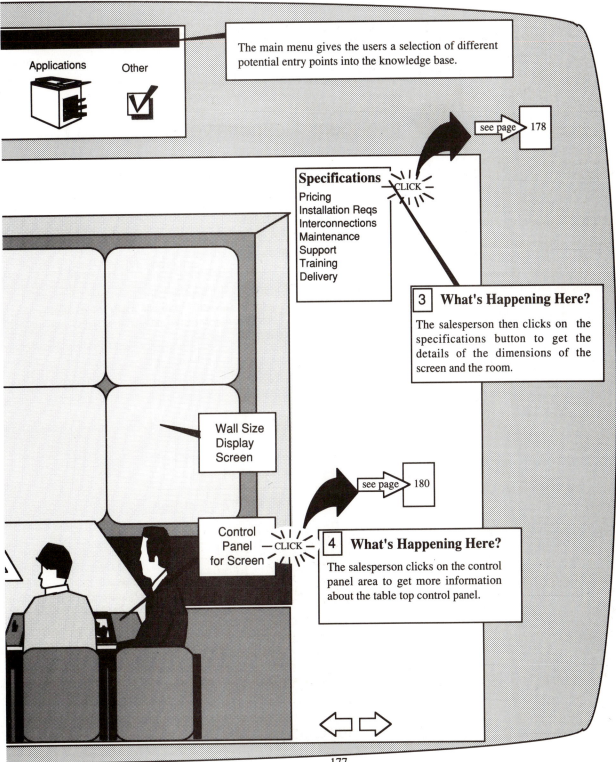

Applications   Other

The main menu gives the users a selection of different potential entry points into the knowledge base.

see page 178

Specifications
—CLICK—

Pricing
Installation Reqs
Interconnections
Maintenance
Support
Training
Delivery

3 What's Happening Here?

The salesperson then clicks on the specifications button to get the details of the dimensions of the screen and the room.

Wall Size
Display
Screen

see page 180

Control
Panel   —CLICK—
for Screen

4 What's Happening Here?

The salesperson clicks on the control panel area to get more information about the table top control panel.

Product Knowledge Case Study: Specifications

Introduction

This is the second display of the case study we began on the previous page. The salesperson here has found the specific data requested by the client.

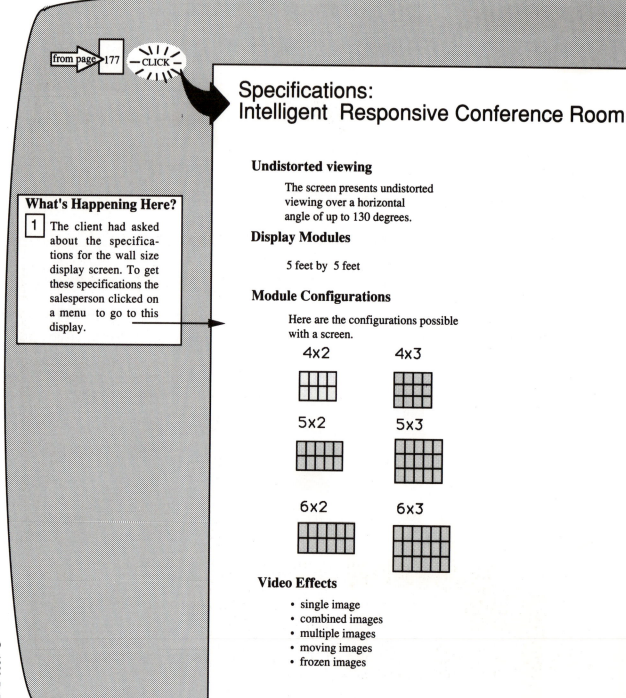

from page 177 — CLICK —

Specifications:
Intelligent Responsive Conference Room

What's Happening Here?

1 The client had asked about the specifications for the wall size display screen. To get these specifications the salesperson clicked on a menu to go to this display.

Undistorted viewing

The screen presents undistorted viewing over a horizontal angle of up to 130 degrees.

Display Modules

5 feet by 5 feet

Module Configurations

Here are the configurations possible with a screen.

4x2   4x3

5x2   5x3

6x2   6x3

Video Effects

- single image
- combined images
- multiple images
- moving images
- frozen images

see page 180

─ CLICK ─

Table Top Control Panel

The screen may be controlled by a single panel or multiple control panels (up to 12).

Accepts Signals From Video and Computer

Displays on the screen may come from

- computer displays of any kind
- special computer displays developed on the CEIC large display controller
- any video source through the CEIC large display controller.

---

2 | ### What's Happening Here?

The salesperson then clicks on the control panel button to get more details of the table top control panel.

Product Knowledge Case Study: Control Panel

Introduction

This is the third display of the case study we described on previous pages. Here the salesperson has asked to see more information on the control panel of the CEIC Intelligent Responsive Conference Room System.

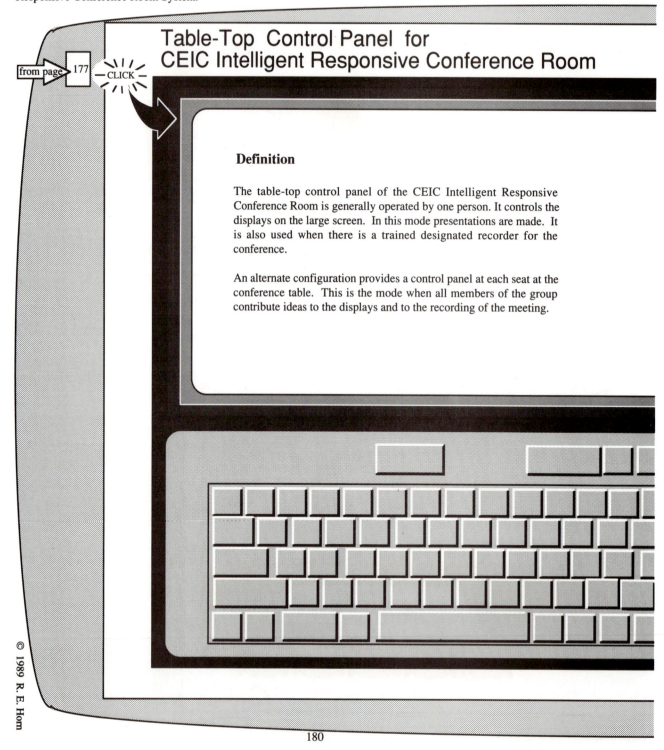

Table-Top Control Panel for CEIC Intelligent Responsive Conference Room

from page 177 —CLICK—

Definition

The table-top control panel of the CEIC Intelligent Responsive Conference Room is generally operated by one person. It controls the displays on the large screen. In this mode presentations are made. It is also used when there is a trained designated recorder for the conference.

An alternate configuration provides a control panel at each seat at the conference table. This is the mode when all members of the group contribute ideas to the displays and to the recording of the meeting.

Control Panel

Access by Task-Driven Procedures

Introduction

One of the ways that the user can move around in a knowledge base of relatively stable subject matter is through task-driven procedures. The user has to do something or decide something. The hypertext system acts as a decision aid, stepping users through each part of the decision. At any point, using other buttons, users can jump off to inspect information that may be useful in helping them make the decision.

Example

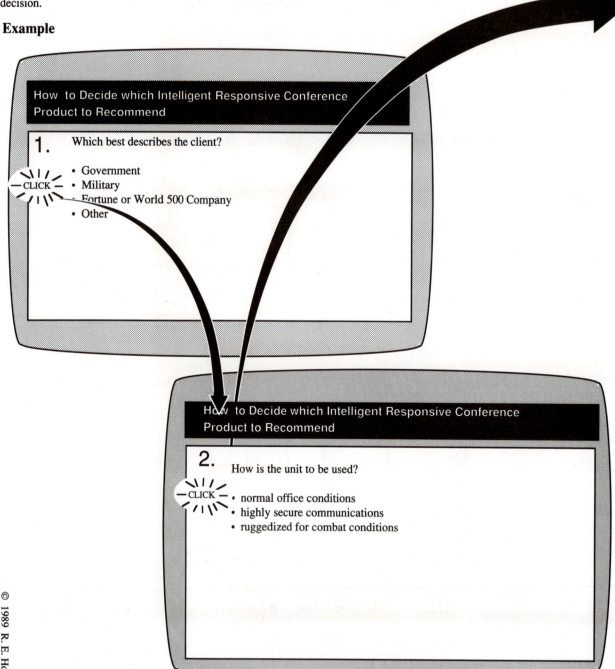

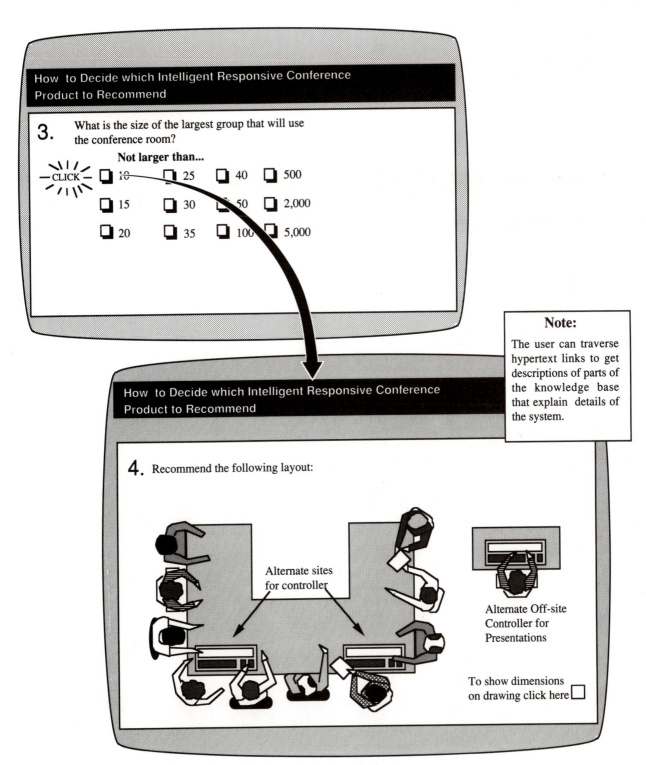

How to Decide which Intelligent Responsive Conference Product to Recommend

3. What is the size of the largest group that will use the conference room?

Not larger than...

CLICK

☐ 10   ☐ 25   ☐ 40   ☐ 500

☐ 15   ☐ 30   ☐ 50   ☐ 2,000

☐ 20   ☐ 35   ☐ 100 ☐ 5,000

Note:

The user can traverse hypertext links to get descriptions of parts of the knowledge base that explain details of the system.

How to Decide which Intelligent Responsive Conference Product to Recommend

4. Recommend the following layout:

Alternate sites for controller

Alternate Off-site Controller for Presentations

To show dimensions on drawing click here ☐

Chapter 7. Disputed Discourse: Argumentation Analysis

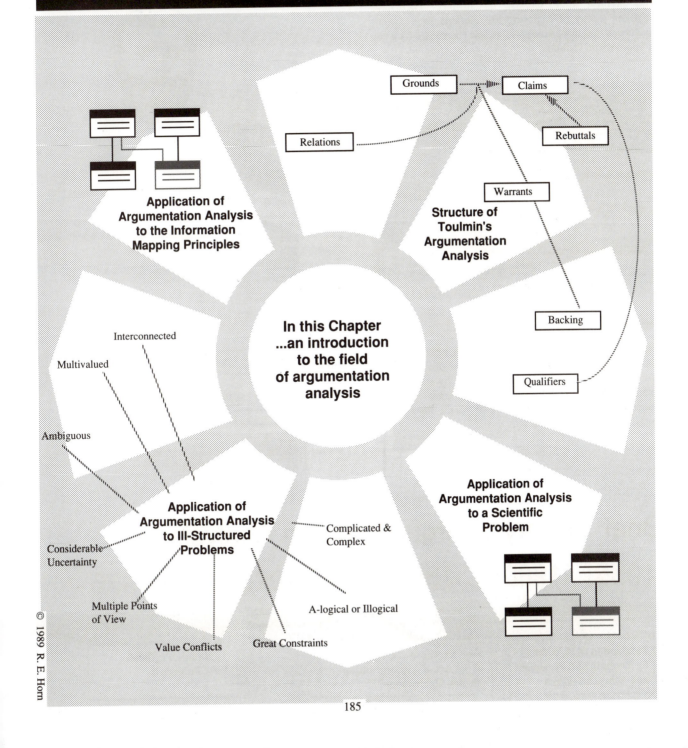

Application of
Argumentation Analysis
to the Information
Mapping Principles

Grounds

Claims

Relations

Rebuttals

Warrants

Structure of
Toulmin's
Argumentation
Analysis

Backing

In this Chapter
...an introduction
to the field
of argumentation
analysis

Qualifiers

Interconnected

Multivalued

Ambiguous

Application of
Argumentation Analysis
to a Scientific
Problem

Considerable
Uncertainty

Application of
Argumentation Analysis
to Ill-Structured
Problems

Complicated &
Complex

Multiple Points
of View

A-logical or Illogical

Value Conflicts

Great Constraints

Overview of This Chapter

Different Kinds of Reasoning Require Different Kinds of Analysis

The British philosopher Stephen Toulmin and the Belgians, Chaim Perelman and L. Olbrechts-Tyeca have claimed that the reasoning process involved in most discussions about policy, ethics, law, and business strategy is more complex than the three part structure of the classic syllogism (i.e., major premise, minor premise, conclusion). They have suggested a way of capturing the subtleties and overall structure of reasoning processes. In this chapter we focus on the approach of Toulmin.

Aristotle

The Three Part Syllogism -- Useful But Limited

The syllogism of Aristotle's classical logic is a time-tested and still very useful way of deductive reasoning. It is, indeed, the basis of contemporary "expert systems" in artificial intelligence.

You start with the...	Example
Major Premise →	All men are mortal.
...then introduce the... ***Minor Premise*** →	Socrates is a man.
...and through deduction, reach the... ***Conclusion*** →	Therefore, Socrates is mortal.

Toulmin pointed out that arguments in public policy, science, ethics, and management are much more likely to sound like this...

Definition: Argumentation Analysis

Argumentation analysis is a sentence-by-sentence examination of the components of an argument or a line of reasoning in order to identify the functions performed by the different sentences. This provides a structure of the argument. In the Toulmin version of argumentation analysis the functions are typically listed as in this diagram:

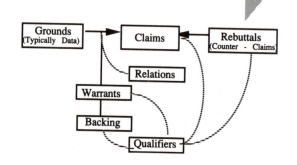

Brief History of Argumentation Analysis

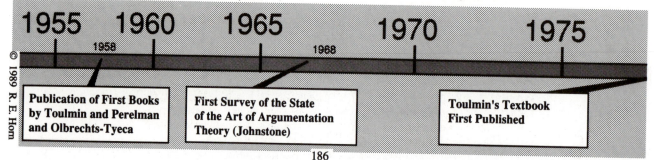

1955   1960   1965   1970   1975

1958

1968

Publication of First Books by Toulmin and Perelman and Olbrechts-Tyeca

First Survey of the State of the Art of Argumentation Theory (Johnstone)

Toulmin's Textbook First Published

Even if attacked, a superpower should not retaliate with nuclear weapons.

Why do you say that?

Because a large nuclear war could destroy most of the life in the Northern Hemisphere or even our entire species.

But how do you get to your conclusion?

Well, no reason or value is important enough to risk the destruction of our entire species.

How do you justify that conclusion?

Human beings must survive if we are to have any other values at all.

But we don't know for sure. It's only a possibility that we would destroy the entire species.

Toulmin has worked on a structure that would help us study reasoning such as this.

For example, he calls this a "claim," and this the "grounds" of the argument. And this he designates as the "warrant," that which enables you to go from the grounds to the claim.

Other parts of his framework include the "backing" which supports the warrant and various rebuttals.

Commentary: Plan of This Chapter

Argumentation analysis has a substantial history separate from hypertext. But a number of groups are computerizing it and considering the linked networks of blocks of information to be similar in intent and structure to other hypertext networks. From the standpoint of this book we place argumentation analysis in a position that helps link the two other discourse domains we deal with. We present the following two abbreviated examples of argumentation analysis in this chapter. (REH)

Relatively well-structured problems

The rationale and research underpinning the 4 principles of Information Mapping's method.

see page 194

Relatively ill-structured problems

A portion of the current dispute over the ethics of using deterrence as a national policy in the era of nuclear weapons.

see page 200

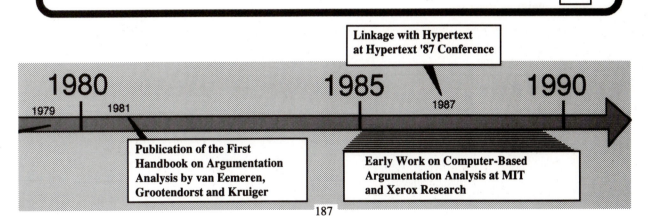

Linkage with Hypertext at Hypertext '87 Conference

1980   1985   1990

1979   1981   1987

Publication of the First Handbook on Argumentation Analysis by van Eemeren, Grootendorst and Kruiger

Early Work on Computer-Based Argumentation Analysis at MIT and Xerox Research

Claims

Introduction

When we begin to examine a policy discussion or an ethical argument, there is always some "destination," some claim that one of the discussants advances.

Definition

Claims are "assertions put forward publicly for general acceptance with the implication that there are underlying 'reasons' that could show them to be 'well founded' and therefore entitled to be generally accepted." (Toulmin, et. al. 1979)

Questions to be asked

What exactly are you claiming?

Where precisely do you stand on this issue?

What position are you asking us to agree to as the outcome of your argument?

Example one: claim as fact

The company is in good financial shape.

Our sales may not be up but we are beginning to sell to the right niche.

Example two: claim as policy proposal

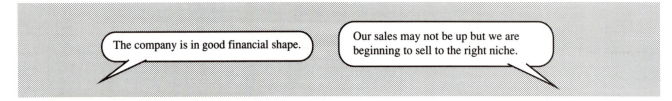

Our best bet is to try to sell to the specialized section of the retail market -- the high end.

We should go after international markets rather than put all of our investment in the domestic market.

Example three: claim as forecast

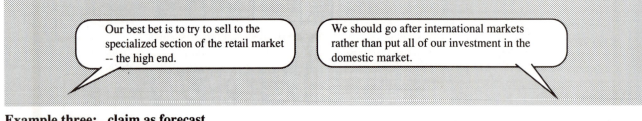

The economy will grow this year at a rate of 3.5 per cent.

Our sales forecast in the retail market is for $25 million.

Form of the sentences

The form of sentences for claims is often one of the following:

- We should follow policy (x).
- We should (or should not) take action (a).
- If we follow policy (x) or action (a), state (s) will follow.
- (x) is a state that exists.

188

Grounds (Data)

Introduction

As we try to understand why somebody believes something, we may ask them exactly why they are making that claim and what they have to go on. Often their reply is in the form of data or facts that they believe to be true.

Definition

"The term 'grounds' refers to the specific facts relied on to support a given claim." Toulmin (1979)

Questions to be asked

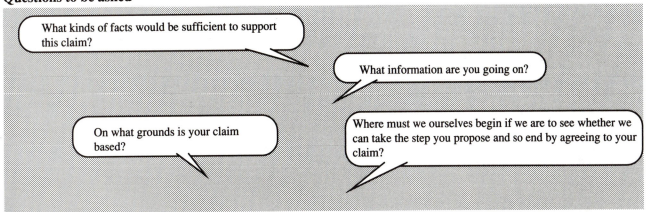

What kinds of facts would be sufficient to support this claim?

What information are you going on?

On what grounds is your claim based?

Where must we ourselves begin if we are to see whether we can take the step you propose and so end by agreeing to your claim?

Example one

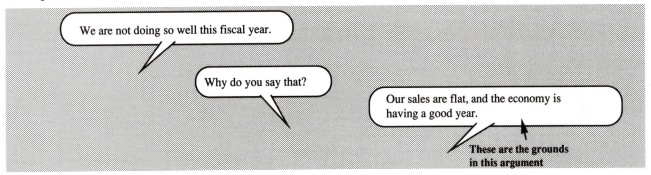

We are not doing so well this fiscal year.

Why do you say that?

Our sales are flat, and the economy is having a good year.

These are the grounds in this argument

Form of the sentences

The form of sentences in grounds is often the following:
- Situation (s) exists.
- (x) is a measurement that is (y).
- (x) is a conclusion drawn from the data collection methods we've used.

Warrants

Background.

"Historically speaking," the warrant "has always had close associations with the notion of a license or permit and also with that of a warranty or guarantee." Toulmin (1979)

Definition

The warrant is the assertion that entitles you to interpret or link the grounds (facts) as support for the claim.

Questions to be asked

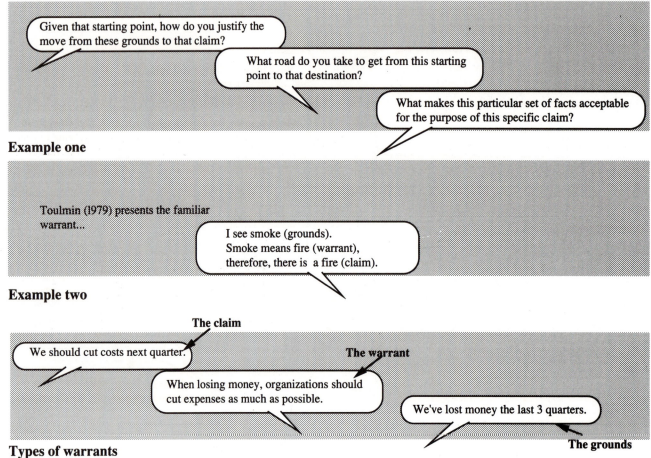

Given that starting point, how do you justify the move from these grounds to that claim?

What road do you take to get from this starting point to that destination?

What makes this particular set of facts acceptable for the purpose of this specific claim?

Example one

Toulmin (1979) presents the familiar warrant...

I see smoke (grounds).
Smoke means fire (warrant),
therefore, there is a fire (claim).

Example two

The claim

We should cut costs next quarter.

The warrant

When losing money, organizations should cut expenses as much as possible.

We've lost money the last 3 quarters.

The grounds

Types of warrants

Warrants usually "take the form of laws of nature, legal principles and statutes, rules of thumb, engineering formulas," moral commandments or principles.

Form of the sentences

The form of sentences of warrants is often one of the following:
• Situation (s) indicates the presence of condition (c).
• When condition (c) exists, do action (a) to obtain goal (g).
• When situation (s) exists, follow policy (p).

Backing

Introduction

Sometimes we are not satisfied with the mere assertion of the warrant. We want more information. We want to understand why that warrant can hold in this situation.

Definition

"The Backing consists of a very general set of background assumptions which, in effect, legitimize the basis for believing in the Warrant. That is, if the Warrant is not accepted on its surface, then the Backing is called into play to add deeper support to the argument."

(Mitroff and Mason, 1980)

Questions to be asked

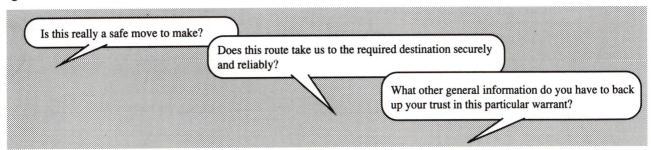

Example

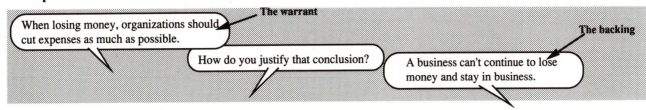

Different kinds of backing

"The warrants relied on to authorize arguments in different fields of reasoning require correspondingly different kinds of backing: legal statutes must have been validly legislated; scientific laws must have been thoroughly checked out..."
Toulmin (1979)

Mitroff and Mason (1980) list four types of backing:

1. Cause-effect (given the truth of the evidence, the claim must follow)

2. Analogy (this situation is sufficiently like another to apply the same argument)

3. Belief in authority (someone powerful or credible argues that he or she believes (x) to be the case where (x) is a warrant)

4. Logical necessity (it is logically inconceivable or impossible that the claim would fail to occur given the evidence)

Rebuttal

Introduction

Rarely are we faced with an "airtight" situation or argument. Therefore, we need to know under what circumstances the current argument might not work.

Definition

The rebuttal presents the possible exceptions or objections as to why the claim, the grounds, the warrants, or the backing may not hold for the situation under discussion.

Questions to be asked

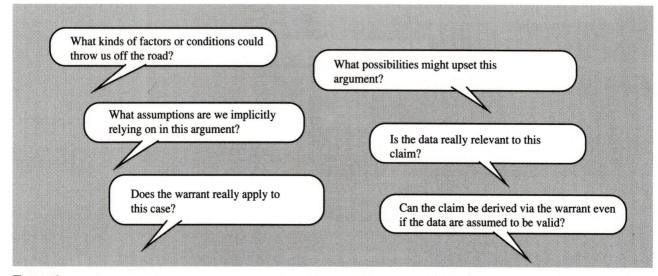

What kinds of factors or conditions could throw us off the road?

What possibilities might upset this argument?

What assumptions are we implicitly relying on in this argument?

Is the data really relevant to this claim?

Does the warrant really apply to this case?

Can the claim be derived via the warrant even if the data are assumed to be valid?

Example

That may be true in general, but not with our customers. Besides that, times have changed; the economy has changed; the dollar has fallen in value.

Rebuttal

Types of rebuttal

There are several types of rebuttal:

1. Grounds. The facts are wrong (Situation (s) is not the case.).
2. Warrants. The warrant does not apply.
   (The warrant is wrong. E.g., do something else.)
3. Backing. False analogy or false belief.
4. Claims. We should take action B, not action A.
   (Situation (s) is not the case, so do some other
   action that is not-A.)

Qualifiers

Introduction

Every argument has a degree of certainty. We often refer to the limits of an argument. We cite its plausibility or degree of certainty.

Definition

Qualifiers are those words that indicate how strongly the claim is being asserted, or how likely that something might occur.

Examples of qualifiers

Here are some qualifiers that one frequently encounters in arguments:

- presumably
- very likely
- in all probability
- always

- certainly
- very possibly
- plausibly

Questions to be asked

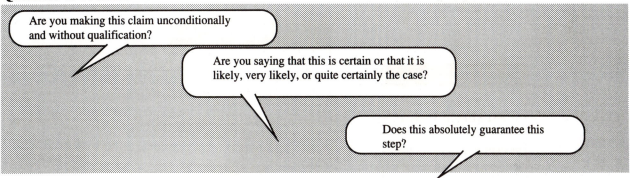

Example

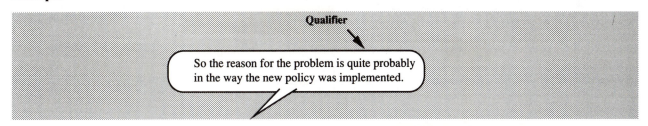

Argumentation Analysis for Four Principles

Application: Some Principles of Information Mapping's Method

We present on this page an analysis of the rationale for using the four principles Δ that we have claimed to be the foundations of Information Mapping's methodology. We use the argumentation analysis methodology Δ presented in this book as a framework for presenting this rationale.

see page 85

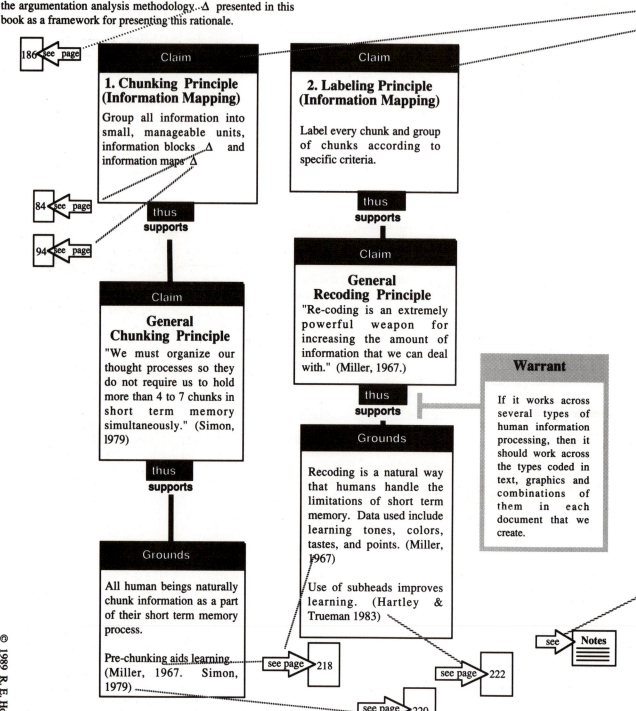

186 see page

Claim

1. Chunking Principle (Information Mapping)

Group all information into small, manageable units, information blocks Δ and information maps Δ

84 see page

thus
supports

94 see page

Claim

General Chunking Principle

"We must organize our thought processes so they do not require us to hold more than 4 to 7 chunks in short term memory simultaneously." (Simon, 1979)

thus
supports

Grounds

All human beings naturally chunk information as a part of their short term memory process.

Pre-chunking aids learning. (Miller, 1967. Simon, 1979)

Claim

2. Labeling Principle (Information Mapping)

Label every chunk and group of chunks according to specific criteria.

thus
supports

Claim

General Recoding Principle

"Re-coding is an extremely powerful weapon for increasing the amount of information that we can deal with." (Miller, 1967.)

thus
supports

Grounds

Recoding is a natural way that humans handle the limitations of short term memory. Data used include learning tones, colors, tastes, and points. (Miller, 1967)

Use of subheads improves learning. (Hartley & Trueman 1983)

Warrant

If it works across several types of human information processing, then it should work across the types coded in text, graphics and combinations of them in each document that we create.

see page 218

see page 222

see Notes

see page 220

Four Principles of Information Mapping

Claim

3. Relevance Principle (Information Mapping)

Include in one chunk only information that relates to one main point based on that information's purpose or function for the reader.

thus

supports

supports

Grounds

Gedänken Experiment △

Think of an experiment where we deliberately and randomly mislabel chunks of information.

Prediction: Tests of speed and error rate in retrieval would be slower for mislabeled information than for systematically labeled group.

Grounds

see Jonnason experiment (1980) and Shaffer (1982)

Comment

Also indirect evidence from the six dissertations with experimental data done on the whole methodology although the factors of relevancy and consistence were not specifically isolated and controlled in the experiments.

Warrant

It is not necessary to conduct every experiment in science that may be possible, particularly if in doing a Gedunken experiment, you can feel relatively certain of the results.

Definition

Gedänken Experiment

From the German, literally a "thought" experiment. A term used in science to describe experiments that are planned in thought but not carried out because of inherent limitations or because science proceeds upon the basis of critical experiments.

Claim

4. Consistency Principle (Information Mapping)

For similar subject matters, use similar words, labels, formats organizations, and sequences.

thus

supports

Grounds

Summary of Research

"For any particular type of data display, maintain consistent format from one display to another... For displayed data and labels, choose words carefully and then use them consistently... Ensure that wording is consistent from one display to another." (Smith and Mosier, 1986; see also Stewart, 1980, Pakin and Wray, 1982)

Note

In the grounds blocks we have typically provided descriptions of one or more papers. Usually there is further research that supports these claims. The reader may consult other sources provided in the bibliography.

Argumentation Analysis for Three More Principles

Application: Information Mapping's Method

On the previous pages, we have presented an argumentation analysis framework supporting the four basic principles that we used to construct all information blocks Δ We present on this page three more principles that we used to guide development decisions in formulating Information Mapping's methodology. We use the argumentation analysis methodology Δ presented in this book as a framework for presenting this rationale.

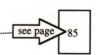 see page 85

 see page 186

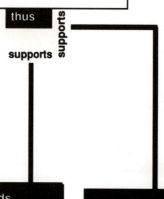

Claim

Hierarchy of Labeling and Chunking Principle (Information Mapping)

Organize all small, relevant units of information into a hierarchy and provide the larger group(s) with label(s).

thus

supports   **supports**

Claim

Integrated Graphics Principle (Information Mapping)

Use diagrams, tables, pictures, etc. as an integral part of the text, not as an afterthought added on when the writing is complete.

thus

supports

Grounds

Chunking Research

All human beings naturally chunk information as a part of their short term memory process. Pre-chunking aids learning. (Miller, 1967. Simon, 1979) Δ

Grounds

Hierarchy Research

Readers construct hierarchical representations of the text they read. (Van Dijk and Kintsch, 1983)

Grounds

Some graphic information structures are better than prose in conveying the same information. (Reid and Wright, 1973) Δ

Survey of graphic research literature (MacDonald-Ross and Smith, 1977, Smith & Mosier, 1985)

 see page 218

 see page 268

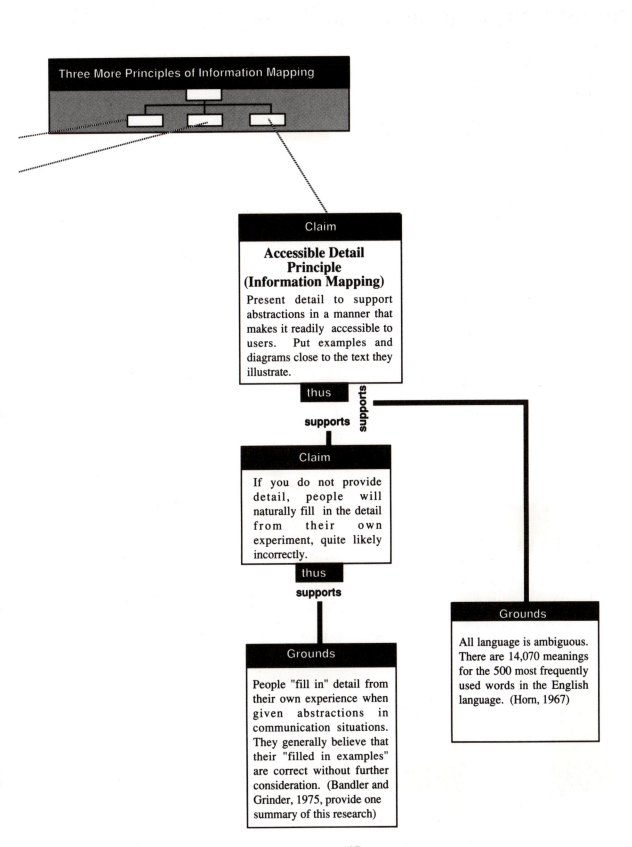

Three More Principles of Information Mapping

Claim

Accessible Detail Principle (Information Mapping)

Present detail to support abstractions in a manner that makes it readily accessible to users. Put examples and diagrams close to the text they illustrate.

thus

supports **supports**

Claim

If you do not provide detail, people will naturally fill in the detail from their own experiment, quite likely incorrectly.

thus

supports

Grounds

People "fill in" detail from their own experience when given abstractions in communication situations. They generally believe that their "filled in examples" are correct without further consideration. (Bandler and Grinder, 1975, provide one summary of this research)

Grounds

All language is ambiguous. There are 14,070 meanings for the 500 most frequently used words in the English language. (Horn, 1967)

Useful in Representing Ill-Structured Problems

Introduction

Only recently have researchers begun to study what can be called ill-structured problems, problems that defy easy definition and boundaries, and have little consensus as to their nature.

Definition: Ill-Structured Problems

Ill-structured problems are those about which different people have very different perceptions and values concerning their nature, their causes, their boundaries, and their solutions. They are the problems that bring out two or more points of view from the first mention of them.

Definition: Well-Structured Problems

Well-structured problems are textbook problems, problems which are most often used in training of scientists and engineers. There is widespread consensus as to their nature. They are logically coherent and consistent.

Characteristics

Ill-structured problems exhibit many of the characteristics shown on these pages.

Example of the Analysis of Part of an Ill-Structured Problem

 On the next few pages we present part of a case study in the ethics of using nuclear weapons. This is a field that is ill-structured. It meets many of the characteristics noted on this page.

see page 200

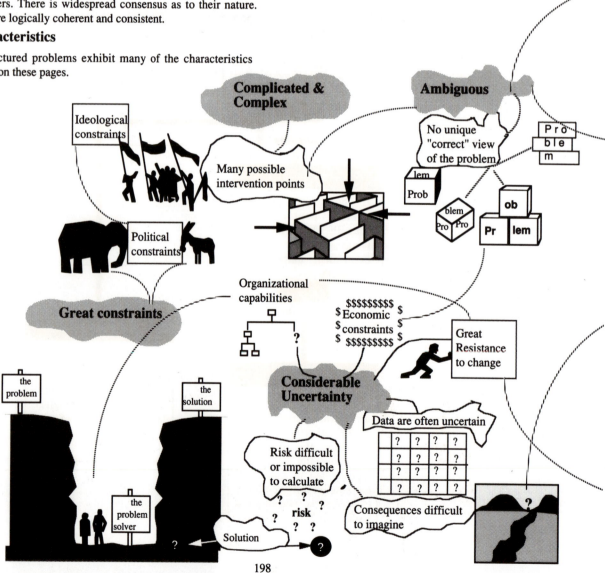

Complicated & Complex

Ambiguous

Ideological constraints

Many possible intervention points

No unique "correct" view of the problem

Problem

Political constraints

Great constraints

Organizational capabilities

$$$$$$$$ $ Economic $ constraints $ $$$$$$$$ $

Great Resistance to change

Considerable Uncertainty

the problem

the solution

the problem solver

Data are often uncertain

Risk difficult or impossible to calculate

risk

Solution

Consequences difficult to imagine

198

Commentary: Visual Structure

On this page I tried to illustrate visually how difficult it is to comprehend an ill-structured problem. I did that by making the visual elements very tangled and disorderly. I hope you get the "feel" of what I am trying to convey about ill-structured problems from this visual device. (REH)

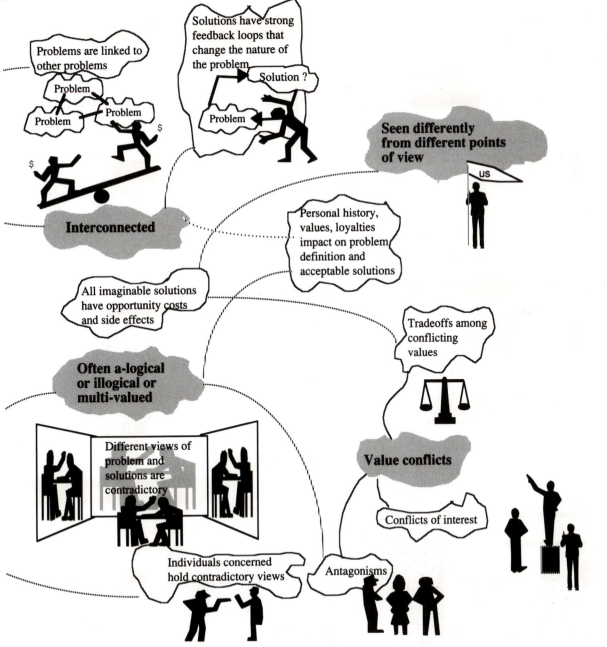

Problems are linked to other problems

Problem

Problem

Problem

Solutions have strong feedback loops that change the nature of the problem

Solution ?

Problem

Seen differently from different points of view

US

Interconnected

Personal history, values, loyalties impact on problem definition and acceptable solutions

All imaginable solutions have opportunity costs and side effects

Tradeoffs among conflicting values

Often a-logical or illogical or multi-valued

Different views of problem and solutions are contradictory

Value conflicts

Conflicts of interest

Individuals concerned hold contradictory views

Antagonisms

Case Study of a Poorly-Structured Problem

Introduction

We present on the following pages the basic arguments that were argued in the 1980's over the ethics of the policy of nuclear deterrence to illustrate the application of argumentation analysis to ill-structured problems.

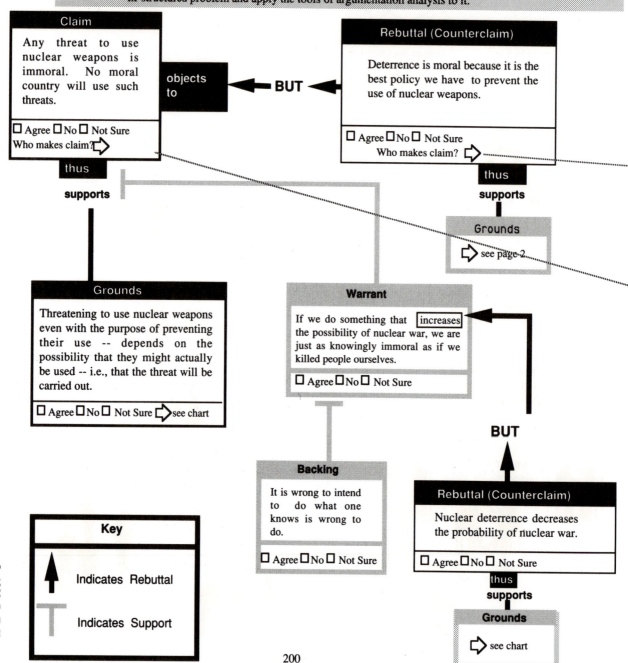

chart 1.

Deterrence △ is an Immoral Policy

The current debate about nuclear ethics is focused in large part on a re-examination of the policy of deterrence. For some people, threatening to use nuclear weapons is an immoral policy. For others, it is the only moral position. With such contradictory positions, we can identify nuclear ethics as an ill-structured problem and apply the tools of argumentation analysis to it.

Claim

Any threat to use nuclear weapons is immoral. No moral country will use such threats.

☐ Agree ☐ No ☐ Not Sure
Who makes claim? ⇨

objects to

BUT

Rebuttal (Counterclaim)

Deterrence is moral because it is the best policy we have to prevent the use of nuclear weapons.

☐ Agree ☐ No ☐ Not Sure
Who makes claim? ⇨

thus
supports

thus
supports

Grounds

⇨ see page 2

Grounds

Threatening to use nuclear weapons even with the purpose of preventing their use -- depends on the possibility that they might actually be used -- i.e., that the threat will be carried out.

☐ Agree ☐ No ☐ Not Sure ⇨ see chart

Warrant

If we do something that [increases] the possibility of nuclear war, we are just as knowingly immoral as if we killed people ourselves.

☐ Agree ☐ No ☐ Not Sure

BUT

Backing

It is wrong to intend to do what one knows is wrong to do.

☐ Agree ☐ No ☐ Not Sure

Rebuttal (Counterclaim)

Nuclear deterrence decreases the probability of nuclear war.

☐ Agree ☐ No ☐ Not Sure

thus
supports

Grounds

⇨ see chart

Key

↑ Indicates Rebuttal

⊤ Indicates Support

© 1989 R. E. Horn

Definition

Nuclear Deterrence

1. a condition of the modern age of nuclear powers such that each superpower realizes that, if they started a nuclear war, the other superpower has sufficient invulnerable weapons to retaliate and potentially destroy their military forces, culture and cities. 2. any policy of a nuclear nation that tends to promote or continue the condition of nuclear deterrence. It is a policy in which both superpowers think: "We will not start a nuclear war because the other side threatens to retaliate and destroy us and we think they could and would do that."

Who Makes This Claim?

"It makes no sense to reject deterrence simply because it may not be infallible; it makes sense to reject it only if it proves more dangerous than the alternatives."

--Charles Krauthammer

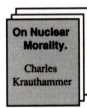

On Nuclear Morality.

Charles Krauthammer

Who Makes This Claim?

In Defense of Creation: The Nuclear Crisis and a Just Peace

By
The Council of Bishops of the United Methodist Church

(1986)

The Bishops of the United Methodist Church said in their pastoral letter (1986): "We have said a clear and unconditional 'no' to nuclear war and to any use of nuclear weapons. We have concluded that nuclear deterrence is a position which cannot receive the church's blessing...the ideology of deterrence must not receive the churches' blessing, even as a temporary warrant for holding on to nuclear weapons. The lingering possession of such weapons for a strictly limited time requires a very different justification: an ethic of reciprocity as nuclear-weapon states act together, in agreed stages, to eliminate their nuclear weapons."

Case Study Brings Together Opposing Viewpoints

Introduction

These two pages are a continuation Δ of the basic arguments that were argued in the 1980's over the ethics of the policy of nuclear deterrence to illustrate the application of argumentation analysis to ill-structured problems.

see page 200

chart 2.

Deterrence Δ prevents war; therefore it is the only morally acceptable policy.

The counterclaim of the immorality of deterrence is that deterrence is moral. The argumentation analysis outlining the main structure of this argument is presented on this page.

Definition

see chart 1.

Rebuttal (Counterclaim)

Deterrence has too many risks in the face of the possibilities of inadvertent outbreak of nuclear war.

☐ Agree ☐ No ☐ Not Sure
Who makes claim? ⇨ see chart___

BUT ➤◄ **BUT**

Claim

Deterrence is moral because it is the best policy we have to prevent the use of nuclear weapons.

☐ Agree ☐ No ☐ Not Sure
Who makes claim? ⇨

thus

supports

Warrant

Pragmatic Argument for Deterrence Policy

Before throwing out what has worked to keep the peace and prevent nuclear war, you must come up with a better moral alternative. Otherwise it is morally better to keep the policy you have.

☐ Agree ☐ No ☐ Not Sure ⇨ see chart

Warrant

Deterrence is less dangerous than its alternatives .

Deterrence may not be perfect as a policy but it is less dangerous than its alternatives.

☐ Agree ☐ No ☐ Not Sure   see chart

Key
⬆ Indicates Rebuttal
⊤ Indicates Support

Grounds

Deterrence prevents nuclear war by making both sides afraid of starting a war because they will surely lose more than they could possibly gain and could conceivably completely destroy their own country.

☐ Agree ☐ No ☐ Not Sure ⇨ see chart

Grounds

The policy of deterrence has worked for 40 years. Since 1945 there has been no nuclear war and no conventional war between superpowers.

☐ Agree ☐ No ☐ Not Sure ⇨ see chart

© 1989 R. E. Horn

Rebuttal
(Counterclaim)

Any threat to use nuclear weapons is immoral. No moral country will use such threats.

☐ Agree ☐ No ☐ Not Sure
Who makes claim? ⇨ see chart 1

BUT ◄

Rebuttal
(Counterclaim)

Nuclear war risks the future of the human species and risking the future of human species is not worth protecting the values claimed to be protected.

☐ Agree ☐ No ☐ Not Sure
Who makes claim? ⇨ see chart___

Who Makes This Claim?

"Nuclear war is such an emotional subject that many people see the weapons themselves as the common enemy of humanity. Nuclear weapons are intrinsically neither moral nor immoral, though they are more prone to immoral use than most weapons. But they can be used to accomplish moral objectives and can do this in ways that are morally acceptable. The most obvious and important way is to use them or their availability to deter others from using nuclear weapons. The second -- of much lower, but still significant priority -- is to use them to help limit the damage (human, social, political, economic, and military) that could occur if deterrence fails. Anything that reduces war-related destruction should not be considered altogether immoral."

--Herman Kahn

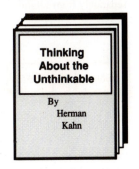

Thinking About the Unthinkable

By
Herman
Kahn

for other quotes ⇨ see chart 1.

Comparing Ill-Structured and "Tame" Problems

Introduction.

Ill-structured problems can best be seen if we look at them in comparison with "tame" or "well structured" problems, as in the chart below.

Characteristics	Tame Problems	Ill-Structured Problems
Ability to formulate the problem	Can be formulated exhaustively and written down definitively. 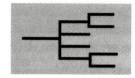	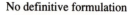 No definitive formulation 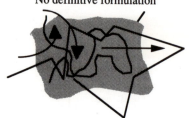
Ability to devise and conduct definitive tests	Can be tested. Mistakes and errors can be identified. 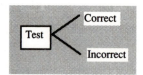	No single criterion to determine correctness. Difficult to determine when a solution is a solution or even whether a test is applicable. 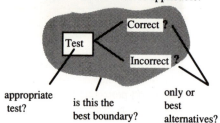
Relationship between problem and solution	Problems can be formulated separately from solutions. 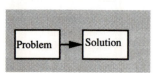	Solving the problem is synonymous with understanding it in the first place.  Each formulation of an ill-structured problem contains a definition of the solution.

Characteristics	Tame Problems	Ill-Structured Problems
Ability to determine whether problem has been solved	Have a clear ending point and a determinable solution. 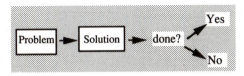 A clear rule or test can be stated to determine completion.	No stopping criteria...the problem may be ongoing and continuously changing, so there is no way of determining completion. 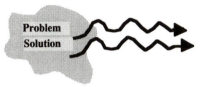
Tractability	Exhaustive list of operations used to solve problem exists. | Step	Procedure	 |---|---| | 1		 | 2		 | 3		 | 4			No list of operations exists for solving ill-structured problems. 
Relationship between explanation and solution	Can be stated as a discrepancy between what is and what could or ought to be, and an explanation exists for every gap. 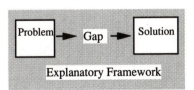	Many possible explanations and each one "contains" or "implies" a different solution. 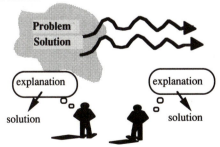

More on this table on next page

Comparing Ill-Structured and "Tame" Problems

Characteristics	Tame Problems	Ill-Structured Problems

Uniqueness or reproducibility of problem

Problems can be abstracted from the real world and similar solutions can be found.

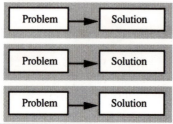

Each problem and each solution is unique.

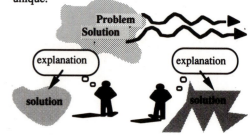

Repeatability of solutions

Attempts to solve can be made repeatedly until one works.

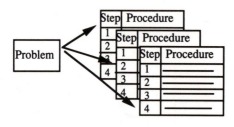

You cannot undo what you have tried, so that each solution is unique and changes the nature of the problem.

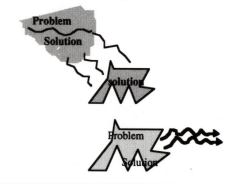

Level of analysis

Identifiable, "natural" form with high degree of certainty...level of detail for solving the problem can be found...and boundaries for the problem are reasonably easy to agree upon.

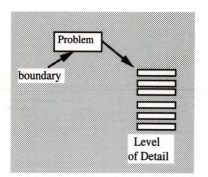

No identifiable causes...every "symptom" is a problem and vice versa...level of detail and approach are not easy to define...little agreement on setting boundaries of the problem.

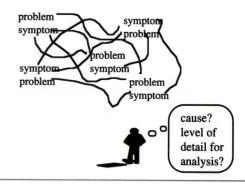

© 1989 R. E. Horn

206

Conclusions: Argumentation and Hypertext

Summary

Argumentation is a different kind of discourse from relatively stable subject matter. We have seen in this chapter that it is useful to clarify the components of a disagreement by identifying exactly what the claims, grounds, warrants, etc., are. And it is useful to use a more graphic way of displaying these components.

Connection With Other Types of Discourse

How does argumentation analysis relate to the other major types of discourse we have presented in this book?   On this page we show the major connections with other types of discourse discussed in this book.

Commentary: Usefulness of Argumentation Analysis

It is quite possible that argumentation analysis, as described in this chapter, will provide a method for slowing down disputes and looking very carefully at the merits of different points of view. Obviously, many disputes can be conducted without it. In other disputes we will be able to use argumentation analysis as a kind of "microscope" to look at the argument quite closely for any flaws or weaknesses. For that, it will become a significant tool. (REH)

3 Many of the statements in textbooks and training manuals arrive there after a process of argumentation and experimentation. This is particularly the case with facts, generalizations, and explanations of process.

see chapter **6**

2 After a scientific experiment has been planned and carried out, it is written up in articles which we describe in the domain of experimental discourse.

see chapter **8**

Scientific Articles and Papers

These results may provide the grounds for new claims that clarify the argument and may provide clear facts or generalizations that find their way into the documents of relatively stable discourse.

1 Disputed discourse arises when individuals disagree with either the claims, grounds, warrants, or backing of a given argument. They propose a rebuttal (or counter claim) which may become the subject of more systematic observation or a scientific experiment.

see chapter **7**

Chapter 8. Experimental Discourse: Scientific Information

Chapter 8
Experimental Discourse: Scientific Information

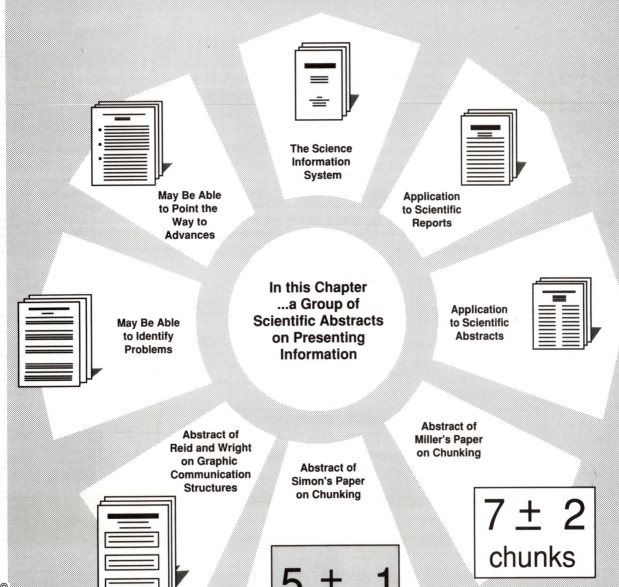

The Science Information System

Application to Scientific Reports

May Be Able to Point the Way to Advances

In this Chapter ...a Group of Scientific Abstracts on Presenting Information

Application to Scientific Abstracts

May Be Able to Identify Problems

Abstract of Miller's Paper on Chunking

Abstract of Reid and Wright on Graphic Communication Structures

Abstract of Simon's Paper on Chunking

7 ± 2 chunks

5 ± 1 chunks

Overview of This Chapter

Introduction

Unlike the relatively stable discourse domain (Chapter 6) which has seen literally tens of thousands of applications of Information Mapping's method, our applications to the discourse of experiment is somewhat speculative and theoretical. We propose that the approach of structured hypertext with Information Mapping's method could be used to approach scientific abstracts and other elements of the science information system. We do this by showing prototype abstracts. It is speculative in that we have only tried this on a pilot basis in our own lab with documents on human factors research and a few other small projects. By extension, we suggest that scientific articles may be written with many of the guidelines and principles of Information Mapping's method, and be accessed through associative hypertext networks.

1	The Science Information System

To provide a context for this discussion, we present a simplified seven level model of how "new" information flows in science from untested theoretical ideas to what is taught in the classroom.

2	Applying Information Mapping Principles to Scientific Reports, Articles, and Presentations

The major difference from current practice in writing scientific reports, articles, and presentations with Information Mapping's approach is a much smaller chunking size (as well as a more useful set of block types).

At this point, we present a list of potential block types for scientific reports.

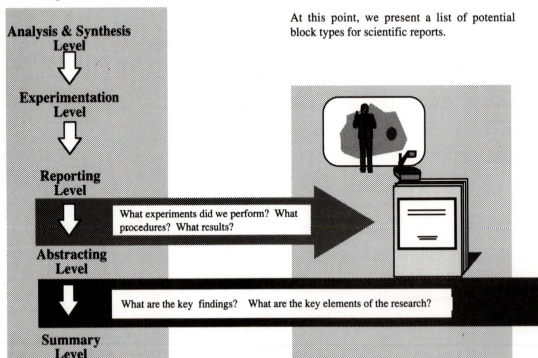

Analysis & Synthesis Level

Experimentation Level

Reporting Level

What experiments did we perform? What procedures? What results?

Abstracting Level

What are the key findings? What are the key elements of the research?

Summary Level

Teaching Level

Definition: Discourse Domain △ of Experimental Knowledge

see page 104

The domain of experimental knowledge discourse consists of descriptions of scientific experiments and the discussion of the results of these experiments in abstracts, state of the art reviews and theoretical papers.

| **3** | **Applying Information Mapping Principles to Abstracts of Scientific Papers** | **4** | **Futuristic Possibilities Suggested by Hypertext and Information Mapping** |

Writing informative abstracts about scientific abstracts is quite similar to the process for scientific papers.

We first present an overview of the kinds of blocks that might be expected in such abstracts.

And then we present five examples of such abstracts on psychological research related to the subject of this book.

Hypertext and Information Mapping may help us explore the frontiers of science and identify the most productive problems and flag them in more visible ways.

We present an outline of one way of looking for productive problems in science and then consider how that might look in a hypertext system.

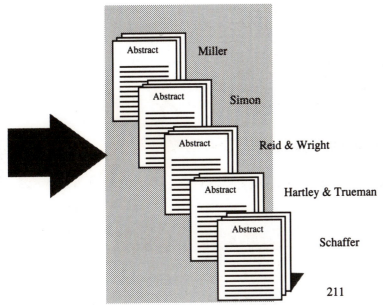

Abstract — Miller
Abstract — Simon
Abstract — Reid & Wright
Abstract — Hartley & Trueman
Abstract — Schaffer

Find and Mark Problems and Opportunities

211

The Science Information System

Introduction

To provide a context for this chapter, we will review on these pages the general structure of the international scientific information system. It is substantially similar for most of the scientific disciplines and subspecialties.

The Levels of Scientific Endeavor

Path
of "New"
Information

Analysis and Synthesis Level

1

At this level of work the scientist is asking questions, formulating new ideas for research, and putting together results from other workers to form new theories.

Experimentation Level

2

At this level of work the scientist carries out the experimental procedures formulated at the previous stage, preparing notes, collecting and processing data.

Reporting Level

3

At this level of the science process, the scientist writes up the results of experiments and presents the data and conclusions in papers and reports.

Abstracting Level

4

At the abstracting level of the science information process, professional writers prepare abstracts and summaries of the reporting level documents.

Summary Level

5

This is the level at which books and articles summarizing advances in the field are written.

Teaching Level

6

At this level the textbooks and other teaching materials are developed.

Documents that are Used at Each Level of Science

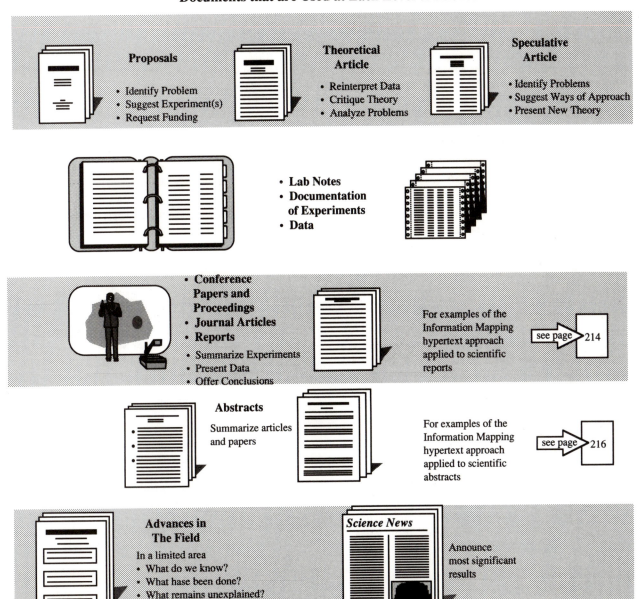

Proposals

- Identify Problem
- Suggest Experiment(s)
- Request Funding

Theoretical Article

- Reinterpret Data
- Critique Theory
- Analyze Problems

Speculative Article

- Identify Problems
- Suggest Ways of Approach
- Present New Theory

- **Lab Notes**
- **Documentation of Experiments**
- **Data**

- **Conference Papers and Proceedings**
- **Journal Articles**
- **Reports**
  - Summarize Experiments
  - Present Data
  - Offer Conclusions

For examples of the Information Mapping hypertext approach applied to scientific reports see page 214

Abstracts

Summarize articles and papers

For examples of the Information Mapping hypertext approach applied to scientific abstracts see page 216

Advances in The Field

In a limited area
- What do we know?
- What hase been done?
- What remains unexplained?
- What might be done?

Science News

Announce most significant results

Textbooks and Handbooks

Integrate what is known in didactic or handbook format

This is the domain of relatively stable subject matter. see page 168

Application: Scientific Reports and Articles

Introduction

If you walk into the offices of most research scientists, you see large piles of scientific papers.   When I ask the scientist about the contents of the stack of reports, I usually get the reply that each pile represents what they have to read before going on to the next experiment or writing the next proposal. These piles are not small.   They often contain 50 or 100 papers.   How many papers can a scientist read in a week? Not many if they are doing other things, writing, doing experiments, and teaching.   There would be a great advantage to a million scientists and engineers if we could improve the scannability of basic scientific reports. If scientists could quickly determine which of the 50 or 100 reports contained information that they needed to read carefully, they could do their jobs better. The principles of Information Mapping's approach are specifically aimed at improving such communication situations.   How would that work?

What is the situation now?

When we look at contemporary primary scientific reports today, we typically see five main divisions: background, method, data, conclusions, and discussion.   Compared to the amount of information in the report, this is not enough chunks. There are typically too few labels to provide rapid scanning.

A preliminary analysis

On these pages, we present our preliminary analysis of reports that contain experimental data.   We suggest a group of information blocks that would provide the working scientist with better guidance for rapidly scanning scientific reports. When we applied the chunking principle, we divided the information in each report into much more fine-grained pieces. The labels focus on a content-independent set of categories that working scientists are interested in.

Status of this work

We should point out that, unlike the results we presented in Chapter 3 for relatively stable subject matter, this information block analysis is preliminary. We have not extensively tested it either deeply in one field or broadly across several fields of science and technology.   We believe that many of the categories would hold up well in such an evaluation, but there are likely to be additions to the set of information blocks from such a test.

Background Information Leading Up to the Research

- Argument (leading up to hypothesis development, background)
  - Related Research
  - Theoretical Propositions
  - Experimental Evidence
  - Implications (for this project)
  - Bibliographic Citations
- Definitions (of novel key terms)
- Definitions of Abbreviations & Notation
- Examples (of novel key terms)
- Prerequisite Technical Terms (not defined but used in this report)
- Main Questions
- Theoretical Model
- Assumptions
- Formal Hypothesis
  - What is New About Hypothesis?
  - Parameters of Theoretical Model to be Varied
  - Independent Variable(s)
  - Dependent Variable(s)
- Controls
  - Conditions of Testing
  - Subjects
  - Selection Procedures

Preliminary Analysis of Blocks Needed for Reporting Experimental Data

Procedure for Conducting the Experiment

- Site
- Year
- Experimental Setup
- Equipment or Apparatus
  - New Apparatus
  - Unusual Aspects of Apparatus
- Experimental Design
- Procedure (Methods of Data Collection)
  - Measures Used
  - New Techniques
  - Unusual or Significant Aspects of Procedure
- Subjects
  - Age
  - Sex
  - Race
  - Income
  - etc.

Outcomes of Experimentation

- Data Collected (results)
- Data Reduction(s)
  - Sample Size
- Mathematics Used for Data Reduction
- Computer Program Used
- Main Conclusions
- Secondary Conclusions
  - Unexpected Findings
  - Intuitive Grasps of the Data or Process
- Significant Negative Results
- Implications
  - Important (to whom?)
  - Utility (for what?)
- Limitations and Shortcomings
  - Limits of Generalization of the Study
  - Technical Flaws Discovered in Doing the Experiment
  - Possible Errors
  - Critical Comments
- Theoretical Implications
- Research Which Needs to be Done as a Result of This Experiment

Bibliographic Information

- Title
- Author(s)
- Affiliation and Location of Author
  - Address (complete, zip)
  - Phone
- Journal
- Citation
- Presentation at Meeting
- Contract Number(s) and Acknowledgement of Financial Support
- Acknowledgements of Assistance
- Document Identification Numbers
- Suggested Indexing Terms

Applying Information Block Analysis to Abstracts

Introduction

On the previous page we provided the results of a preliminary examination of scientific reports. Here we examine, in similar fashion, the scientific abstract. We ask, what types of blocks are essential to restructuring the scientific abstract? If standard block types can be developed for different types of scientific abstracts, the abstracter will be able to provide information that can be easily scanned and summarized by investigators who use the abstracts. Our research in this area is preliminary, but suggestive of how we might proceed.

Standard Information Blocks for Scientific Abstracts

On these pages we present a list of the information blocks that appear to be important for all scientific abstracts presenting experimental data. We would encourage the abstracter to use them unless there are overriding reasons for not doing so. To be regarded as fully following the principles of Information Mapping's method, we would have to develop and test specific standards, guidelines, and rules for construction for each of the twenty-five or thirty blocks that abstracts might contain.

Examples

On the following pages we present examples of several abstracts developed with this approach.

About the experiment

- Purpose
- Method
- Results (Findings)
- Conclusions

These blocks also appear to be important in describing the experiment in longer abstracts

- Implications
- Data (i.e., a simplified data table, chart or graph of the data collected)
- Limits of Study
- Instrumentation Modification
- New Techniques or Equipment
- Controls
- Other Observations
- Background (theoretical or other setting for experiment)
- Caution
- Consequences
  - Benefits
  - Safety
  - Cost
  - Convenience

Information Blocks for Abstracts

- Risk
- Status
- Criteria
- Recommendations
- Installation Requirements
- Environmental Factors
- Advantages/Disadvantages
- Trade-offs
- Feasibility
- Promising Lines of Research

For Specific Specialties

Specific scientific specialties would require blocks for important information items that always or frequently appear. For example, in psychology or education the following would be useful:
- Subjects (with additional sub-blocks such as number and characteristics)
- Time Span
- Task
- Treatment of Groups

Bibliographic Information

- Author
  - Affiliations
- Address
- Title of Publication
- Citation (include citation in the convention of the field)

About the Abstract

- Abstracter
- Data

Next Level of Detail

Examples of abstracts written using this approach

see page 218

Miller: Short Term Memory Limits and Chunking

Problem

What are the limitations on the amount of information that we can receive, process, and remember?

Background

Psychology and Information Theory

Information theory can provide a quantitative approach to questions raised in the psychology of communication. What psychology calls experiments in absolute judgment, information theory calls experiments on the capacity of people to transmit information. In a communication system, the term "amount of information" is used to express what psychology would call the "variance" in either input (stimuli) or output (response). "Amount of transmitted information" is the term used for the relationship between input and output.

Information Measurement

In experiments on absolute judgment, the capacity to transmit information, the experimental problem is to increase the amount of input information and to measure the amount of transmitted information. Input can be increased in rate or in amount. An increase in the amount of information is an increase in the number of alternative stimuli. The observer is considered a communication channel, and has a "channel capacity" -- the upper limit on the extent to which the observer can match response to stimuli. That is, there is a limit to the capacity to accurately transmit received information. As information input is increased, the observer's transmitted information will at first increase, then level off at some asymptotic value as errors in transmission increase.

Bits

To test accuracy of transmission, the observer is given a discrimination task; a judgment must be made between alternatives. To describe this judgment quantitatively: The amount of information needed to make a decision between two equally likely alternatives is one bit. For instance, to decide if a man is less than 6 feet tall or more than 6 feet tall, if we know that the chances are 50/50, requires one bit of information.

2 alternatives require 1 bit of information
4   "   2 bits   "
8   3
16   4
32   5

Each doubling of alternatives requires one additional bit of information.

Research

In experiments of absolute judgment using unidimensional stimuli -- pitch or loudness of auditory tones, saltiness, position of a pointer on a line -- channel capacities had a mean of about 2.6 bits, or about 6.5 alternative categories. Channel capacity increases when dimensions are added. In experiments for two-dimensional stimuli -- dots in a square, saltiness and sweetness, loudness and pitch -- capacity was about 3 to 5 bits. For multidimensional stimuli, capacity varies; capacity for colors that vary in size, hue, and brightness was around 4 bits; for 6 different acoustical variables, capacity was about 7 bits.

While adding variables increases total capacity, it decreases the capacity for any particular variable. In other words, we can make relatively crude judgments of several things simultaneously.

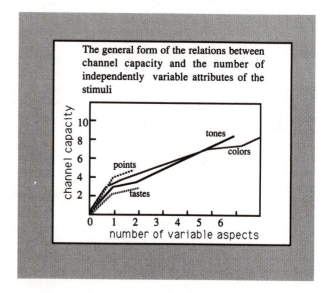

The general form of the relations between channel capacity and the number of independently variable attributes of the stimuli

Analysis

The number seven recurs in various experiments. The "span of absolute judgment" (limit to accuracy in identifying the magnitude of a unidimensional stimulus variable) is about 7 alternatives. The span of immediate memory is about 7 items in length. The span of attention encompasses about 6 items. While it is easy to postulate that a single process underlies these three spans, that is not the case. There appears to be a difference between the process of absolute judgment and the process of immediate memory. Absolute judgment is limited by amount of information, or bits. Immediate memory is limited by number of items, or chunks. A chunk is a coding unit which groups bits. The span of immediate memory seems to be almost independent of the number of bits per chunk, though chunks themselves are limited to about 7.

Importance of Miller's Paper

Miller's paper is a classic and changed the way of studying short term memory.

7 ± 2
chunks

New Definition: Chunks

Chunks are familiar units -- a word is a chunking of phonemes. In Morse code, dit and dah can be separate chunks for the beginner, but they are only part of larger chunks -- letters, words, phrases -- for the experienced operator. In communications theory such ordering of information is called recoding. Input is recoded into another code that contains fewer chunks, with more bits per chunk.

Conclusions

The span of absolute judgment and the span of immediate memory impose severe limitations on the amount of information that we are able to receive, process, and remember. By organizing the stimulus input simultaneously into several dimensions and successively into a sequence of chunks, we manage to break (or at least stretch) this information bottleneck.

The process of recoding is a very important one in human psychology and deserves much more explicit attention than it has received. Information concepts have already proved valuable in the study of discrimination and of language; they promise a great deal in the study of learning and memory. It has even been proposed that they can be useful in the study of concept formation. There may be something deep and profound behind the "magical number seven," or there may only be a "Pythagorean coincidence."

Author

George A. Miller

Citation

"The Magical Number Seven, Plus or Minus Two: Some Limits on Our Capacity for Processing Information" *Psychological Review,* Vol. 63, No. 2, March 1956, pp. 81-89

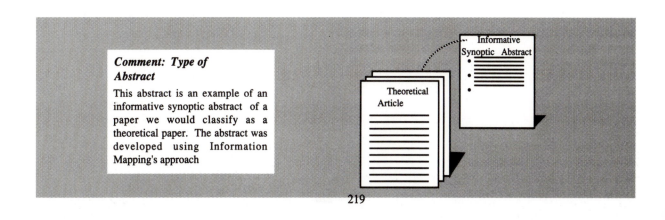

Comment: Type of Abstract

This abstract is an example of an informative synoptic abstract of a paper we would classify as a theoretical paper. The abstract was developed using Information Mapping's approach

Simon's Tests Show Chunking Size to be 5 to 7

Problem

How can the parameters of the human information processing system be determined?

Background

Shift in Experimental Approach to Memory: The examination of problem-solving processes is part of the attempt to understand complex cognitive behaviors. Short term memory and the transfer of information to long term memory (fixation) is crucial to problem solving. To examine memory, experimental psychology is taking a new view of experiments. Traditionally, an experiment tests a hypothesis by focusing on the relation of a dependent variable to independent variables manipulated over a set of experimental conditions. Such an experiment produces one bit of information for instance, that the ease of learning nonsense syllables is related to their meaningfulness. It does not give the strength of the relation -- the parameters that tell whether running up the scale of meaningfulness from 0 to 100 reduces learning times by 5%, 50%, or 100%.

Now experiments are shifting from hypothesis testing to parameter estimating.

Analysis

The Chunk

Studies cited by George A. Miller in 1956 pertaining to short term memory were mostly of the parameter estimating type. He postulated the "chunk" as the unit held by short term memory, and found that the capacity of short term memory, measured in chunks, appears constant. The capacity is also apparently independent of the content of the chunks -- whether words, digits, colors, poetry, or prose. However, unless chunk size can be measured independently of memory span, the assertion of a fixed chunk span loses all empirical content. Instead, there is a definition: a chunk of any material is what short term memory will hold five of.

Determining the Size of the Chunk:

The chunk is then not a directly observable quantity. However, if the hypothesis of the unobservable chunk is combined with a hypothesis of an observable quantity, such as learning time, empirical evidence for the chunk can be derived.

1st hypothesis: The span of immediate recall is a constant number of chunks.

2nd hypothesis: Learning time is proportional to the number of chunks to be assembled.

For instance, take the short term memory span for a particular test situation, e.g., for nonsense syllables, and compare it with the memory span for another test situation, e.g., simple words. Using Brener's data, the ratio of word span to syllable span is 2.2. This ratio can then be compared to learning-time ratios for the same materials. It is commonly observed that there is a 2.5 to 1 advantage in learning simple words over nonsense syllables, for fixation of information in long term memory. The near agreement of these ratios lends support to the hypothesis that there is a chunk of constant size underlying the process of short term memory and the process of fixation of information in long term memory. Not all experiments show such agreement, however; e.g., the comparison of nonsense syllables with the digits.

Quick Summary

Simon's work essentially confirms Miller's hypothesis. The exact number of chunks is less important than that we know that the size of short term memory is approximately 5.

5 ± 1
chunks

5 to 10 seconds per chunk to fix in long term memory.

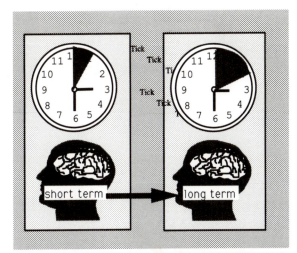

Implications

The chunking hypothesis has implications for the increase in digit memory span with age (possibly due to shortening of encoded strings by use of learned chunks). The chunking hypothesis has been used to explain the ability of chess grand masters to reproduce the pattern of pieces on a chessboard after a brief exposure. This may not be an extraordinary perceptual ability, but a "vocabulary" of chunks similar in size to an educated adult's vocabulary in his native language. The chunking hypothesis can be related to the strategy of using paradigms estimated for simple tasks to predict performance on complex tasks.

Conclusions

To summarize, the estimates of relative chunk size for nonsense syllables, words, and prose obtained from immediate recall experiments agree very well with the estimates obtained from rote learning (long term memory) experiments. There is serious disagreement, however, between the two estimates of digit chunk size; data for estimating chunk size for colors and geometric figures are apparently not available from the rote learning paradigm. The psychological reality of the chunk has been fairly well demonstrated, and the chunk capacity of short term memory has been shown to be in the range of five to seven. Fixation of information in long term memory has been shown to take about five or ten seconds per chunk. These two basic constants organize, systematize, and explain a wide range of findings about both simple tasks and more complex cognitive performances that have been reported in the psychological literature over the past 50 years or more.

Author

H. A. Simon

Citation

"How Big is a Chunk?" in *Models of Thought*, New Haven: Yale University Press, 1979 pp. 50-61

Biographical Note

Herbert Simon won the Nobel Prize in economics for his studies in decision making.

Comment: Type of Abstract

This abstract is an example of an informative synoptic abstract of a paper we would classify as an experimental paper. The abstract was developed using the Information Mapping approach.

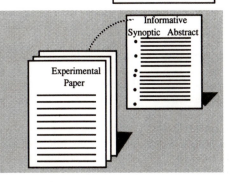

Hartley and Trueman: Headings Aid Retrieval

Problem

How does presence or absence of text headings affect recall, search, and retrieval?

Definitions

Recall -- amount of information recalled.
Search -- time taken to find information in an unfamiliar text.
Retrieval -- time taken to retrieve information from familiar text.

Material Used

Text was adapted from the *Sunday Observer Magazine*, approximately 1,000 words. Topic was television viewing habits in the United Kingdom. Text was a report on a questionnaire, and contained a large number of facts and figures. Text was typed with one and a half spacing on about 3 1/2 pages. There were 2 versions: one with headings and one without. Both versions had 12 paragraphs. Text with headings had either marginal or in-text headings approximately every 2 paragraphs. Headings were either questions or statements. Flesch reading ease score of text: 55, regarded as "fairly difficult" or suitable for 15- to 17-year olds.

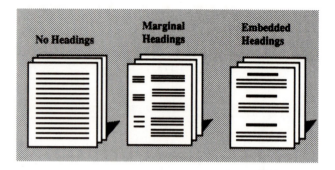

Theoretical Model

" . . . work . . . conducted from an a-theoretical position."

Task

To read text and answer questions about it on a short-answer test with 12 items. Task was structured toward either recall, search, or retrieval.

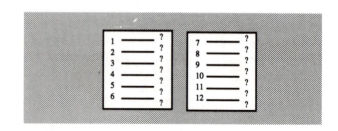

Evaluative Criteria

Test questions required specific answers: "What percentage of viewers were dissatisfied with BBC 1 programs?"

Method of Presenting Task

Recall studies: Participants read through material carefully once, and then answered test questions without referring back to the text.

Search studies: Participants first did a practice task as a group and then did the main task individually. Task in both cases was to find and circle in the text the answer to each of the test questions.

Retrieval studies: A practice task preceded the main task. Both times, participants *read the material first,* found and circled the answers to each of the test questions in the text.

Task not timed.

Task was timed.

Task was timed.

Subjects

1,270 fourth-year British comprehensive school students, 14 and 15 years old, male and female.

Experiments took place in classes, usually "organized by the school into different ability groups." No remedial students took part. Participants were allocated randomly, but approximately equally by sex, to each condition of the experiment.

Results

Headings aided recall, search and retrieval.

Headings or not: The average participant who read material with headings "performed better than 66 percent of the participants in the no-headings groups."

General or specific effect of headings: Could not be determined for search and retrieval. For recall tasks, effects were general.

Position of headings: Whether marginal or embedded had no significant effect.

Kind of heading: questions or statements. Could be directly compared in only 1/3 of the experiments. No significant effect.

Other Findings

Ability: " . . . a suggestion that different tasks might have produced different results with the low-ability participants." Data inconclusive.

Conclusions

━━━ **Comment** ━━━

In later studies, (Hartley 1989, personal communcation) the results with low-ability participants was *not* confirmed. (REH)

"Headings thus proved effective for aiding recall, search and retrieval. This was the case whether or not headings were embedded in the text or positioned in the margin, and whether or not headings were written in the form of statements or in the form of questions."

Authors

J. Hartley and M. Trueman, Department of Psychology, University of Keele

Citation

"The Effects of Headings in Text on Recall, Search and Retrieval,"*British Journal of Educational Psychology*, 1983, 53, pp 205-214,

Schaffer: Information Mapping's Methodology

Problem

What is the value of a "structured modular writing technique (Information Mapping)" in the utilization of instruction?

Background: Information Mapping

"Information Mapping (IM) is a structured modular writing technique." Informational needs of users, content specification, and guidelines for writing and formatting are essential components of the method.

Purpose

To determine the "potential benefit" from the revision of an instruction by trained professionals utilizing IM.

Subjects

Ten subjects: 7 female, 3 male
Age: Average 38.6
Job Type: 5 clerical, 4 management
Average Length of Employment: 10.2 years
Knowledge of Tasks: Subjects were screened to prevent inclusion of individuals familiar with the specific time reporting instruction tested on IM.

Materials Used

Original Version   "140 page Time Reporting Instruction" "The selection was based upon the high quality of the existing document, its technical complexity, and the size of the user population. The current version has few errors in content and an exceptionally clear writing style. Also, the widespread use of the instruction multiplies the importance of the human performance characteristics of the document."

Information Mapping Version   "185 page revised version" developed by Information Mapping, Inc.

Tasks

"The tasks were generated by randomly selecting time reporting deviation codes from a pool of codes that are not generally known. The selected codes were then inserted at random into one of two formats. One question format involved the determination of a code's meaning using a multiple choice presentation. The other question format involved the determination of the appropriate code for a given situation. After each item a space was provided for the subject to record the time. In this way, two equivalent sets of tasks were developed, each containing three multiple choice items followed by three code determination items."

Other Tasks

A pre- and post-semantic differential evaluation form to assess perception of task format and feelings about the material.

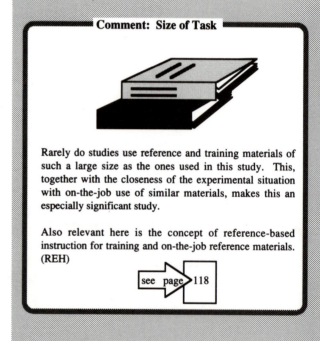

Comment: Size of Task

Rarely do studies use reference and training materials of such a large size as the ones used in this study. This, together with the closeness of the experimental situation with on-the-job use of similar materials, makes this an especially significant study.

Also relevant here is the concept of reference-based instruction for training and on-the-job reference materials. (REH)

see page 118

Method of Presenting Task

Group testing: Subjects were asked to evaluate two different versions of the materials.

1st phase: "Equal numbers of the two versions of the instruction were then distributed in a random fashion."

2nd phase: First semantic differential.

3rd phase: "A second trial was then conducted following the above procedure with each subject evaluating the other version of the instruction and performing the second set of tasks."

Analysis

Time and error data compiled. Semantic differential scaled on 1-7 scale.

Results

Time: "The instruction version had no significant effect on the time required to complete the tasks."
Errors: "Subjects made 54.5% fewer errors in the tasks when using the Information Mapping version of the instruction."

Subjectivity rating: The Information Mapping version was reported to be more 'modern,' 'clear,' 'not frustrating,' 'friendly,' and 'good.'

"Of the 25 items on the final evaluation instrument, 12 revealed significant differences between the versions of the instruction (P<.05)."
"The Information Mapping version was described as . . .

- text rambles less
- more broken into logical parts
- table of contents easier to use
- type font less 'too small'
- more 'trustworthy' and 'friendly'
- made subject feel more 'satisfied,' 'confident,' and 'in control'
- more 'easy to use'
- more 'easy to learn from'
- more of a 'good quick reference.'"

Conclusions

"Although the current version is generally considered by management to be in 'good shape' the Information Mapping version was significantly superior. Although the scope of the study is limited the importance of writing quality is clearly demonstrated."

Author

Eric M. Schaffer

Citation

"The Potential Benefits of the Information Mapping Technique" *NSPI Journal* , February 1982, p. 34 - 38.

Reid and Wright: Superiority of Visual Structuring

Introduction

To what degree can we make an abstract visual? And will addition of visual material aid in the rapid comprehension of the abstract.? We present an experiment here for readers to judge.

Problem

How do alternative ways of presenting technical information affect reader ability to determine the outcome of complex contingencies?

Materials Used

The same basic instructional information was presented in four formats:
- bureaucratic prose
- algorithm (flow chart)
- list of short sentences
- row and column table.

"Fictitious material was invented so that subjects had no option but to read the written information to solve each problem; the problems could not be solved from any previous knowledge."

Prose

When time is limited, travel by Rocket, unless cost is also limited in which case go by Space Ship. When only cost is limited an Astrobus should be used for journeys of less than 10 orbs, and a Satellite for longer journeys. Cosmocars are recommended, when there are no constraints on time or cost, unless the distance to be travelled exceeds 10 orbs. For journeys longer than 10 orbs, when time and cost are not important, journeys should be made by Super Star.

Short Sentences

Where only time is limited travel by Rocket.
Where only cost is limited travel by Satellite if journey more than 10 orbs. Travel by astrobus if journey less than 20 orbs.
Where both time and cost are limited', travel by Space Ship
Where time and cost are not limited travel by Superstar if journey more than 10 orbs. Travel by Cosmocar if journey less than 10 orbs.

Task

36 Problems

Easy

Difficult

Typical Problem

Determine the appropriate mode of travel, given information on the traveler's available time, affordable cost, and the journey's distance.

Subjects

68 adults,
17 in each of the
4 experimental groups.
32 were male,
36 female.

Prose Group

Short Sentences Group

Algorithm (Flow Chart) Group

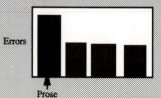

Data

Errors

Type of Problem	Prose	Algorithm	Short Sentences	Table
Straightforward	34.4	18.1	19.1	14.7
Difficult	41.7	26.0	41.7	35.8

Conclusions

More Errors with Prose on Straightforward Problems

Errors

Prose

Commentary: Conclusions about graphic communication

Does such evidence hold across different kinds of visual communication devices? Yes. (See Smith and Mosier, 1986, for a summary of many of the research findings.) (REH)

Algorithm (Flow Chart)

Is time limited?
- Yes → Is cost limited?
  - Yes → travel by Space Ship
  - No → travel by Rocket
- No → Is cost limited?
  - Yes → Is traveling distance more than 10 orbs?
    - Yes → travel by Satellite
    - No → travel by Astrobus
  - No → Is traveling distance more than 10 orbs?
    - Yes → travel by Superstar
    - No → travel by Cosmocar

Table

	If journey less than 10 orbs	If journey more than 10 orbs
Where only time is limited	travel by Rocket	travel by Rocket
Where only cost is limited	travel by Astrobus	travel by Satellite
Where time and cost are not limited	travel by Cosmocar	travel by Super Star
Where both time and cost are limited	travel by Space Ship	travel by Space Ship

Method of Presenting Task

"An independent group design was used, each subject working with only one of the information formats. Subjects were tested individually." For each of the three sections of the experiment, problems were given at two levels of difficulty. Simple problems gave information on time, cost, and distance directly; difficult problems gave the information implicitly.

Judgment Criteria

Success of subjects was judged according to the accuracy of their problem-solving, since "Clearly the most important datum is error rate. If information cannot be used accurately there is little value in it being used speedily."

Table Group

Author

Reid, F. , and Wright, P.

Citation

"Written Information: Some Alternatives to Prose for Expressing the Outcomes of Complex Contingencies," *Journal of Applied Psychology*, 1973, Vol. 57, No. 2, 160-166

Note

This summary covers one of two experiments reported in this paper.

Fewer Errors with Algorithms on Difficult Problems

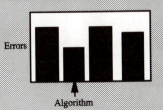

Errors

Algorithm

Commentary: Conclusions about Abstracts

In this section, we have presented five scientific abstracts. They demonstrate how Information Mapping's method can be used to improve the scannability and ease of use of this kind of document. (REH)

Facilitate Identifying Problems at Science Frontiers

Introduction

Science advances by identifying "productive problems" on which experimental or theoretical work can be accomplished. Scientists ask: What are the big problems now? What are the "tractable" problems on which we can work? What are the frontiers that appear a little beyond our capabilities now? An important property of a fully useful scientific hypertext would be the ability to describe the frontiers of science.

Problem of Problems

Root-Bernstein (1982) describes the following nine types of problems as ones which characterize opportunities for advances in science.

Nine Types of Potentially Fruitful Problems

(1) problems of definition

How shall we classify the phenomena?

(2) problems of theory

How well does a given theory explain the data?

(3) problems of data

Do we have sufficient data in sufficient quality to verify the hypothesis?

(4) problems of methodology or technique

How adequate are the tools and techniques of data collection?

(5) problems of criteria

How adequate is the "interpretation, meaning or validity" of items 1 through 4 of this list?

(6) problems of integration

How can we integrate two or more theories or collections of data?

(7) problems of extension

How can we borrow ideas, data, techniques or tools from other branches of science for this problem?

(8) problems of comparison

How comparable are two or more definitions, theories, or data collection techniques?

(9) artifactual problems

Are the tools and methods used in an experiment appropriate to the question being asked?

Hypertext Application

Structured hypertext may help in providing the facilities for individuals and groups to analyze and communicate the frontiers of particular scientific problems through webs of text and graphics such as the logical trees linked to abstracts as shown in this chapter.

Example of Annotations of Frontiers

What would a survey of the frontiers of science look like?

see page 230

Logical Tree Technique for Visualizing Problem Linkages at Scientific Frontiers

Root-Bernstein is interested in how to pick "big problems" to work on, i.e., those which have major implications or which include several problems at once. He suggests that scientists build "logical trees" of problems (rather than solutions) that will better give them a picture of the strategic selection of problems.

Example of a Logical Tree (Immune System)

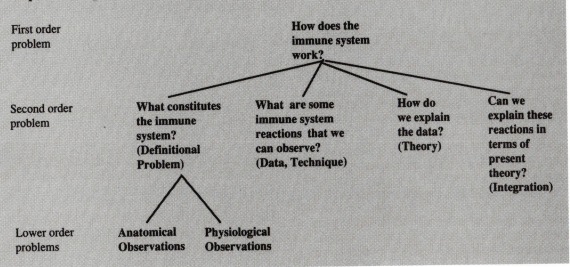

Get the Right Tree

Scientific "problems may only be solved when the techniques, data, theories, or concepts exist for solving them," says Root-Bernstein. "The trick of problem solving, then, becomes the ability to propose a tree of logically connected (i.e., 'nested') problems so constructed that one or more branches or twigs connect with the known. The solution of one or more subproblems may then provide the basis for the solution of the problem next in the 'order.' In a very well-connected 'logical problem tree,' the solution of a single minor problem may create a 'domino effect' or 'chain reaction' leading to the solution of an entire problem area."

Graft Trees

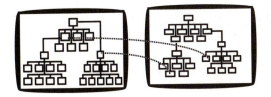

"Logic is not sufficient to the resolution of problems... To resolve one problem requires knowledge that raises another problem that requires knowledge that raises another problem...In such instances, infinitely regressing 'problem trees' will only be useful if the 'tree' may be grafted at some point onto another 'tree' that connects to the known. One way of making such grafts is by analogy: 'This problem, about which we know nothing, is like that problem which can be solved; perhaps, therefore, the solution to that problem provides an analogy by which this problem may be resolved.'"

Linked Comments Will Highlight Deficiencies

Introduction

Scientists advance knowledge by noticing the deficiencies, errors, omissions in particular theories, data, technique, interpretations. One of the most powerful capabilities suggested for hypertext facilities will be the ability for analysts to add comments to other workers' presentations. On these pages we present a schematic which shows a portion of a subfield of science with annotations attached to the Information Mapped hypertext.

Ability to See Holes in Arguments

"Perhaps the most important (yet least vivid) benefit of hypertext will be a new ability to see absences. To survive the coming years, we must evaluate complex ideas correctly, and this requires judging whether an argument is full of holes. But today we have trouble seeing holes."

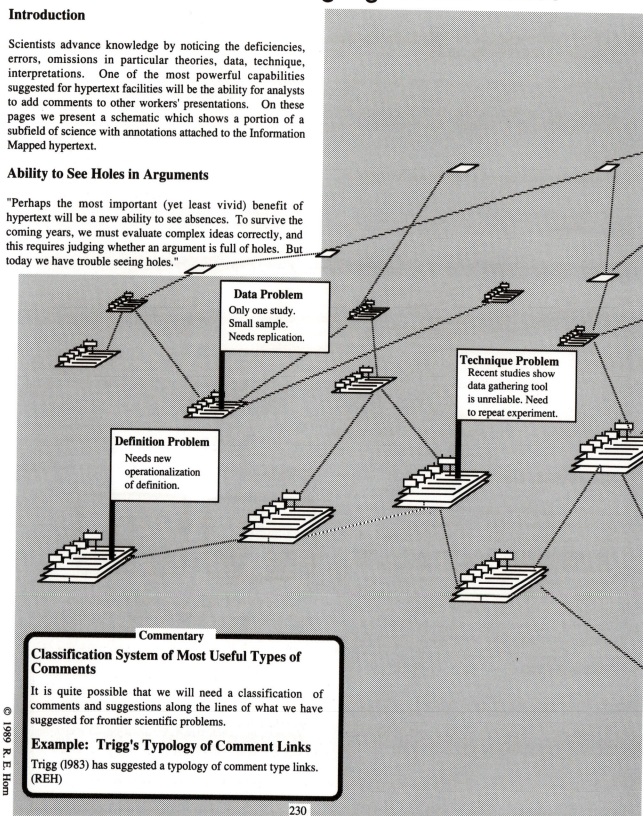

Data Problem
Only one study.
Small sample.
Needs replication.

Technique Problem
Recent studies show data gathering tool is unreliable. Need to repeat experiment.

Definition Problem
Needs new operationalization of definition.

Commentary

Classification System of Most Useful Types of Comments

It is quite possible that we will need a classification of comments and suggestions along the lines of what we have suggested for frontier scientific problems.

Example: Trigg's Typology of Comment Links

Trigg (1983) has suggested a typology of comment type links. (REH)

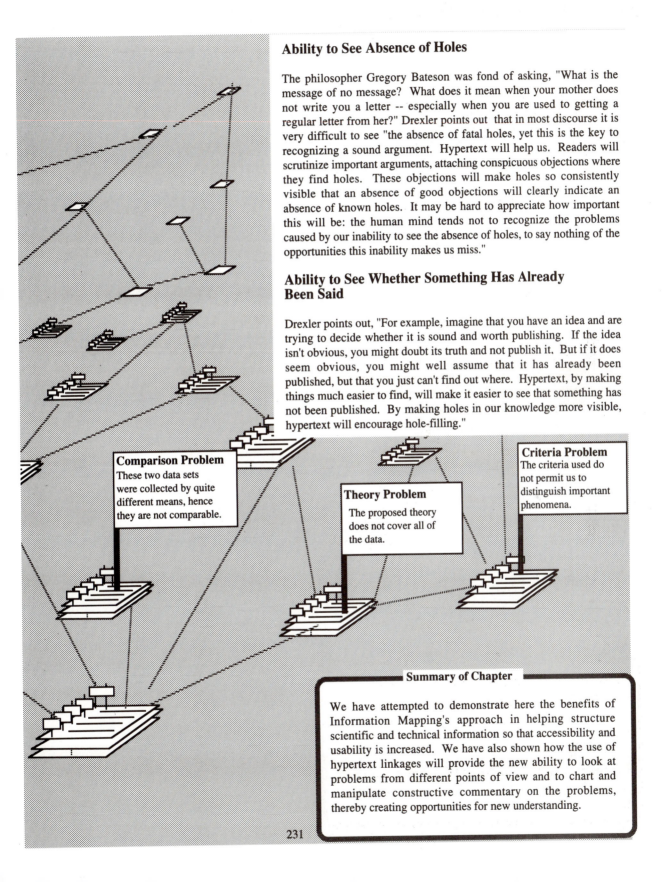

Ability to See Absence of Holes

The philosopher Gregory Bateson was fond of asking, "What is the message of no message? What does it mean when your mother does not write you a letter -- especially when you are used to getting a regular letter from her?" Drexler points out that in most discourse it is very difficult to see "the absence of fatal holes, yet this is the key to recognizing a sound argument. Hypertext will help us. Readers will scrutinize important arguments, attaching conspicuous objections where they find holes. These objections will make holes so consistently visible that an absence of good objections will clearly indicate an absence of known holes. It may be hard to appreciate how important this will be: the human mind tends not to recognize the problems caused by our inability to see the absence of holes, to say nothing of the opportunities this inability makes us miss."

Ability to See Whether Something Has Already Been Said

Drexler points out, "For example, imagine that you have an idea and are trying to decide whether it is sound and worth publishing. If the idea isn't obvious, you might doubt its truth and not publish it. But if it does seem obvious, you might well assume that it has already been published, but that you just can't find out where. Hypertext, by making things much easier to find, will make it easier to see that something has not been published. By making holes in our knowledge more visible, hypertext will encourage hole-filling."

Comparison Problem
These two data sets were collected by quite different means, hence they are not comparable.

Theory Problem
The proposed theory does not cover all of the data.

Criteria Problem
The criteria used do not permit us to distinguish important phenomena.

Summary of Chapter

We have attempted to demonstrate here the benefits of Information Mapping's approach in helping structure scientific and technical information so that accessibility and usability is increased. We have also shown how the use of hypertext linkages will provide the new ability to look at problems from different points of view and to chart and manipulate constructive commentary on the problems, thereby creating opportunities for new understanding.

Chapter 9. Mapping Future Infospace: Summary and Trends

Chapter 9
Mapping Future Infospace: Summary and Trends

In this
Chapter
we sum up
and
look at
the trends

Summary of the Argument

We have made the case in this book that

Hypertext will help us get our on-line text organized in a new way, following associative trails that are more like the way human memory operates.

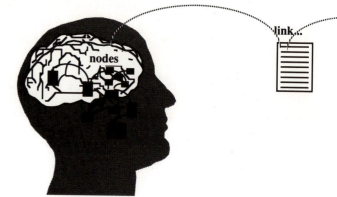

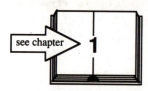

Information Mapping's method is mature technology for analyzing, organizing, writing, sequencing and formatting of information. We have shown how it forms an appropriate rhetoric for the writing of hypertext and hypermedia databases.

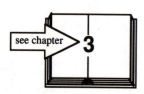

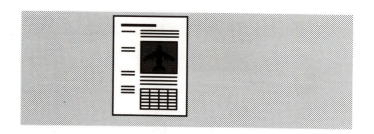

Argumentation analysis, a still evolving methodology of understanding disputes, helps in particular ways when we are looking at important issues.

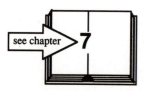

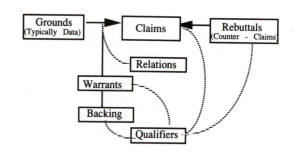

Putting these three emerging technologies together may very well help the science information system with its problems of complexity and information overload.

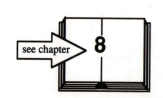

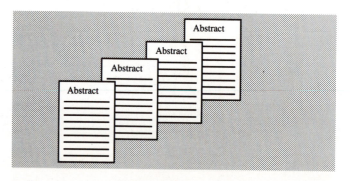

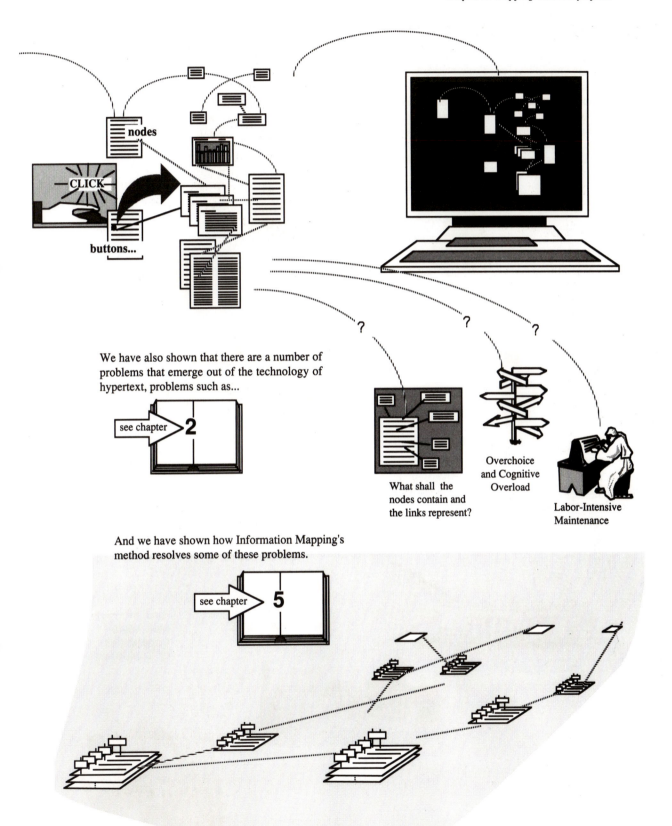

nodes

CLICK

buttons...

We have also shown that there are a number of problems that emerge out of the technology of hypertext, problems such as...

see chapter **2**

What shall the nodes contain and the links represent?

Overchoice and Cognitive Overload

Labor-Intensive Maintenance

And we have shown how Information Mapping's method resolves some of these problems.

see chapter **5**

Trend: Integrate Communication and Computing

Introduction

We can see the increasing integration of a number of technologies, hardware, software, and "mindware" that will bring about a much more flexible, convenient, and fertile medium for knowledge workers in the next decade and beyond. Much of the discussion in this book has been about the "mindware" aspects of these developments. But they all interact. What visionaries have "seen" twenty or thirty years ago is coming to pass.

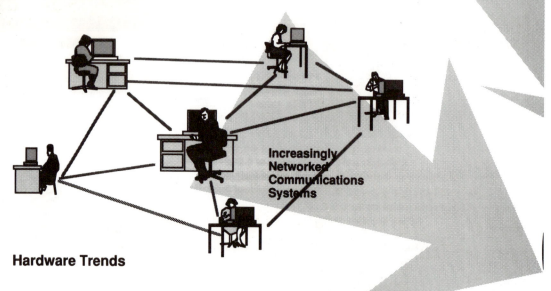

Increasingly Networked Communications Systems

Hardware Trends

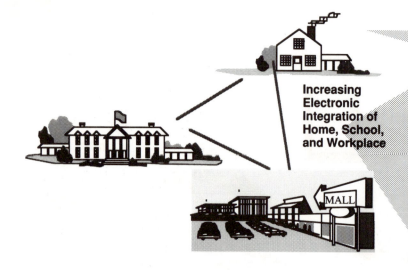

Increasing Electronic Integration of Home, School, and Workplace

New Interactive Multi-Media Capabilities of Computers

Software Trends

Increasingly Powerful Workstations and Personal Computers

Increasingly "Intelligent" Software

Better Understanding of How Computer Screens and Interaction Can Be Designed to Make Them Easier to Use

On-Line Help

Everything Needed for Widespread Use of Hypertext and Hypermedia

Ability of Knowledge Workers to Manage Large Amounts of Information Through Analytic Techniques

Increasingly Visual Language Approach to Communication

Mindware Trends

237

Navigating Through Whole Subject Matters

Introduction

On the next few pages we will present a simulation of what it might be like to use some of the capacities of a future hypertext system with hypertrails. This wall-sized conference room is described in a previous chapter.

see page 176

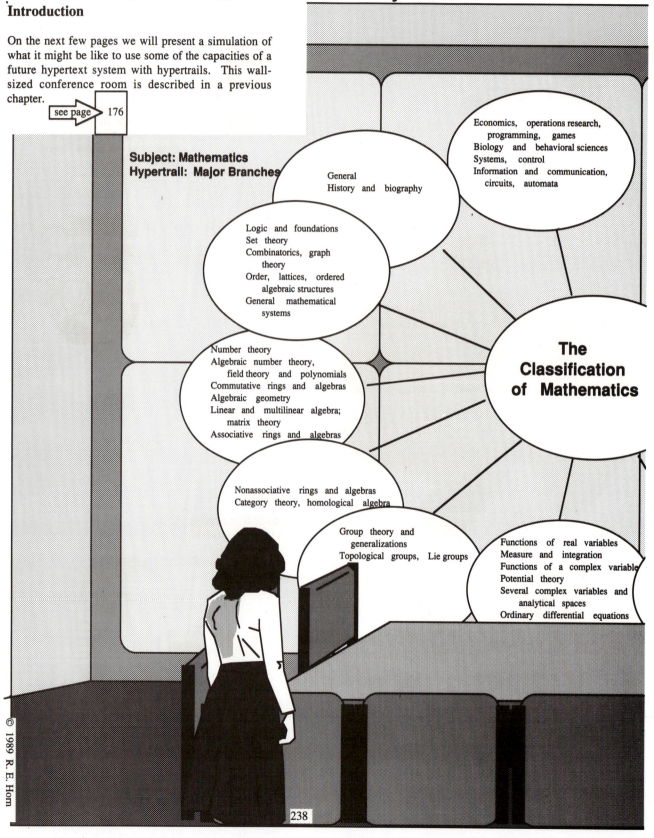

Subject: Mathematics
Hypertrail: Major Branches

General
History and biography

Economics, operations research, programming, games
Biology and behavioral sciences
Systems, control
Information and communication, circuits, automata

Logic and foundations
Set theory
Combinatorics, graph theory
Order, lattices, ordered algebraic structures
General mathematical systems

Number theory
Algebraic number theory, field theory and polynomials
Commutative rings and algebras
Algebraic geometry
Linear and multilinear algebra; matrix theory
Associative rings and algebras

The Classification of Mathematics

Nonassociative rings and algebras
Category theory, homological algebra

Group theory and generalizations
Topological groups, Lie groups

Functions of real variables
Measure and integration
Functions of a complex variable
Potential theory
Several complex variables and analytical spaces
Ordinary differential equations

238

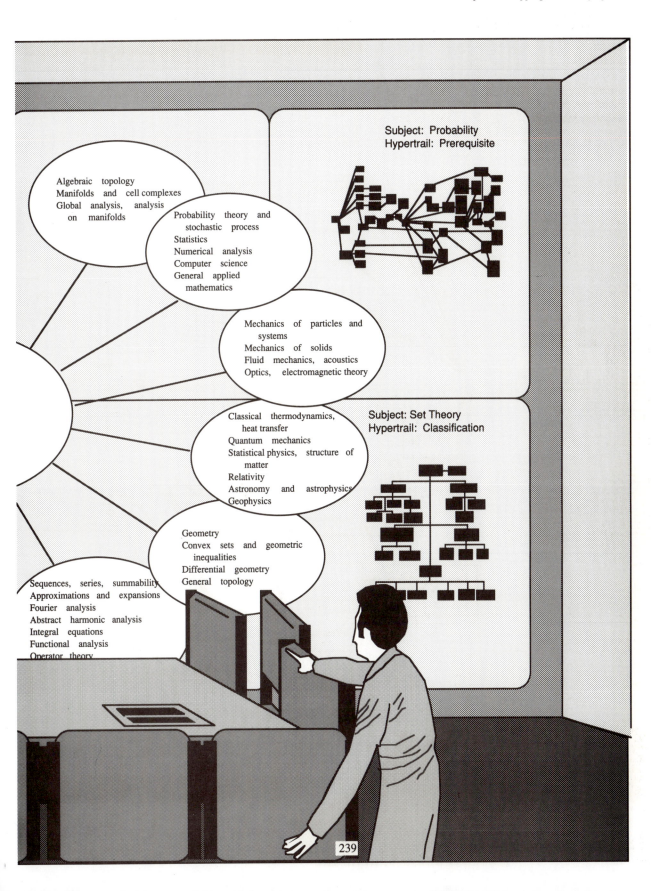

Algebraic topology
Manifolds and cell complexes
Global analysis,   analysis
    on   manifolds

Probability   theory   and
    stochastic   process
Statistics
Numerical   analysis
Computer   science
General   applied
    mathematics

Mechanics   of   particles and
    systems
Mechanics   of   solids
Fluid   mechanics, acoustics
Optics,   electromagnetic theory

Classical   thermodynamics,
    heat transfer
Quantum   mechanics
Statistical physics, structure of
    matter
Relativity
Astronomy   and   astrophysics
Geophysics

Geometry
Convex sets and geometric
    inequalities
Differential   geometry
General   topology

Sequences, series, summability
Approximations and expansions
Fourier   analysis
Abstract   harmonic   analysis
Integral   equations
Functional   analysis
Operator theory

Subject: Probability
Hypertrail: Prerequisite

Subject: Set Theory
Hypertrail: Classification

239

Navigating Along Hypertrails

Introduction

This is a prerequisite hypertrail of part of the subject matter of basic sets and probability theory. For more information on prerequisite hypertrails see page 128

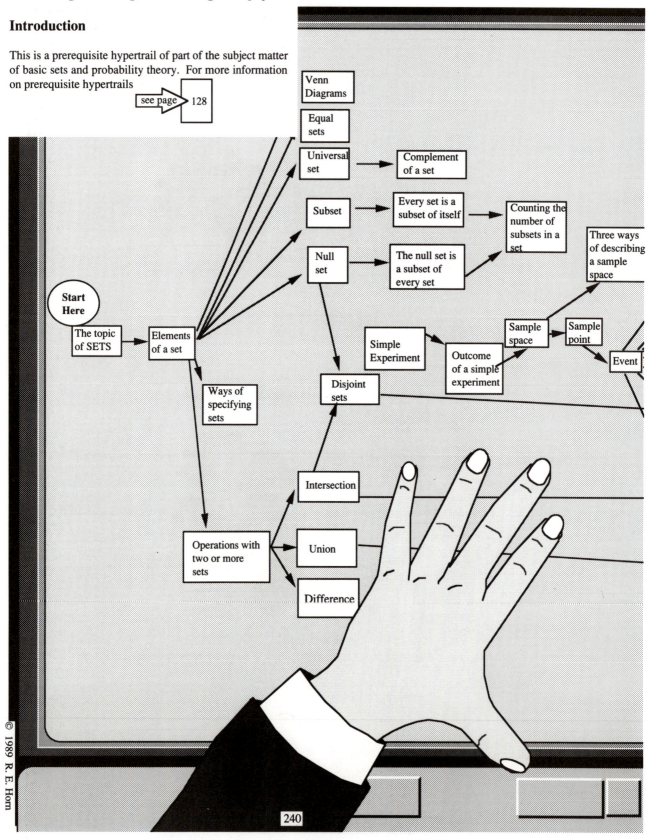

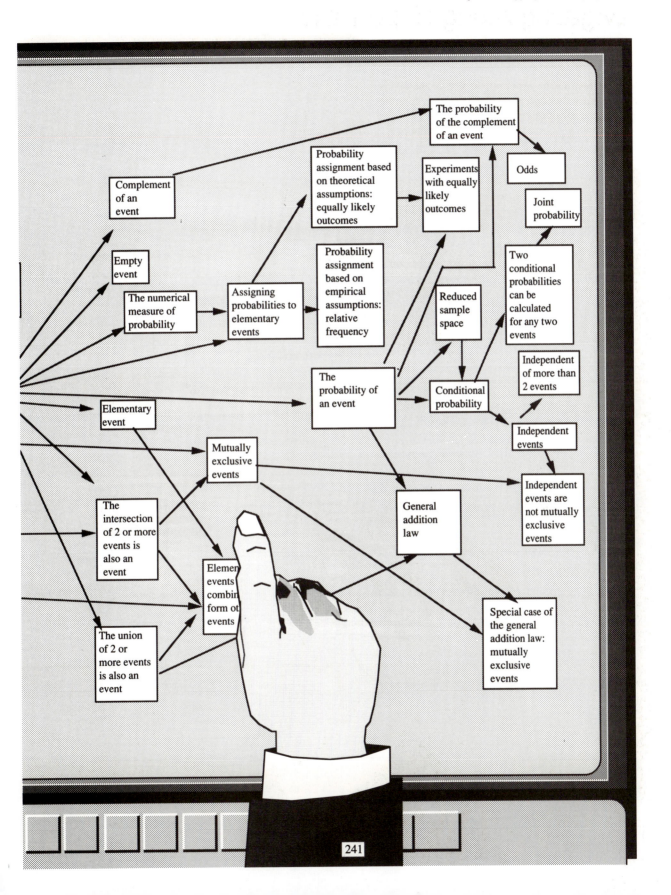

Looking from Multiple Points of View

Introduction

This is a classification hypertrail of part of the subject matter of basic sets and probability theory. For more information on classification hypertrails

see page 130

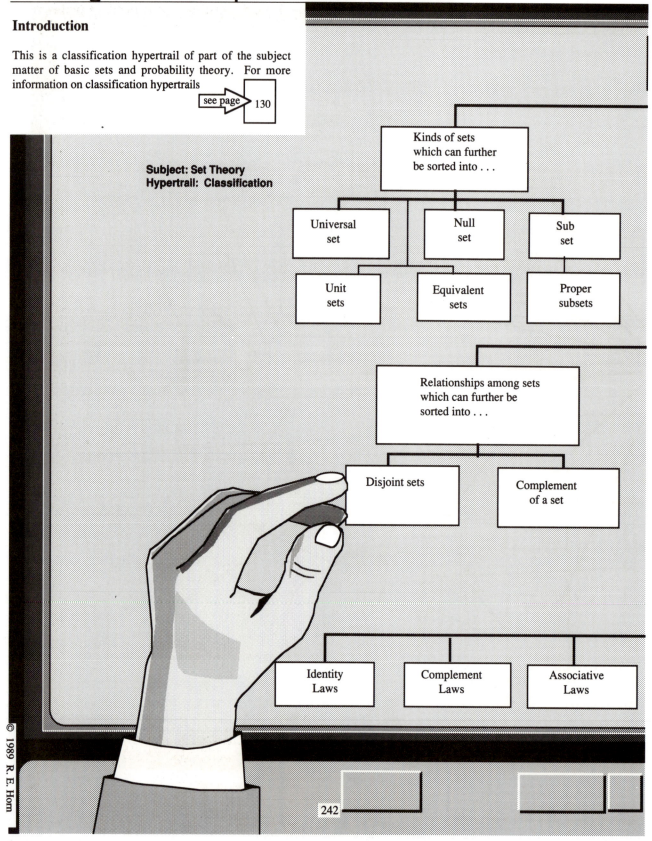

Subject: Set Theory
Hypertrail: Classification

Kinds of sets which can further be sorted into . . .

| Universal set | Null set | Sub set |

| Unit sets | Equivalent sets | Proper subsets |

Relationships among sets which can further be sorted into . . .

| Disjoint sets | Complement of a set |

| Identity Laws | Complement Laws | Associative Laws |

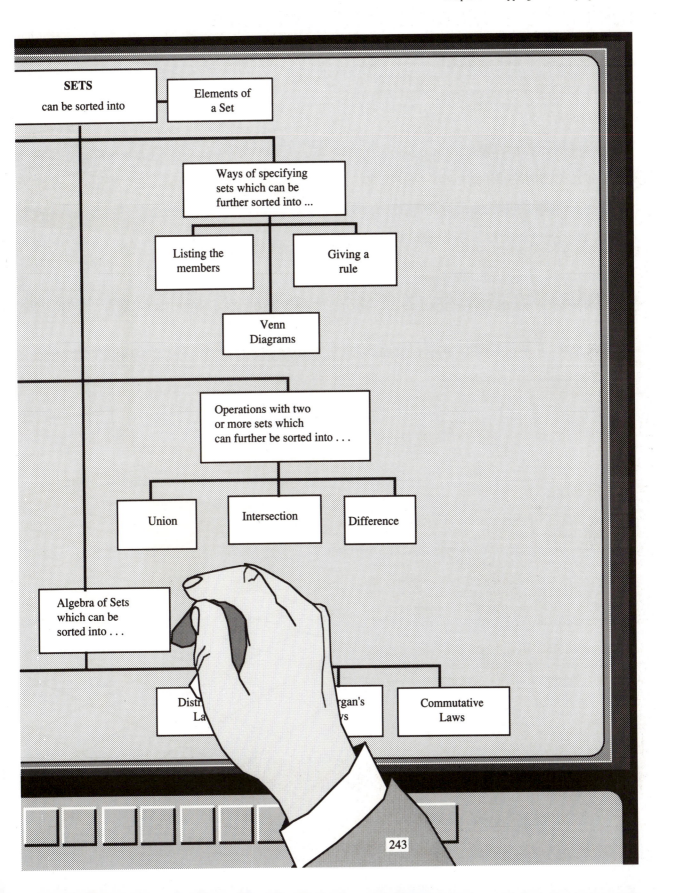

SETS

can be sorted into

Elements of
a Set

Ways of specifying
sets which can be
further sorted into ...

Listing the
members

Giving a
rule

Venn
Diagrams

Operations with two
or more sets which
can further be sorted into . . .

Union

Intersection

Difference

Algebra of Sets
which can be
sorted into . . .

Distr...
La...

...rgan's
...ys

Commutative
Laws

Virtual Reality -- A New Tool

Human-Computer Interaction

Virtual Reality is another newly emerging technology which will significantly change the way people interact with computers. Still in the prototype stage, virtual reality interfaces will impact the design of hypertext and hypermedia systems.

Virtual Reality -- The Basics

Virtual reality provides the illusion to users that they are inside a three dimensional world rather than observing an image. The minimum virtual reality hardware-software system consists of
• stereoscopic screens mounted in front of the eyes that project computer created images in 3-D
• a sensing system that recognizes the user's head position and as the head turns, rapidly updates the picture
• some means of interacting with virtual objects that appear in the virtual space (in one such system a gesture glove is worn by the user and appears as a hand-like object moving in virtual space). Several versions of virtual reality hardware are available today. Illustrated here are the helmet and the glove.
• a navigational system which can be as simple as pointing gestures with the glove.

Inexpensive displays of reality currently are "wire frame" representations (shown here). But technicolor geometric shaded solids are also available in much more expensive versions.

Virtual Reality -- The Next Step

You put on goggles, earphones, and a glove and you are suddenly transported into another reality. Whatever you can imagine can be made to seem real ... literally anything. As John Walker, a founder of Autodesk, the CAD firm says, virtual reality "is an amusement park where anything that can be imagined and programmed can be experienced. The richness of the experiences that will be available ... can barely be imagined today."

And these virtual realities can be shared by more than one person interactively, the so-called "reality built for two" experience. We will experience Alice in Wonderland and beyond!

Examples

We will soon be able to display large networks of structured information mapped by visual landscapes in virtual reality and we will be able to move around in them.

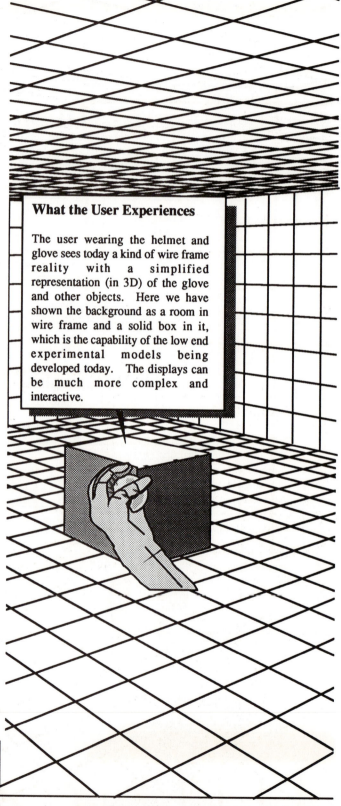

What the User Experiences

The user wearing the helmet and glove sees today a kind of wire frame reality with a simplified representation (in 3D) of the glove and other objects. Here we have shown the background as a room in wire frame and a solid box in it, which is the capability of the low end experimental models being developed today. The displays can be much more complex and interactive.

see page 246

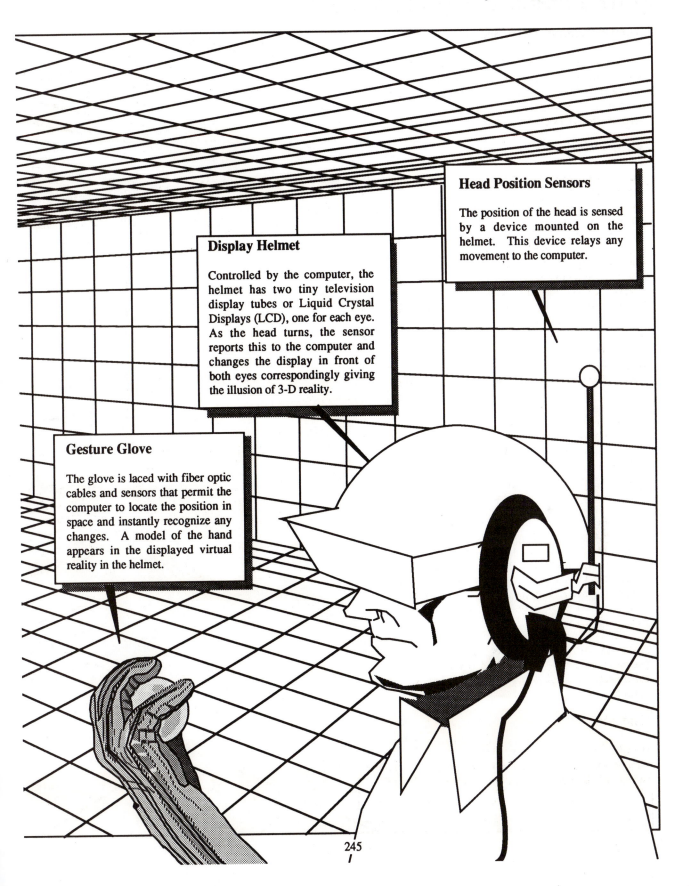

Head Position Sensors

The position of the head is sensed by a device mounted on the helmet. This device relays any movement to the computer.

Display Helmet

Controlled by the computer, the helmet has two tiny television display tubes or Liquid Crystal Displays (LCD), one for each eye. As the head turns, the sensor reports this to the computer and changes the display in front of both eyes correspondingly giving the illusion of 3-D reality.

Gesture Glove

The glove is laced with fiber optic cables and sensors that permit the computer to locate the position in space and instantly recognize any changes. A model of the hand appears in the displayed virtual reality in the helmet.

245

Travelling in Large Visual Landscapes

Complex Systems Require Adequate Displays

Comprehending the important interrelationships of complex systems requires increasingly more sophisticated display. Virtual reality spaces that portray 3-D models of projects, organizations, development of product lines, markets and processes will be developed.

Such visual landscapes will enable us to see the bigger picture of what we are doing, its context and its details. They will enable us to unfold in a quasi-animated fashion how a process has developed over time.

Example

Shown on these pages is a large visual landscape of how a project is unfolding. What cannot be shown in a fixed printed page display is that the observers in virtual reality might well have rolled time backward to when the project began and looked at each part of the process as it developed. In this way they would not be overwhelmed by the complexity of the visual structure. The virtual reality user could "fly around" in the display to inspect detail. Any of the individual locations, which are distinct phases in the process, could be opened up and looked at in detail.

We might note that, in this example, we are looking at a 3-D version of a cognitive or diagrammatic reality, rather than attempting to create facsimiles of actual realities such as building interiors.

We should also remind ourselves that this is only a very simple example of what may become possible with the virtual reality goggles as research and implementation continue. The putting together of hypermedia and virtual reality is a fertile field for creativity.

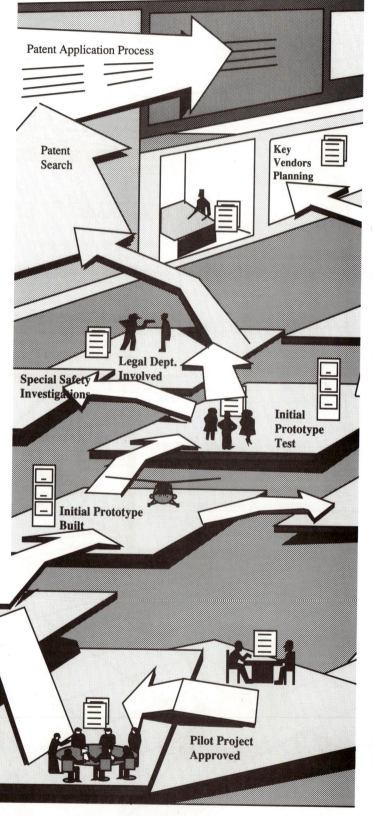

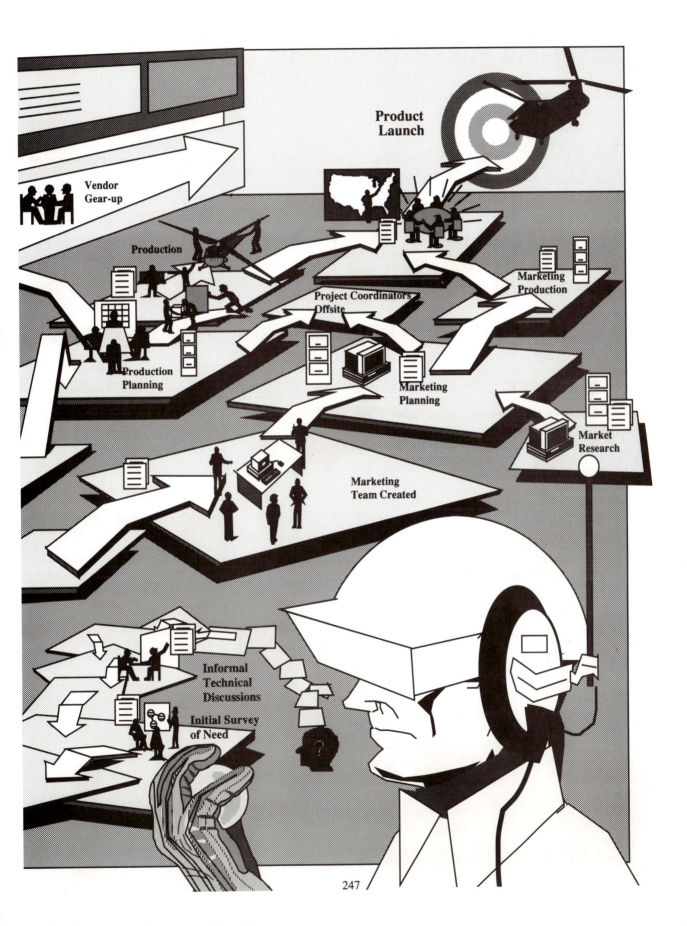

Product
Launch

Vendor
Gear-up

Production

Project Coordinators
Offsite

Marketing
Production

Production
Planning

Marketing
Planning

Market
Research

Marketing
Team Created

Informal
Technical
Discussions

Initial Survey
of Need

247

Heading into Future Information Landscapes...

Introduction

Where are we headed? As we have shown in this book there are many creative people working on the ideas of hypertext. There are still problems unresolved. There are many doorways into the future, a future with extraordinary horizons.

Appendix A: Some Historical Notes

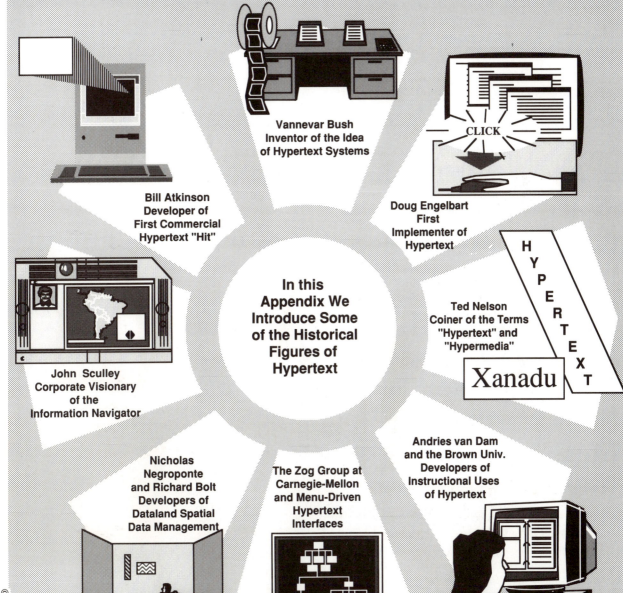

Vannevar Bush
Inventor of the Idea
of Hypertext Systems

CLICK

Bill Atkinson
Developer of
First Commercial
Hypertext "Hit"

Doug Engelbart
First
Implementer of
Hypertext

In this
Appendix We
Introduce Some
of the Historical
Figures of
Hypertext

Ted Nelson
Coiner of the Terms
"Hypertext" and
"Hypermedia"

HYPERTEXT

Xanadu

John Sculley
Corporate Visionary
of the
Information Navigator

Nicholas
Negroponte
and Richard Bolt
Developers of
Dataland Spatial
Data Management

The Zog Group at
Carnegie-Mellon
and Menu-Driven
Hypertext
Interfaces

Andries van Dam
and the Brown Univ.
Developers of
Instructional Uses
of Hypertext

Bush: Inventor of the Concept of Hypertext

Introduction

World War II is over. The Director of the U.S. Government's Office of Scientific Research and Development, science advisor to the President, writes an article in the *Atlantic Monthly* in which he sketches his vision of a tool that will aid individual knowledge workers. "Consider a future device for individual use, which is a sort of mechanized private file and library. It needs a name, and, to coin one at random, memex will do. A memex is a device in which an individual stores all his books, records, and communications, and which is mechanized so that it may be consulted with exceeding speed and flexibility. It is an enlarged intimate supplement to his memory." With these words, Dr. Vannevar Bush describes what is to become the personal computer and hypertext systems of today and tomorrow. All quotes are from Bush's 1945 article "As We May Think."

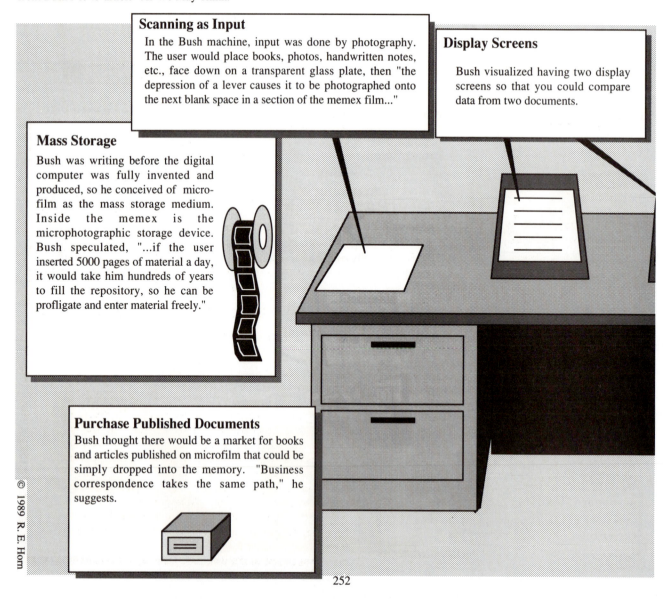

Scanning as Input

In the Bush machine, input was done by photography. The user would place books, photos, handwritten notes, etc., face down on a transparent glass plate, then "the depression of a lever causes it to be photographed onto the next blank space in a section of the memex film..."

Display Screens

Bush visualized having two display screens so that you could compare data from two documents.

Mass Storage

Bush was writing before the digital computer was fully invented and produced, so he conceived of microfilm as the mass storage medium. Inside the memex is the microphotographic storage device. Bush speculated, "...if the user inserted 5000 pages of material a day, it would take him hundreds of years to fill the repository, so he can be profligate and enter material freely."

Purchase Published Documents

Bush thought there would be a market for books and articles published on microfilm that could be simply dropped into the memory. "Business correspondence takes the same path," he suggests.

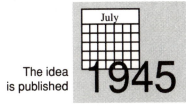

The idea
is published

Vannevar Bush

Rapid Browsing

Part of the attractiveness of the idea of the memex for Bush was rapid access to the scientific and technical literature. "There is, of course, provision for consultation of the record by the usual scheme of indexing. If the user wishes to consult a certain book, he taps its code on the keyboard, and the title page of the book promptly appears before him... On deflecting one...lever...to the right he runs through the book before him, each paper in turn being projected at a speed which just allows a recognizing glance at each."

Adding Personal Links

Bush also foresaw the idea of user-created links. "A special button transfers him immediately to the first page of the index. Any given book of his library can thus be called up and consulted with far greater facility than if it were taken from a shelf. As he has several projection positions, he can leave one item in position while he calls up another. He can add marginal notes and comments, taking advantage of one possible type of dry photography..."

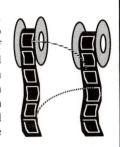

Keyboard Input

"There is a keyboard, and a set of buttons and levers. Otherwise it looks like an ordinary desk."

Retrieving Trails of Links

Bush had a vivid idea of how the retrieval of links would take place. He wrote, "...associative indexing, the basic idea of which is a provision whereby any item may be caused at will to select immediately and automatically another....When the user is building a trail, he names it, inserts the name in his code book, and taps it out on his keyboard. Before him are two items to be joined, projected onto adjacent viewing positions... The user taps a single key, and the two items are permanently joined... Thereafter, at any time, when one of these items is in view, the other can be instantly recalled merely by tapping a button... Moreover, when numerous items have been thus joined together to form a trail, they can be reviewed in turn, rapidly or slowly, by deflecting a lever...."

Engelbart's Augment: First Operational Hypertext

Introduction

Douglas C. Engelbart, then with Stanford Research Institute, built the first working and usable hypertext system. His Augment hypertext system, currently marketed by McDonnell Douglas, has supported a group of a thousand or more knowledge workers over 20 years. It provides the most sophisticated demonstration of the structured hypertext principles as well as the idea of an on-line community of knowledge workers that has been implemented. Here we present a brief overview of the Augment system and salute Engelbart for his accomplishments.

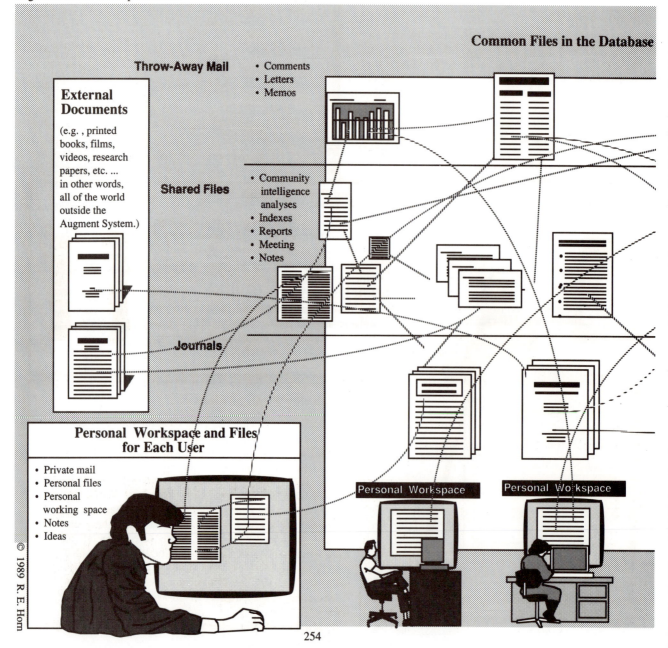

First
Implementation
of Hypertext

1962-75
Douglas C. Engelbart

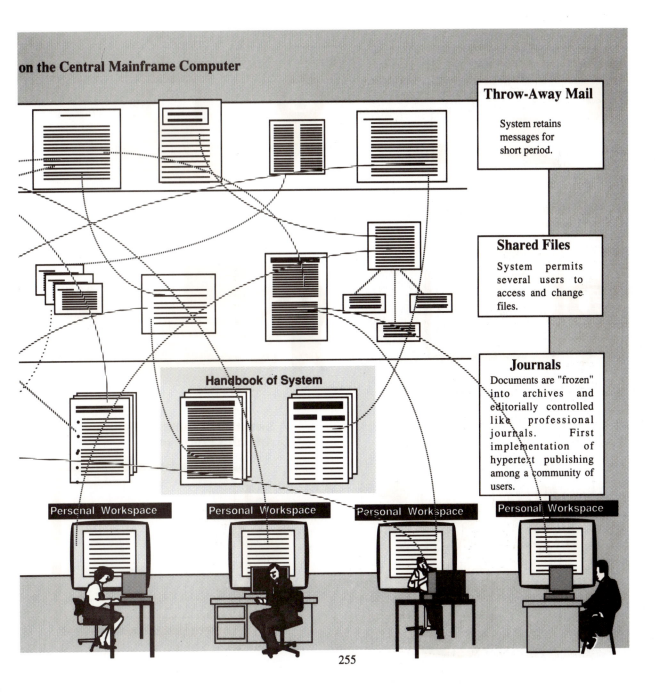

on the Central Mainframe Computer

Throw-Away Mail

System retains
messages for
short period.

Shared Files

System permits
several users to
access and change
files.

Journals

Documents are "frozen"
into archives and
editorially controlled
like professional
journals. First
implementation of
hypertext publishing
among a community of
users.

Handbook of System

Personal Workspace   Personal Workspace   Personal Workspace   Personal Workspace

Engelbart: Edison of the Personal Computer

Introduction

Doug Engelbart is the Edison of the personal computer. He not only invented many of the familiar devices we have on our PC's and workstations, but also was the first builder of a working hypertext system. His research program was built on an extraordinarily broad vision of "augmenting human intelligence." Here we record just some of the major accomplishments of Engelbart and his colleagues at Stanford Research Institute. His Augmentation Research Laboratory began in 1962 and had a working personal computer with the hypertext system and on-line group work environments by the mid-sixties. Among the accomplishments of Doug and the Laboratory are the following:

Invention of the Mouse

First Major Implementation of Electronic Mail

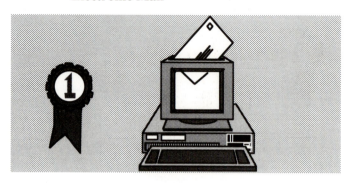

Invention of Multiple Window on Computer Screen

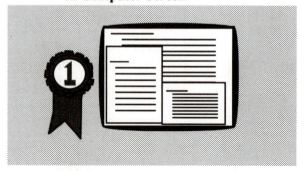

First Implementation of Word Processing

Invention of On-Line Integrated Help Systems

Invention of Outlining Software And Idea Processors

Invention of Computer Supported Group Conferences

First Implementer of Hypertext Links and Nodes

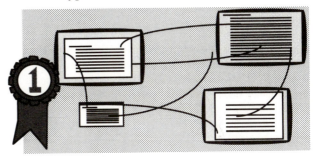

Invention of Composite Text-Graphic Files

Invention of Shared Screen Teleconferencing

Invention of Many Interface Elements Including a Very Efficient 5-Finger Input Device

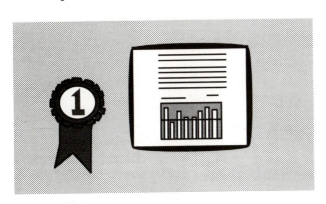

Invention of Remote Procedure Call Protocol for Efficient "Reach Through" Integration of Functions

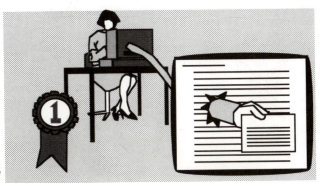

Nelson: Name-Giver of the Word "Hypertext"

Introduction

Ted Nelson coined the terms "hypertext" and "hypermedia" in 1965 and has acted as an evangelist for the concepts ever since. His definition of hypertext is "computer-supported non-sequential writing." His visionary idea of a "docuverse" containing all of humankind's documents linked has inspired a generation of researchers and educators.

The Xanadu Vision

Xanadu® is Nelson's plan for a "world-wide network, intended to serve hundreds of millions of users simultaneously from the corpus of the world's stored writings, graphics, and data."

"Xanadu is not a large centralized software system but rather an idea for software for running a decentralized network." As Nelson says, "It is a design for a new literature and a system of order to make such a network understandable, usable, and readily expansible to any degree...."

Storage System

Xanadu is a concept of a storage system that permits documents to be stored only once in a "universal data structure to which all other data may be mapped."

Address and Linking System

The address and linking system permits "any spans of bytes in any document or file, on any server, (to be) linked to any other spans of bytes, in any document or file, on any server, by a link type which is unique or used elsewhere in the system."

Authoring

The system would permit

1. allocation of credit of authorship and publishing

2. allocation of payment of royalties based on the reader's use of documents

3. quotability of any document, yet easy tracing to the source of the quotation via hypertext links.

"Imagine everything available and tied together. Grand visions come to mind of what things will be like when 'it's all there and linked.' The thought of that great body of material calls to us, calls to us like the ocean."

"But the ocean of universal hypertext is not enough: we want free sailing on it.... A world of open hypertext publishing promises extraordinary new freedom for the mind, a new empowerment of humanity."

The
Words
Hypertext
and
Hypermedia

1965

Theodor Holm Nelson

"Everything is deeply intertwingled."

"Imagine making your own notes and connections any way you choose in this great interconnected corpus; so that any time you want to reopen this great hypertext world at any of these private annotations that make it your own, it will be like opening a book to a bookmark."

"Universal or grand hypertext, then, means a new publishing system -- an accessible great universe of linked documents and graphics (and audio recordings and video and movies). This is an idea many people now share -- the idea that we can get to everything, keep track of everything, add to everything, tie everything together, that we can have it all."

"By 'hypertext'
I mean
non-sequential
writing."

Van Dam and Brown: First University Instruction

Introduction

Since the late 1960's, Andries van Dam and a team at Brown University have created several generations of experimental hypertext and hypermedia systems. Their focus has been on the use of these systems in college instruction.

English Poetry

One system was used in the early 1970's to teach an English poetry class. Students worked together on the same hypertext document, reading and writing on computer terminals that displayed the hypertext consisting of poetry and commentary.

Biology and English Literature

Two more classes largely supported in hypertext have been developed. The Brown team has in the last few years built a group of multi-media workstations and taught courses in cell biology and English literature on the system.

Prototype sections of other courses have also been implemented. This work has produced important information on how to integrate hypertext documents into normal teaching-learning environments.

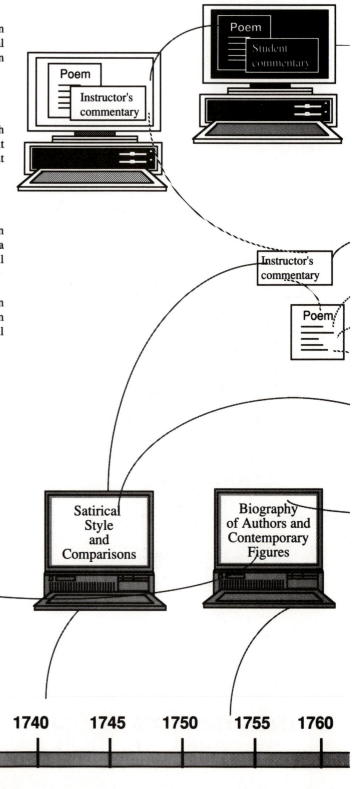

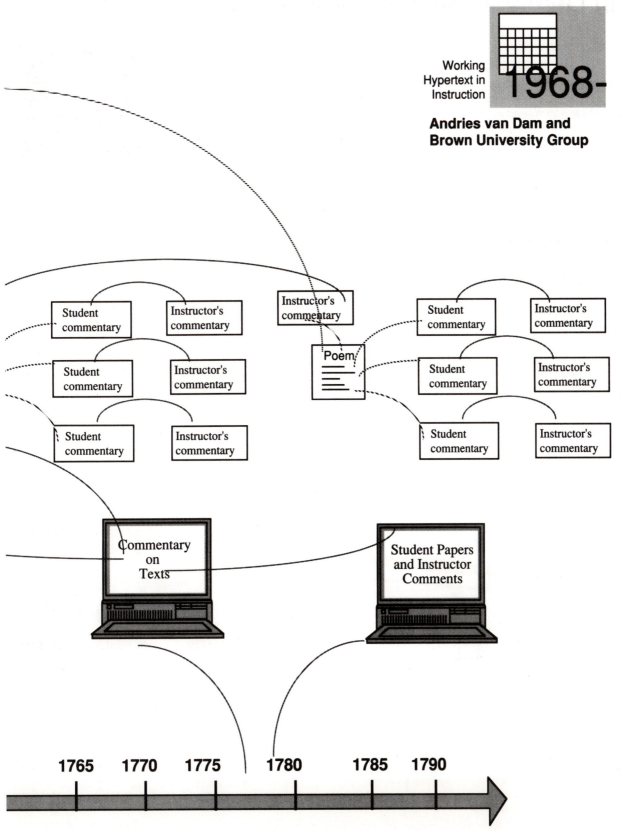

Working
Hypertext in
Instruction

1968-

**Andries van Dam and
Brown University Group**

| Student commentary | Instructor's commentary | | Instructor's commentary | | Student commentary | Instructor's commentary |

| Student commentary | Instructor's commentary | | Poem | | Student commentary | Instructor's commentary |

| Student commentary | Instructor's commentary | | | | Student commentary | Instructor's commentary |

Commentary
on
Texts

Student Papers
and Instructor
Comments

1765   1770   1775   1780   1785   1790

Zog Group at Carnegie-Mellon: Menu Interfaces

Menu-Driven Interfaces for Hypertext

In 1972, a group at Carnegie-Mellon University that has included Allen Newell, Donald L. McCracken, Robert M. Akscyn, and George G. Robertson began building a series of experimental hypertext systems that were given the collective name Zog. Their work was focused on making a system that would produce rapid response in large networks through a simple menu selection interface. Zog was designed to serve a large community of users.

Nuclear Aircraft Carrier Application

The group was given the opportunity in 1980 to implement its work on the new U. S. Navy nuclear-powered carrier, USS Carl Vinson. They developed a new version that supported the ship's organization and regulations manual and a planning and evaluation application.

Knowledge Management System

Out of the work on the USS Vinson, a commercial version of the Zog system has been marketed since 1983 under the name Knowledge Management System (KMS). It is implemented on Sun workstations.

Current Version of KMS

The current version of KMS is particularly well suited to the joint creation of documents on different workstations in a network, such as when many engineers have to work on a single proposal.

Screen-Sized Frames

The database in KMS consists of screen-sized frames which may contain "any mixture of text, graphics and image items, each of which may be linked to another frame or used to invoke a program." These frames may be stored in the memories of different workstations on the network. Here we show displays of different frames on the screens of several workstations.

Multi-User
Menu-Driven
Interfaces
with Large
Database

The Zog Group

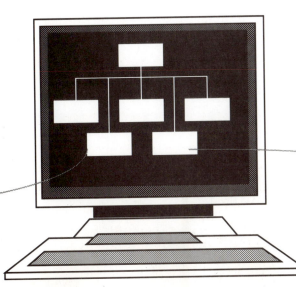

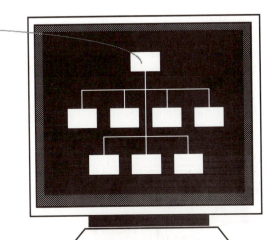

Hierarchical Structure Emphasized

KMS emphasizes hierarchical structures and retains fairly
conventional implementations of tables of contents, menus,
and indexes as key interface devices. Non-hierarchical links
are possible.

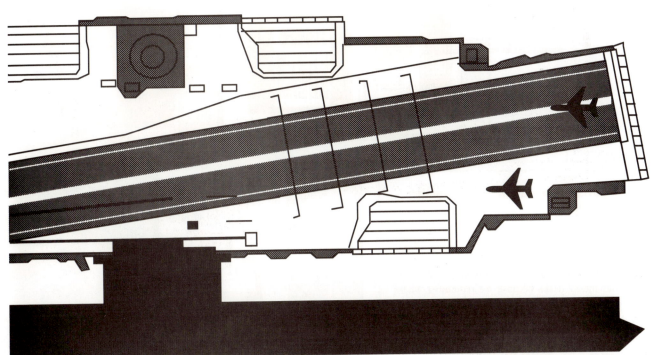

Negroponte and Bolt: Spatial Dataland

Managing Information Spatially in Dataland

The Architecture Machine Group at MIT in the late 1970's build a number of experimental information environments that expanded the vision of what the possibilities of interacting with the computer can be. They called their information space "Dataland" and it operated in a room where almost everything was manipulatable information. The room, noted Bolt, is the computer terminal. Many of the functions, such as calendars and calculators, that we routinely use on our visual computer interfaces were first demonstrated in Dataland. Strictly speaking, the experiment was not about hypertext but about hypermedia. The ability to switch media and move around in an information environment was the key demonstration. We diagram the room-terminal on these pages.

Cursor

The "You Are Here" cursor located on the monitor.

Touch sensitive TV monitors

for "touch travel." They enable users to point to places on "key maps" to navigate in the information space, for example, to control types of functions such a telephone or calculator.

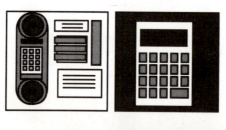

Spatial Information Management Principle

One major concept used by the dataland experiment is called the "managing things spatially" principle. People "have a place" for information, suggested George Miller. We keep our messy desks because we remember where things are. If we straighten it up, we lose our spatial memory cues.

Joy Stick

on each armrest for directing travel around the screen.

The
MIT Architecture
MachineGroup
Managing
Information
Spatially

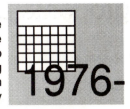

1976-

**Nicholas Negroponte
and Richard A. Bolt**

Each Object On Display Can Be Activated

Each of the objects displayed can be "zoomed in" on
for greater detail.

Display Screen
Whole wall is
display screen.

Voice Activated Commands

User wears a speech recognition microphone
for voice travel. User can say things like
"go to the book in upper left," "create a
green circle...there," "move data A to green
circle," and so on for "copy, delete, make
smaller...larger, call that...,"etc.

Loudspeakers

Four loudspeakers located in
wall provide wrap-around
sound.

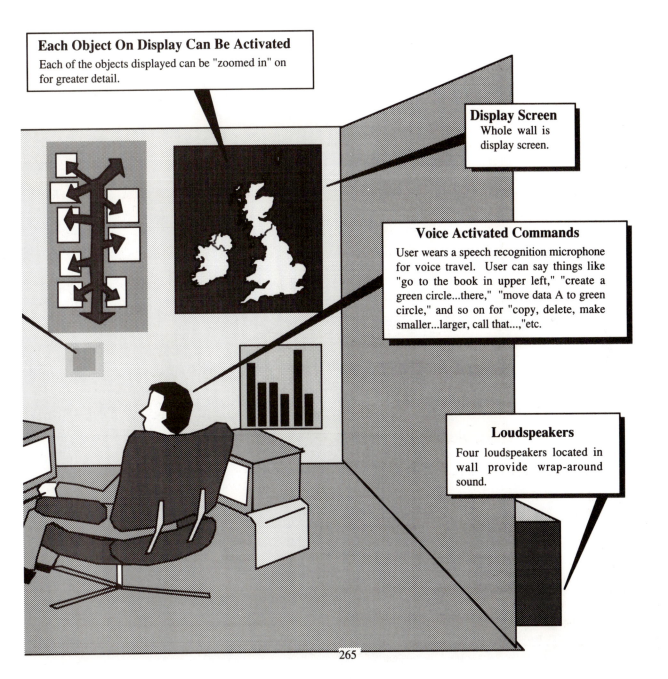

Brown and Guide: Hypertext for PC and Macintosh

First Commercial System for Two Major Personal Computer Systems

To Owl International, Inc., which was founded in 1985, goes the credit of bringing out the first hypertext system to work on both of the major personal computer platforms, the IBM PC and Apple's Macintosh. Peter Brown of the University of Kent (U.K.) was the inventor of the Guide system.   The products are based on further development work at Office Workstations Limited of Edinburgh, Scotland.

Owl has continued to increase the flexibility of Guide and to equip it with a family of support products including Guidance, which provides a context-sensitive environment for online reference and tutorials and Guide Reader, a low cost version that permits reading hypertext, but not authoring.

Guide also supports multi-media connections and the ability to link not only between documents but also between applications so that, for example, a user can link a text document with a spreadsheet.

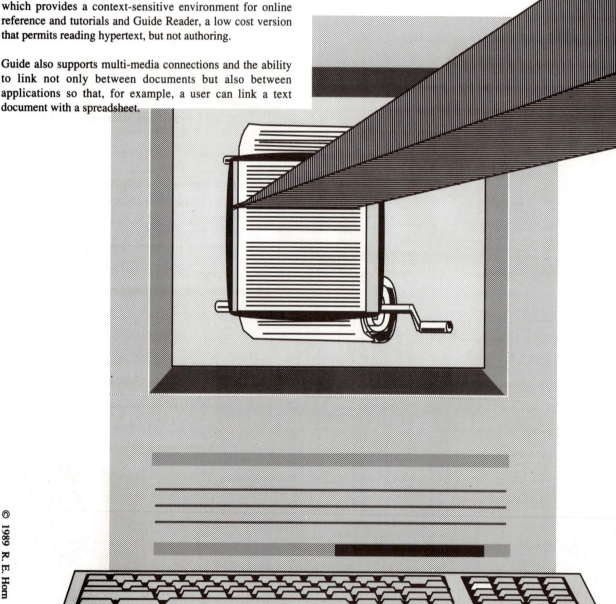

Hypertext
for Apple
Macintosh
and IBM PC
DOS
Computers

1986

**Peter Brown and
Owl International, Inc.**

Scroll and Outline Architecture

Guide relies heavily on a software architecture of scrolls of variable length, an outline structure of the document, and user-controlled expansion of that outline, which are revealed by clicking on portions of the outline. Other link types, such as the ability to link to other places in the text to pop-up notes and to activate other media are also part of the system design.

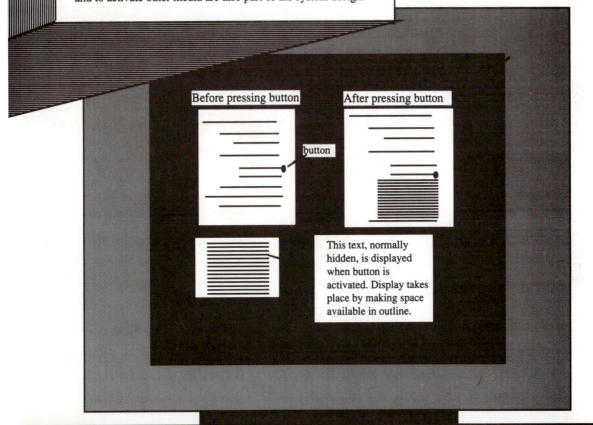

Before pressing button

After pressing button

button

This text, normally hidden, is displayed when button is activated. Display takes place by making space available in outline.

Sculley: Vision of the Knowledge Navigator

Introduction

John Sculley is a different kind of visionary. He is CEO of a major computer corporation. Yet many of his speeches have dealt with how we must change ourselves and our information environments in order to compete in the new information age.

Sculley inspired and sponsored futuristic work at Apple on the Knowledge Navigator, which describes the possibilities for personal computing in the years beyond 2010. The computer as envisioned by Sculley is driven by voice-activated commands. The computer responds with computer-created speech through the little moving picture of the man in the bow tie. We picture here a sketch of the Knowledge Navigator, which is a book-sized personal computer which has access to large knowledge bases of information.

The original Knowledge Navigator scenario was made into a videotape that simulated the functions of the computer and showed how the computer took its owner through a day that included an exploration of the problems of the destruction of the Amazon rain forests.

Impact of the Knowledge Navigator on Education

Sculley suggests, "Education will not simply be a prelude to a career, but a lifelong endeavor. Some of the important elements that will promote this new paradigm for lifelong learning are: (1) the development of conceptual skills, and the ability to test reality against multiple points of view; (2) the nourishment of individual creativity and the encouragement of exploration; (3) the encouragement of collaboration, and an emphasis on clear communication."

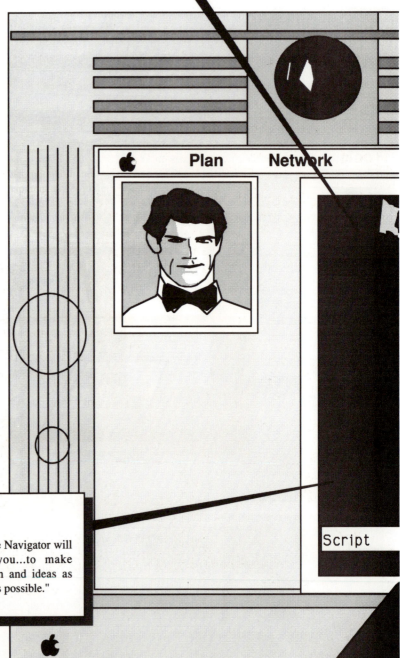

Large, Flat, Full Color Screen

"Large, flat display screen...full color, high-definition, television-quality images, full pages of text, graphics, computer-generated animation."

Plan   Network

Script

Customize Knowledge

"Most important, the Knowledge Navigator will customize knowledge for you...to make navigating through information and ideas as interesting and understandable as possible."

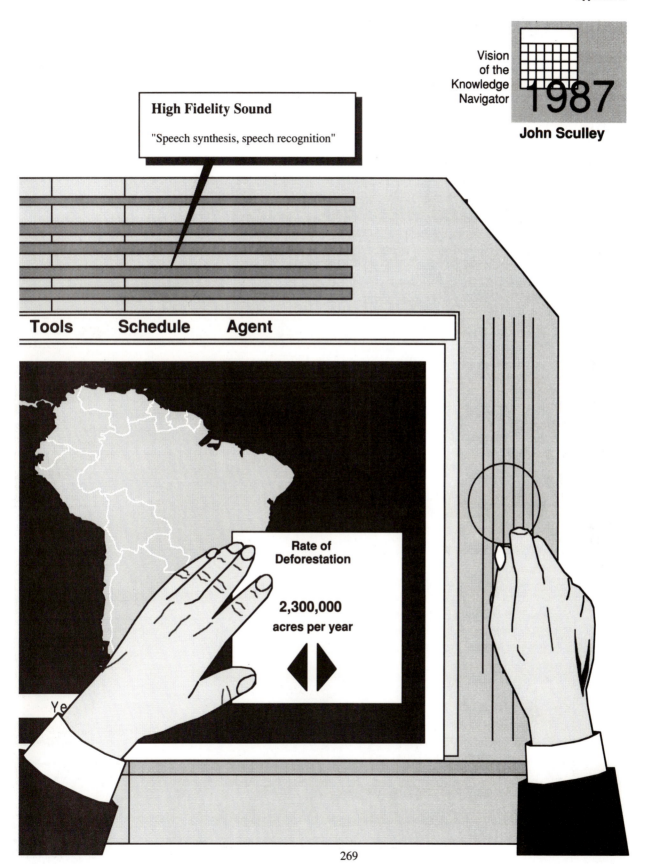

Atkinson: First Commercial Hypertext "Hit"

Introduction

HyperCard, developed by Bill Atkinson, is a multi-functional
software tool that includes many hypertext properties. Apple
Computer made it the first hypertext "hit" by deciding to give
it away with the purchase of a computer.

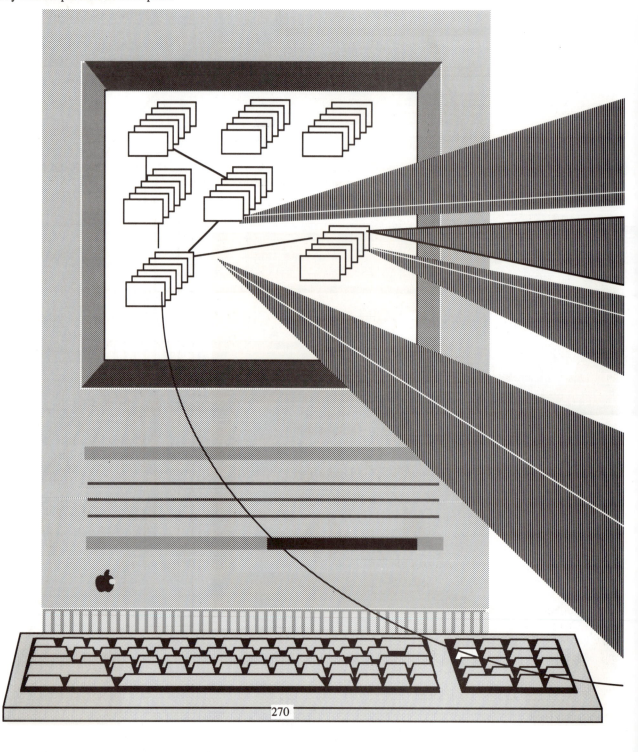

One
Million
HyperCard
Programs
in One Year

1987

Bill Atkinson

HyperCard

HyperCard rapidly became the hit of 1987, far outstripping competing hypertext systems and enabling enthusiasts and commercial applications to hook up to laser disks and CD/ROM's to tap enormous text and graphics files.

Card Architecture

As the name implies, HyperCard relies on a software architecture and interface that appears to the user as a stack of index cards. However these cards are linked in a great variety of ways that give considerable flexibility in the final development of hypertext and hypermedia on it.

HyperCard's Key Components

Atkinson had the genius to put the metaphor of hypertext together with an easy-to-use programming language, a simple word processor, a painting program and an elegant, inviting interface. The ease of use and the combination of functions of HyperCard provided a significant jump for hypertext.

HyperCard Focused Attention

HyperCard almost singlehandedly brought the idea of hypertext into the minds of well over a million people in one stroke, when Apple Computer's John Sculley decided to give it away with each purchase of a Macintosh computer. While HyperCard is much more than hypertext software, it put hypertext on the map.

Notes

Chapter 1. Introduction to Hypertext and Hypermedia

p. 6. What is Hypertext? "Hypertext is both an . . ." Brown University (1985).   "By 'Hypertext' I mean non-sequential writing." Nelson (1974).

p. 16. The Navigation Through Information Space Metaphor. "Ted Nelson's gigantic vision . . ." Nelson (1974).

p. 20. Hypermedia Application: New Product Marketing. Lou Casabianca of *Hypermedia Magazine* first showed me an application like this.

p. 22. Case Study: Hypermedia for Shakespeare. This discussion of hypermedia for Shakespeare was inspired by an implementation at Brown University and by a similar one at Stanford University

p. 29. Dimensions of Hypertext Systems. "Theodore Nelson has suggested . . ." Nelson (1974).

Chapter 2. Current Issues With Hypertext

p. 47. Where to Put How Many Buttons of Which Kind.   The seductive buttons were inspired by a slide from Theodor Nelson's dynamic slide show on hypertext.

p. 48-51 Inadequate (and Missing) Reading Cues. Material on these four pages follows the excellent paper by Charney (1987) and summarizes this paper.

p. 52. Branching Difficulties of Serialist Readers. see Pask (1976)

p. 56. Lost in Hyperspace. These issues were most compellingly raised by Conklin (1987).

p. 58 . Overchoice and Cognitive Overload. These issues are also well put in Conklin (1987).

p. 60.   Chaos in Titles for Documents and Their Parts. The author thanks Michael J. Steinback for formulating commandment number 7.

Chapter 3   Introduction to Information Mapping's StructuredWriting Method

p. 76. Overview of This Chapter. Information Mapping, Inc. (for further information on the products and services of the company and licensing of the methodology for software or training, contact Information Mapping, Inc., 303 Wyman Street, Waltham, MA. 02154 or call 617-890-7003) **Brief History of Information Mapping.**   See items listed under Horn in the bibliography. Other Examples of Applications. **Application of Information Mapping's Methodology to Philosophy.** Several authors in Horn, ed., (1983) use the methodology in essays on metaphysics, cybernetics, and logic.

p. 82. The Problem of Human Short Term Memory. For further information on these pages see Miller (1956) and Simon (1979).

p. 96-97. Examples of Maps Displayed on Paper. The author acknowledges the permission of Information Mapping Inc. to reproduce these two sample pages of Information Mapping and other example material in this chapter.

p. 107. A Brief Discourse Analysis (Stable Subjects). The data in the two examples are from unpublished data of Horn.

p. 110. What are the information types?   Six of seven of these were first suggested by Horn (1965). See also Horn (1969), (1971, 72, 76) for further information.

p. 122. Meeting Criteria for Better Communication. Among the data supporting these claims are eleven doctoral and two masters dissertations on the Information Mapping Method. See references: Burrell (1978), Cheung (1980), Falk (1980), Fields (1982), Hauck (1985), Mcclung (1985), Olivares-Guerrero (1985), Reid (1984), Romiszowski (1977), Skelly (1982), Soyster (1980), Stelnicki (1980), Stuart (1979). Other research conducted on the method has been reported by Webber (1979), Jonassen (1979, 1981), Jonassen and Falk (1980) and Schaffer (1982). Other studies have focused on components used in the method (for example, see Smith and Mosier, 1986). In addition, approx. 20,000 people have been trained in the methodology through courses given by Information Mapping, Inc.

Chapter 4 Navigating Structured Hypertrails

p. 128. Prerequisite. Mathematics example adapted from Kemmeny (1965) see also Horn et. al. (1969)

p. 144. Example Hypertrails. Example One (on dreams), see Bonime (1982) "Example of example hypertrail" is from an article which first appeared in Horn (1976).

Chapter 5 Resolving Some Hypertext Problems

p. 152. At the Nodes, Blocks and Maps Structure Hypertext. The author acknowledges permission of Information Mapping, Inc. to publish the map on the example of an information map.

p. 158. Addressing The Major Reading Cues Problem. The best sources are Horn (1976) currently used as course manuals in Information Mapping's courses.

Chapter 6 Relatively Stable Discourse: Documentation and Training

p. 170-171. Operations and Technical Manuals. The author acknowledges permission of Information Mapping, Inc. to reproduce these two maps.

p. 172-173. Personnel Manuals and Policy Manuals. The author acknowledges permission of Information Mapping, Inc. to reproduce these two maps.

Chapter 7 Disputed Discourse: Argumentation Analysis

p. 186-187. Overview of This Chapter. The discussion on this page is from Toulmin (1958) as well as the discussion on the next three pages of claims, grounds, warrants, backing, rebuttal, and qualifiers. Extensive use was also made of Toulmin et. al. (1979).

p. 200-204. Case Study. The example is from an unpublished study of using argumentation analysis in examining the ethics of using nuclear weapons done at the Lexington Institute. The most extensive use of Toulmin structures in hypertext has been done by Cathy Marshall (1987).

p. 204-206. Comparing Ill-Structured and "Tame" Problems. The material on these pages is from an excellent discussion in Mitroff et. al. (1983).

Chapter 8 Experimental Discourse: Scientific Information

p. 218. Miller: Short Term Memory Limits and Chunking. The chart is from Miller (1956). The author gratefully acknowledges permission of the American Psychological Association to reproduce it.

p. 224. Schaffer: Information Mapping's Methodology. The quotes are all from Schaffer (1982). The author gratefully acknowledges permission of the NSPI Journal to reproduce the quotes.

p. 226. Reid and Wright: Superiority of Visual Structuring. The four diagrams are from Reid and Wright (1973). The author gratefully acknowledges the permission of the *Journal of Applied Psychology* to reproduce the four examples in the "material used section."

p. 228. Hypertext May Facilitate Identifying Problems. The two quotes are from Root-Bernstein (1982).

p. 230. Linked Comments Will Highlight Deficiencies. The references made are to Drexler (1986).

Chapter 9 Mapping Future Infospace

p. 238-239. Navigating Through Whole Subject Matters. Subjects of Mathematics. The categorization of mathematics on this page and the following page is adapted into graphic form from Davis and Hersh (1981) who attributed it to a report in the *Mathematical Reviews* (1979).

p. 241. Navigating Along Hypertrails. Prerequisite Hypertrail . The diagram on this page is from Horn (1969).

p. 244. Virtual Reality--A New Tool . The quote is from Walker (1988).

p. 246. Travelling in Large Visual Landscapes. The graphic possibilities of large landscapes like this have been suggested to me by Jim Channon and David Sibbet. I have taken their 2-D work and applied it to the 3-D world of virtual reality.

Appendix A: Some Historical Notes

p. 252. Bush: Inventor of the Concept of Hypertext. All the quotes from this page are from Bush (1945). The author gratefully acknowledges permission of *Atlantic Magazine* to reproduce these quotes.

p. 258. Nelson: Name-Giver of the Word "Hypertext." The quotes on this page are from Nelson (1988) and Nelson (1974)

p. 260. van Dam and Brown: First University Instruction. This account is from Yankelovich (1985).

p. 262. The Zog Group at Carnegie Mellon. This discussion is based on Newell et. al. (1981).

p. 264. Negroponte and Bolt: Spatial Dataland. Details of the material on this page can be found in Bolt (1984).

p. 268. Sculley: Vision of the Knowledge Navigator. The quote on this page is from Sculley (1989). Other quotes are from Sculley (1987).

References

Hypertext

A Critical Assessment of Hypertext Systems, (1988) *ACM CHI '88 Proceedings*

Akscyn, R., McCracken, D., Yoder, E. (1987) KMS: A Distributed Hypermedia System for Managing Knowledge in Organizations. *Hypertext '87 Papers.* November 13-15 1987

Barrett, E., ed. (1988) *Text, ConText, And Hypertext.* Cambridge, MA: MIT Press.

Beeman, W.O., Anderson, K.T., Bader, G., Larkin, J., McClard, A.P., McQuillan, P., Shields, M. (1987) Hypertext and Pluralism: From Lineal to Non-lineal Thinking. *Hypertext '87 Papers.* November 13-15, 1987

Binder, Carl. (1988) Hypertext: Features and Benefits. *Managing End-User Computing* Vol. 1, No. 9. April, 1988

Binder, Carl. (1988) Hypertext: Sorting Out the Software Options. *Managing End-User Computing* Vol. 1, No. 9. April, 1988

Binder, Carl. (1987) The Promise of a Paperless Workplace. *Optical Insights* Fall 1987

Boston Computer Society, Hypermedia Group, Hypermedia Resource Base, Available as indexed bibliography (paper or on disk) BCS, Hypermedia Group, One Center Plaza, Boston, MA, 02108

Brown, P. J. (1987) Turning Ideas into Products: the Guide System. *Hypertext '87 Papers.* November 13-15 1987

Bush, V. (1945) As We May Think. *Atlantic Monthly* 176.1 (July 1945): 101-108

Charney, D. (1987) Comprehending Non-Linear Text: The Role of Discourse Cues and Reading Strategies. *Hypertext '87 Papers.* November 13-15 1987

Conklin, J. (1987) Hypertext: An Introduction and Survey *IEE Computer* Sept, 1987

Drexler, K. E. (1986) *Engines of Creation* New York: Anchor Press, Doubleday

Drexler, K. E. (1987) Hypertext Publishing and the Evolution of Knowledge. Unpublished paper

Ehrmann, S.C. (1987) Hypertext as a Medium for The Three Academic Conversations Unpub. Paper Nov. 24, 1987

Engelbart, D. C. (1984) Authorship Provisions in Augment *COMPCON '84 Digest, Proceedings of the 1984 COMPCON Conference.* Feb. 27-March 1, 1984. 465-472

Engelbart, D. C. (1963) A Conceptual Framework for the Augmentation of Man's Intellect *Vistas in Information Handling, Vol. 1.* editors. P. D. Howerton and D. C. Weeks. Washington, D.C., Spartan Books, 1963 1: 1-29

Frisse. M.E. (1987) Searching for Information in a Hypertext Medical Handbook *Hypertext '87 Papers* November 13-15 1987

Gans, D. (1988) Ted Nelson And The Ultimate Information Machine *Microtimes* April, '88

Glushko, R.J., Weaver, M. D., Coonan, T.A., Lincoln, J.E. (1988) "Hypertext Engineering": Practical Methods for Creating A Compact Disc Encyclopedia. ACM Conference on Document Processing Systems. Santa Fe. Dec. 5-8, 1988

Goodman, D. (1987) *The Complete HyperCard Handbook* New York, Bantam Books

Halasz, F. G. (1987) Reflections on NoteCards: Seven Issues for the Next Generation of Hypermedia Systems *Hypertext '87 Papers.* November 13-15, 1987

Hanson, R. (1987) Toward Hypertext Publishing Unpublished paper, August, 1987

Nelson, T.H. (1988) The Call of the Ocean: Hypertext Universal and Open *HyperAge,* Vol. 1, No. 2, May-June, 1988

Nelson, T. H. (1974) Dream Machines: New Freedoms through Computer Screens - A Minority Report. *Computer Lib: You Can and Must Understand Computers Now* Chicago IL., Hugo's Book Service (reprinted by Microsoft Press, 1988)

Nelson, T. H. (1981) *Literary Machines* Swathmore, PA

Oren, T. (1987) The Architecture for Hypertexts *Hypertext '87 Papers.* November 13-15, 1987

Raskin, J. (1987) The Hype in Hypertext: A Critique *Hypertext '87 Papers* November 13-15, 1987

Remde, J.R., Gomez, L.M., Landauer, T.K. (1987) SuperBook: An Automatic Tool for Information Exploration - Hypertext? *Hypertext '87 Papers.* November 13-15, 1987

Rheingold, H. (1985). *Tools For Thought* New York: Simon and Schuster.

Schecter, G. (Ed) (1967) Getting It Out of Our System Nelson, T. *Information Retrieval: A Critical View* Wash. D.C. Thompson, 1967

Schneiderman, B. (1987) User Interface Design for the Hyperties Electronic Encyclopedia *Hypertext '87 Papers* Nov. 13-15. 1987

Scully, John (1987) *Odyssey* New York, Harper and Row

Slatin, J. M. (1988) *Toward a Rhetoric for Hypertext* Presentation for Hypermedia '88, Univ. of Houston, Clear Lake, Johnson Space Center, NASA, 1988

Trigg, R. H. (1983) *A Networked-based Approach to Text Handling for the On-line Scientific Community* College Park, MD, Univ. of Maryland, 1983. Univ. Microfilms #8429934

Walker, J. H. (1987) Document Examiner: Delivery Interface for Hypertext Documents *Hypertext '87 Papers* Nov. 13-15, 1987

Waller, R. (1986) What electronic books will have to be better than. *Information Design Journal*, Vol. 5, No. 1, 1986

Weyer, S. A. (1982) The Design of a Dynamic Book for Information Search *International Journal of Man-Machine Studies* 17.1 (July 1982): 87-107

Yankelovich, N., L. N. Garrett and K. E. Smith et al. (1988) Issues in Designing a Hypermedia Document System: The Intermedia Case Study *Interactive Multimedia* Redmond, WA. Microsoft Press

The Information Mapping Method

Burrell, L. O. (1978) *Effectiveness of self-assessment guides as a method of teaching critical care nursing to professional students.* Unpub.Ph.D. dissertation. Univ. of Georgia, l978

Cheung, Raymond Yuk-Ming, (1980) *Development of and Information Mapped Text on Basic* Unpublished M.A. Thesis, Concordia University. Montreal, Canada

Falk, L.M. (1980) *Retrieval of information from self study texts*, Unpub. Ph.D. dissertation, Temple University

Fields, Alan, (l982) *An empirical and conceptual investigation of Information Mapping® techniques.* Unpub. Ph. D. dissertation, the Open University (U. K.)

Hartley, J. and Trueman, M. (1983) The Effects of Headings in Text on Recall, Search and Retrieval *British Journal of Educational Psychology,* 53, 205-21

Hauck, L. S. *Differences in Information Mapping®* strategies in left and right brain learners, (1985) Unpub. Ed. D. dissertation, Pennsylvania State Univ.

Horn, R. E. (1966) A Terminal Behavior Locator System Programmed Learning (U.K.) Feb. 1966

Horn, R. E. (1969) Come Along With Me Into My Custom-Made It's-Up-To-You Browsing-Learning-Growing Move-Around Information Environment (If You Want To) reprinted shorter version as "Experiment in Programmed Learning" in Runkel, Harrison, and Runkel (Eds) *The Changing College Classroom: Some Innovations in the Teaching-Learning Process,* San Francisco, Jossey, Inc.,

Horn, R. E., Nicol, E., Kleinman, J., and Grace, M.(1969) *Information Mapping for Learning and Reference* Cambridge, I.R.I. (A.F. Systems Command Report ESD-TR-69-296)

Horn, R. E., Nicol, E., Roman, R., et.al.(1971) *Information Mapping for Computer-Learning and Reference* Cambridge,I.R.I.(A.F. Systems Command Report ESD-TR-71-165)

Horn, R. E.,(1972) Interview with R.E. Horn in *Industrial Training International* (U.K.) pp. 232-234

Horn, R. E., (1972) Information Mapping: New Tool for Learning and Research *Improving Human Performance*: A Research Quarterly Vol.1, No.2, June 1972

Horn, R. E.(197_) Information Mapping *Japanese Journal of Educational Technology Spring*

Horn, R. E.(1971) Information Mapping: New Training Technology for the 1970's, a speech presented to the First National Conference on Technology of Higher Education Rio de Janeiro, June 1971

Horn, R. E.(1974) Briefing on Information Mapping *Training Magazine* March 1974, Vol.II, pp. 27-30

Horn, R. E. (1974) Information Mapping: New Tool to Overcome the Paper Mountain *Educational Technology* Vol.XIV, No.5, May 1974, pp. 5-8

Horn, R. E.(1975 Information Mapping, *Datamation* January 1975 pp. 85-88

Horn, R. E. (1975) Is Information Mapping for Me? *Training Magazine* 1975

Horn, R. E. (1976) *Developing Instructional Materials and Procedures:* 1967. Waltham, MA: Information Mapping 2nd edition, 1979; 3rd edition, (new title: Developing Procedures,Policies, and Documentation)

Horn, R. E. (1977)*Writing Reports* , Waltham, MA, Information Mapping. 2nd edition 1978; 3rd edition retitled *Effective Reports, Proposals, and Memos*

Horn, R. E. (1979) Information Mapping, A presentation to the National Society for Performance and Instruction National Convention, April 1979

Horn, R. E.(1985) Results with Structured Writing Using the Information Mapping Writing Service Standards, an invitational presentation at Designing Usable Text, a conference sponsored by the Open University, Nov. 3-7, 1980 *Toward More Usable Text: an Applied Research Perspective,* Duffy, T.M. and Waller, R. Academic Press, 1985

Horn, R. E.(1980) *Information and Decision Management through Structured Writing*, a concept paper for Delta Force, U.S. Army War College

Horn, R. E.(1980) Structured Writing Possible Solution to Documentation Problems, a presentation to the IBM Guide UsersConference, Nov. 13, 1980. Miami, Florida

Horn, R. E. and John N. Kelly (1981) Structured Writing--An Approach to the Documentation of Computer Software) *The Newsletter of the Special Interest Group on Documentation of the Association for Computing* Machinery.

Horn, R. E.(1982) Structured Writing and Text Design, in Jonassen, D.H. *The Technology of Text: Principles for Structuring, Designing, and Displaying Text* Englewood Cliffs, N.J. Educational Technology Press, 1982

Horn, R. E.(1985) *Recent Perspectives on the Information Mapping Method* Waltham, MA. Information Mapping, Inc.

Horn, R. E.*The Engineering of Documentation--The Information Mapping Approach* (1987) Waltham, MA. Information Mapping, Inc.

Horn, R. E. (1987) *Twelve Myths That Lead to Poor Documentation* Waltham, MA. 1987, Information Mapping, Inc.

Jonassen, D. H. (1979) *Recall and Retrieval from Mapped and Programmed Text,* Paper presented at AECT Convention, New Orleans, LA, Feb. 1979.

Jonassen, D.H., and Falk, L.M. (1980) Mapping and Programming Textural Materials *Programmed Learning and Educational Technology.* Feb., 1980

Jonassen, D. H. (1981) Information Mapping: A Description, Rationale and Comparison with Programmed Instruction, *Visible Language* , XV, 1, 55-66.

Jonassen, D. H., ed. (1985) *The Technology of Text* Englewood Cliffs, N. J.: Educational Technology Publications

Mcclung, L. G. (1985)*The church growth/church planning study guide: a two-phase reading and self-study course* unpub. D.Miss.dissertation, Fuller Theological Seminary

Olivares-Guerrero, R. A., (1985) *Manual for the evaluation of the teacher education programs in Chile* Unpub. Ed. D.dissertation, Columbia University Teachers College

Reid, U.V. (1984) *Instructional systems development: a new approach to education planning in the health systems of the commonwealth caribbean* Unpub. Ed. D. dissertation, Columbia University Teachers College

Romiszowski, A.J. (1977) *A study of individualized systems for mathematics instruction at the post secondary levels* Unpub. Ph.D.dissertation. Loughborough University of Technology (U.K.)

Romiszowski, A.J. (1981) *Designing Instructional Systems* New York: Nichols Publishing

Romiszowski, A.J. (1986) *Developing Auto-Instructional Materials* New York: Nichols Publishing

Romiszowski, A.J. (1984) *Producing Instructional Systems* New York: Nichols Publishing

Ross, B. (1987) Reference-Based Training *Managing End-User Computing.* Information Mapping Dec. 1987

Schaffer, E. M., (1982) "The Potential Benefits of the Information Mapping Technique" *NSPI Journal* February 1982, p. 34 - 38

Skelly, W. H. (1982)*The effects of a comparative advance organizer on knowledge acquisition and retention and its interaction with ninth grade male and female students of differing academic abilities in a unit utilizing the Information Mapping® approach to instructional design* Unpub. Ed.D. dissertation. Temple Univ.

Soyster, Thomas G. (1980)*A comparison of the effects of programmed instruction and the Information Mapping® method of instructional design on learning and retention of students with different mental abilities* Unpub. Ed.D. dissertation. TempleUniv.

Stelnicki, Michael. (1980) *The effects of information-mapped and standard text presentations with fact and concept levels of learning on low general ability adult learner cognition* Unpub. Ed. D.dissertation. Northern Illinois Univ.

Stuart, Teresa Habito. (1979) *The effectiveness of Information Mapping® compared with the conventional paragraph in communicating technical information* Unpublished M.A. Thesis. University of the Philippines at Los Banos

Webber, N. *Some results of Using the Information Mapping Writing Service Standards at Pacific Telephone Co, Paper* presented at NSPI Conference, Washington, D.C. 1979

Argumentation Analysis

Marshall, C. C. (1987) Exploring Representation Problems Using Hypertext. *Hypertext '87 Papers.* November 13-15, 1987

Mitroff, I. I., Mason, R.O., Barabba, V.P. (1983) *The 1980 Census: Policymaking Amid Turbulence.* Lexington, MA Lexington Books

Perelman, C., Olbrechts-Tyteca, L. (1958) *La nouvelle rhetorique: traite de l'argumentation.* Bruxelles, l' Universitete Bruxelles

Perelman, C., Olbrechts-Tyteca, L. (1958) *The New Rhetoric. A Treatise on Argumentation.* South Bend IN., University of Notre Dame Press

Smolensky, P, B. Bell and B. Fox, et al. (1987) Constraint-based Hypertext for Augmentation. *Hypertext '87 Papers* Nov. 13-15. 1987

Toulman, S., Rieke R., Janik, A. (1979) *An Introduction to Reasoning.* New York: Macmillan Publishing Co. Inc.

Toulman, S. (1980) *The Uses of Argument.* London: Cambridge University Press

van Eemeren, F.H., Grootendorst, R., Kruiger, T. (1987) *Handbook of Argumentation Theory.* Dordrecht, Holland Foris Publications

Other Works Cited

Ambron, S., Hooper, K. eds. (1988) *Interactive Multimedia.* Redmond, WA. Microsoft Press

Bandler,R. and Grinder, J., *The Structure of Magic: A book About Language and Therapy,* (1975) Palo Alto: Science and Behavior Books

Bates, M. J. (1980) Idea Tactics. *IEEE Transactions on Professional Communication*, Vol. PC-23, No. 2, June, 1980

Bates, M. J. (1979) Information Search Tactics. *Journal of the American Society for Information Science*, July, 1979

Bolt, R.A. (1984) *The Human Interface.* Belmont, CA: Lifetime Learning Publications

Bonime, W. (1982) *The Clinical Use of Dreams*, DaCapo

Davis, P.J. and Hersh, R. (1981)*The Mathematical Experience,* Boston, Houghton Mifflin

Foley, J. D. (1987), Interfaces for Advanced Computer, *Scientific American,* October 1987, 127-132

Greif, I., ed. (1988) *Computer-Supported Cooperative Work: A Book of Readings* San Mateo, CA: Morgan Kaufmann Publishers, Inc.

Horn, R. E. (1967) Language and Change and Communication, Chicago,S.R.A.

Horn, R. E. (1976) *The Guide to Simulations/Games for Education and Training (Ed)* Cambridge: I.R.I.

Horn, R. E., editor, (1983) Trialectics: Toward a Practical Logic of Unity, Lexington, MA I.R.I. (now distributed by the Lexington, Institute, 80 Marrett Road, Lexington, MA, 02173)

Lanier, J. Virtual Reality -- An Interview with Jaron Lanier, *Whole Earth Review*, Fall 1989, 108-119

Macdonald- Ross, M. and Smith, E. (1977) *Graphics in Text: A Bibliography,* Milton Keynes, Open Univ. Institute of Educational Technology, Monograph No. 6

Miller, G. A. (1956) "The Magical Number Seven, Plus or Minus Two: Some Limits on Our Capacity for Processing Information" *Psych.Rev.*, 63, 2, March 1956, 81-96.

Pask, G. (1976) *Conversation Theory.* Amsterdam: Elsevier

Reid, F. and Wright, P.Written Information: Some Alternatives to Prose for Expressing the Outcomes Complex Contingencies *Journal of Applied Psychology* 1973, Vol. 57, No. 2, 160-166

Root-Bernstein, R.S. (1982) *The Problem of Problems* J. Theor. Biol. 99, 193-201

Simon, H. A. (1979) "How Big is a Chunk?" in *Models of Thought* New Haven: Yale University Press pp. 50-61

Smith, S.L., and Mosier, J. N. (1986) *Guidelines for Designing User Interface Software* Bedford, MA: Mitre

Walker, J. (1988) Through the Looking Glass: Beyond "User Interfaces" Sausalito, Sept 1, 1988

Acknowledgments

A book like this could not have been written without the help of many people. First, I want to acknowledge the encouragement and support of the people of Information Mapping, Inc., who have by their quality work, made the company and the methodology what it is today. Especially, I want to thank the old timers there, especially Nancy Fohl, Tim Burke, George Coufos, Mary Ann Cluggish and Jerry Paradis for their spirit and their excellence. Discussions with Doug Gorman, President of Information Mapping, have always been challenging and useful. And I have also learned a lot from Barb Ross, Vice President, who has pioneered in applying Information Mapping's approach to on-line text, and from Carol Vallone, Vice President, who is now leading Information Mapping in its computer-based applications. Specific acknowledgment and thanks is given to the company for permission to use copyrighted materials.

I have learned something that eventually found its way into this book almost every time I got together with my friends David Sibbet, Bob Weber, Jim Channon, Bill Verplank, Michael Cone, and Paul Foraker.

For reading earlier versions of the book, certain chapters, or offering suggestions on particular aspects of the book, I want to thank Carl Binder, Michael J. Steinbach, Bob Weber, John Kelly, Scott Kim, Aaron Marcus, Paul Bellerive, Doug Gorman, Don Cook, Barbara Ross, Jeff Beegle, and Jan Walker.

And thanks to my typist, Gail Sheehan for putting up with my experiments and my many revisions and to Jeanne Beegle and Ming Kendall for proofreading the book and a second round of thanks to Ming Kendall for doing the index. Thanks also go to Patricia D'Andrade for preparing initial drafts of a few of the abstracts in Chapter 8 and for insightful discussions on improving the usefulness of abstracts. And also thanks to Mrs. Betty Anne Cross and Mrs. Vicky Feteris of the reference section of the Lexington Library without whose help, especially in the inter-library loan area, this book would have taken much longer to get out. I also want to acknowledge the inspiration of my long time acquaintanceship with Doug Engelbart since 1970, and to Ted Nelson, whom I didn't meet until recently, but whose ideas and visions have always sparked my imagination.

Robert E. Horn
Lexington, Massachusetts
December 1989

Index

Mapping Hypertext

The Analysis, Organization, and Display of Knowledge for the Next Generation of On-Line Text and Graphics

a new book by

Robert E. Horn

Contents

® Information Mapping and Info-Map are registered trademarks of Information Mapping, Inc.

Early Comments on *Mapping Hypertext*

I am convinced that the future of man's knowledge production and utilization will be deeply emplanted in the structure, conventions and methods associated with the descendants of today's hypertext. Bob Horn has produced a notable step toward that end.
--*Doug Engelbart, Bootstrap Project, Stanford University; first person to implement hypertext on a computer system*

Mapping Hypertext is a thoughtful and provocative overview of both hypertext and Information Mapping, full of useful advice and interesting bits of history. It is a must read for anyone concerned about how computers can become effective tools for human communication--*Paul Saffo, The Institute for the Future; columnist, Personal Computing*

This book will change the way people think about their current information and the hypertext revolution.
--*Ken Blanchard, co-author of the best selling The One Minute Manager*

Bob Horn suggests an antidote for the problem of disorientation that often comes with navigating through hypertext...
-*Patricia Seybold, founder of Patricia Seybold's Office Computing Group and sponsor of the Seybold Office Computing Conferences. Quotes are from Paradigm Shift: Patricia Seybold's Guide to the Information Revolution.*

Mapping Hypertext by Robert E. Horn is a tour de force in several respects. First, it is an amazing example of "graphic language...Mapping Hypertext is a unique and seminal work, covering the history and conceptual underpinnings of hypertext, suggesting applications and design principles capable of stimulating hypertext and hypermedia design for years to come...
--*Carl Binder, Performance and Instruction, October 1991*

Boy, do I wish we'd had this book when we were designing the CD-ROM Electronic Whole Earth Catalog.... This book is the most thorough survey of solutions thus far. And it is organized in a highly visual hypertext-like format which effectively illustrates many of the principles being discussed. An absolutely first-rate work. --*Keith Jordan, Whole Earth Review, Summer 1991*

Send to: INFORMATION MAPPING, INC.
300 Third Avenue
Waltham, MA 02154

Now available via MASTERCARD or VISA!
Call (617) 890-7003 to order

☐ Please send me ___copy(ies) of *Mapping Hypertext* at $39.50 each, plus $3.00 shipping and handling. I've enclosed a check. (Add $1.73 state tax per copy)

☐ Please use my Mastercard or VISA for payment. (Circle which one)
Card #_____
Exp. Date_____

OR CALL (617) 890-7003

Name_____
Title_____
Department _____
Company_____
Address_____
City,State_____Zip_____
Business Phone_____